the population
Myth

PRAISE FOR THE BOOK

'*The Population Myth* has come at a time when unfounded apprehensions of Muslims emerging as a dominant population group in India are being propagated for political gain. Based on empirical evidence and government data, S.Y. Quraishi busts such a divisive discourse and convincingly shows how population growth among different communities and groups is a function of poor access to basic goods such as education, family planning services and incomes. Beautifully written, this unique book is a must read to understand the complex interrelationships between, population dynamics and fertility, development choices and politics.'

–Sujatha Rao, former Health Secretary of India

'S.Y. Quraishi's remarkable career in government saw him work in child development, AIDS control, sports, and finally in the conduct of elections, all involving huge sections of the population and calling for an understanding of crucial issues in democratic governance. He now turns his attention to family planning among the Muslim community, the myths, the prejudices and the facts. This book is important reading not only for demographers but for all those interested in public health administration, health policy and the future of a democratic India.'

–Keshav Desiraju, former Health Secretary, India,
currently Chairman, Population Foundation of India

'*The Population Myth* explodes the myth with demographic evidence and support from the Islamic tenets that Islam is against family planning. The authentic account presented in this valuable contribution must dispel misgivings among those who spread falsehood and ignite communal tensions in India.'

–Professor Leela Visaria, former President, Asian
Population Association, and Director, Gujarat Institute of
Development Research

'I fully endorse the work because it presents a balanced view and applies Islamic principles to the current situation in a logical manner. It will make a positive impact on the Muslim couples regarding their approach towards family planning.'

–Dr Jawed Jamil, Professor of Islamic Studies,
Yenepoya University, Mangalore, Karnataka

'This is a must-read book, which provides compelling evidence to understand family planning perspectives and practices adopted by different religions across countries and in India. Importantly, it also provides convincing pathways to effectively counteract misconceptions, increase behaviour change and reach out family planning services to those in Muslim communities who are still untouched by them.'

–Poonam Muttreja, Executive Director,
Population Foundation of India

'This book approaches the vexed issue of religious demography very objectively and more scientifically. A serious assessment from varied dimensions.'

–Professor K.S. James, Director and Senior Professor,
International Institute for Population Sciences

'The book has unique contest to religious demography of India. The author places the data and arguments in a comparative perspective especially between religions, which is rare. There is a chapter on family planning practice in Muslim countries which is highly informative. The book also covers the complex aspects of "politics of population" and lays out a communication strategy for promoting family planning among Muslims as well as other citizens of India.'

–Abusaleh Shariff, President, Centre for Research and Debates in
Development Policy, New Delhi and Bengaluru

'Rather than religion, population growth of any group depends on factors such as poverty, status of women, and availability of health facilities. An obvious example is Bangladesh – its rate of population growth has fallen drastically, even more so than India's, because of better gender and health indicators. In India too, the rate of growth of Muslim population in Kerala is far less than the similar rate of growth of Hindu population in UP or Rajasthan. It is generally not known that despite poverty, infant and child mortality among Muslims is lower than the rate among Hindus. These figures persist despite poverty and lower levels of female schooling among Muslims. The practice of "within-kin" marriage and lower dowry might explain why the girl child is not considered so much of a burden in Muslim households. I am sure Dr Quraishi's book would help in clarifying prejudicial views on the population issue that unfortunately persist – and are publicized by the vested interests.'

–Dr N.C. Saxena, former Member,
Planning Commission of India

'*The Population Myth* demystifies issues related to Islam on Family Planning. It provides right direction for Family Planning Policy in India. Must read if you are working on this issue.'

–Dr R.K. Srivastava, former DG, National Institute of
Health and Family Welfare, New Delhi

the
population
Myth

Islam, Family Planning and Politics in India

S. Y. QURAISHI

HarperCollins *Publishers* India

First published in India by
HarperCollins *Publishers* in 2021
A-75, Sector 57, Noida, Uttar Pradesh 201301, India
www.harpercollins.co.in

2 4 6 8 10 9 7 5 3 1

P-ISBN: 978-93-9035-154-1
E-ISBN: 978-93-9035-150-3

Typeset in 11/15.7 Adobe Caslon Pro at
Manipal Technologies Limited, Manipal

Printed and bound at
Thomson Press (India) Ltd

To the unity in diversity – India's unique identity

Contents

Tables and Figures

Tables

Figures

Foreword

POPULATION explosion is an age-old issue in India, but it gained traction in 2019 after Prime Minister Narendra Modi mentioned it in his Independence Day speech that year. PM Modi, known to generally celebrate India's 'demographic dividend', expressed concern at a *'betahasha jansankhya visphot'*[1] (reckless population explosion) and stressed the need for government action to control the situation. The announcement drew mixed reactions. Congress leader P. Chidambaram welcomed it;[2] a few BJP leaders applauded

---

1 Qubul Ahmed, 'Modi ke bhaashan mein jansankhya niyantran par zor, Sanjay Gandhi ke tariqey per uththey sawaal', Aaj Tak, 15 August 2019, https://www.aajtak.in/india/story/independence-day-2019-narendra-modi-population-control-sanjay-gandhi-family-planning-policy-tpt-954875-2019-08-15, accessed on 6 October 2020.

2 'Chidambaram hails PM Modi's announcements on population control, respect for wealth creators', *Economic Times*, 16 August 2019. https://economictimes.indiatimes.com/news/politics-and-nation/p-chidambaram-hails-pm-modis-vision/articleshow/70696356.cms, accessed on 6 October 2020.

it, seeing the announcement as a signal of the government's intention
to enact some kind of legislation to control the Muslim population.[3]
The BJP and RSS leaders have, for years, been blaming Muslims for
the purported spurt in the country's population and raising the bogey
of the community, eventually outnumbering Hindus in the country.[4]
In fact, a few politicians from the ruling party have used the PM's
speech to exhort Hindu women to give birth to at least four children.[5]

Based on the official data, especially the four National Family
Health Surveys (NFHSes: 1992-93, 1998-99, 2005-06, 2015-16),
however, this narrative does not hold water.

Let us consider some facts.

Will Muslims outnumber Hindus in India in the near future?

The Census 2011 data shows that since Census 1951, the share of
Hindus has dropped by 4.3 percentage points, that from 84.1 per
cent to 79.8 per cent of the total population in 2011, while the share
of Muslims has risen by 4.4 percentage points, that from 9.8 per
cent (no Census was conducted in the Jammu and Kashmir in 1951)
to 14.2 per cent in the corresponding period. It is interesting to
note that the projected figure shows a slight increase in the share of

---

3   Financial Express, 'BJP Leaders Hail PM Narendra Modi's Speech,
    Applaud Him for Advocating Population Control', 15 August 2019,
    https://www.financialexpress.com/india-news/bjp-leaders-hail-pm-
    narendra-modis-speech-applaud-him-for-advocating-population-
    control/1676664/; Nikhil Rampal, 'New-gen Muslim Women are Better
    at Family Planning', 23 August 2019, https://www.indiatoday.in/diu/
    story/muslim-women-family-planning-india-1590955-2019-08-23,
    accessed on 6 October 2020.

4   A note on the growing demographic imbalances in the Indian
    subcontinent, Dr M.D. Srinivas, Centre for Policy Studies, Chennai,
    1999.

5   Rampal, 'New-gen Muslim Women are Better at Family Planning'.

Hindu population in 2021 as compared to 2011: 80.3 per cent versus 79.80 per cent.

There is a sense of paranoia that if the Muslim population is allowed to increase, it will overtake the population of Hindus in coming years. Before we resolve the issue, let us discuss what has happened in the first decade of the twenty-first century.

The population growth rate of various religions has come down in the decade spanning 2001–2011. The rate of population growth among Hindus reduced to 16.76 per cent during 2001–2011 from 19.92 per cent during the previous decade. The rate of population growth among Muslims, too, saw a sharp fall: from 29.52 per cent in the previous decade, it came down to a 24.60 per cent in 2001–2011. The latter was most unexpected, since the scenario was unlike any in the last six decades.[6]

The population growth rate among Hindus is projected to go down further to 15.7 per cent from 16.8 per cent of the earlier decade, while the population growth rate among Muslims may witness another steep fall to 18.2 per cent from the previous figure of 24.60 per cent in the decade 2011–2021.[7] Clearly, the gap between the Hindu and Muslim population is closing fast. I believe it will decrease further in the Census of 2031.

So, to say that Muslims will overtake Hindus does not make sense. As the 2019 Economics Nobel Prize winner Abhijit Banerjee puts it, 'minorities in India, much like in the United States, "are not really anywhere close to being dominant"'. Fearing any '"Muslim

---

6   'Population by Religious Communities', Census of India 2011. https://www.census2011.co.in/religion.php#:~:text=Religion%20 Census%202011&text=Population%20Growth%20rate%20of%20 various,%25%20(1991%2D2001).

7   Projected figures for the year 2021 are based on various sources like NFHS-4 (2015-16), Population Reference Bureau and United National Population Division.

takeover in India" is baseless,' according to him.[8] 'I don't think there
is any real fear that there is going to be a Muslim takeover of India,'
he said.[9]

Why is the Muslim population growing slowly?

There are many factors behind this unexpected trend but there are
two that are important: an emerging middle class and declining
fertility.

An analysis of data from NFHS (1992–2016)[10] has shown that
over the past twenty-five years, new-generation Muslim families
have done a better job at family planning, though their statistical
figures still trail the Hindu families.

In India, a small and emerging, yet visible, Muslim middle class
has surfaced, 'breaking the perception of a monolithic impoverished
community', as noted by Ashwaq Masoodi, Nieman Fellow at
Harvard University.[11] For example, the NFHS-4 shows that even

---

8   Rohit Khanna, 'Any fear of "Muslim takeover in India" baseless:
     Abhijit Banerjee', *Times of India*, 28 January 2020, http://
     timesofindia.indiatimes.com/articleshow/73682076.cms?utm_
     source=contentofinterest&utm_medium=text&utm_campaign=cppst,
     accessed on 1 October 2020.

9   Sambit Saha, 'A talk to demonise Muslims: Banerjee', The
     Telegraph Online, 27 January, 2020, https://www.telegraphindia.
     com/west-bengal/a-talk-to-demonise-muslims-abhijit-banerjee/
     cid/1740140?utm_source=facebook&utm_medium=social&utm_
     campaign=ttmetro_daily, accessed on 6 October 2020.

10   National Family Health Survey-1 (1992–93), Mumbai: International
     Institute for Population Sciences (IIPS); National Family Health
     Survey-2 (1998–99), National Family Health Survey-3 (2005–06),
     National Family Health Survey-4 (2015–16).

11   'Joining the India Story: Rise of the Muslim Middle', *Mint*, 24 January
     2019,   https://www.livemint.com/politics/news/joining-the-india-
     story-rise-of-the-muslim-middle-1548262657277.html, accessed on
     6 October 2020.

though, among all religions, the presence of Muslims in the highest wealth quintile (top 20 per cent) of the country was still the lowest, the share had gone up (from 17.2 per cent to 18.8 per cent by 2015–16). Even though in the mid-1990s the community realized the importance of education, as documented by several researchers including Anwar Alam, senior fellow at the Policy Perspectives Foundation (a Delhi-based think tank), it wasn't a dramatic move.[12] Instead some chose hybridized education, which meant that more and more madrasas had to slowly modernize to include English and computer training in their curriculum.

A widely used measure of fertility levels is the 'total fertility rate' (TFR), that is, the average number of children a woman will have in her lifetime. According to NFHS-1 (1992–93), this figure was 4.3 children for Muslims and 3.3 children for Hindus, or a fertility gap of 30.3 per cent or one child per woman. The NFHS-4 data shows that this gap reduced to 20.5 per cent in 2015–16, a difference of half a birth on average per woman, even as both communities were having fewer children than before.[13]

While fertility among Muslims is declining, the fertility gap will not come down until the Hindu fertility level reaches the replacement level. In demography, the TFR is considered to be 2.1 children per woman. In 2011, P.N. Mari Bhat, former director of International Institute of Population Science (IIPS) and a renowned demographer, had estimated that Hindus would achieve replacement fertility by 2021 and a stable population by 2061; that Muslims would achieve replacement fertility by 2031 and population stabilization by 2101,

---

12 'Emergence of Muslim Middle Class in Post-Independence India and Its Political Orientations', *Journal of Muslim Minority Affairs* 35, no. 1 (2015): 123–40, DOI: 10.1080/13602004.2015.1007664.

13 National Family Health Survey (NFHS-4), 2015-16: India. Mumbai: IIPS.

and would account for 18.8 per cent of India's population then. Bhat's projections are extremely close to the NFHS-4 figures.[14]

So, what should the agenda be? The only major religion left out of the demographic transition in India is Islam. And this group could be helped by being provided family planning services specific to their needs, as happened in Bangladesh and Indonesia. Muslim scholars believe that the permanent method of contraception is not permitted in Islam. Therefore, India has to diversify its approach to include other modern methods of contraception in its programme, as done in Bangladesh and Indonesia.

India has to find a way to talk about religious demographics as other nations do – mostly without fuss, resentment or wild policy suggestions. It is because Indian Muslims want to be part of the mainstream. Doubtless, Muslims have a higher rate of fertility rate than those in other religious groups. But, in India, there is no clash of civilizations. Indian Muslims are very much a part of the Indian culture, as argued by the noted Islamic scholar Mahmood Madani.[15] He writes: 'This is because of both India's culture and its historical legacy. Muslim heritage is a part of a larger tradition of multiculturalism and mutual tolerance.'

In spite of poverty and illiteracy, the prevailing unmet need for modern family planning services is surprising, especially among Muslims. As compared to Hindu women, Muslim women have a higher level of unmet need for family planning services (12 per cent

---

14 Kartik Kwatra, 'What a Narrowing Hindu-Muslim Fertility Gap Tells Us', *Mint*, 21 February 2019, https://www.livemint.com/news/india/what-a-narrowing-hindu-muslim-fertility-gap-tells-us-1550686404387.html, accessed on 6 October 2020.

15 'Islamic State Vs Islamic Ideals: There Is No Clash of Civilizations and Terrorism Isn't Jihad', *Times of India*, Blogs, 4 December 2015, https://blogs.timesofindia.indiatimes.com/toi-edit-page/islamic-state-vs-islamic-ideals-there-is-no-clash-of-civilizations-and-terrorism-isnt-jihad/, accessed on 6 October 2020.

versus 16 per cent).[16] It means that Muslim women in general do not want more children, yet they have them due to several other factors. I believe that the Government of India must address this issue squarely, and the authorities must accept that there is a problem in the management of family planning programmes and resolve it.[17] There are sound indicators that Hindu and Muslim fertility rates are merging.

I am delighted that Dr S.Y. Quraishi, a distinguished scholar in his own right, has taken up the challenging task of writing this book. This work will do yeoman's service to the nation by attempting to break the long-perpetuated myths which have become the fulcrum of dangerous communal polarization. He has done well to get two great mathematicians to prepare a mathematical model of population growth which conclusively demolishes the myth that Muslims will overtake the Hindus in the near or distant future.

This book is unique in many other ways too. It convincingly shatters the misconception that Islam is against family planning. In one of the chapters in the book, he explains how all other religions of the world view family planning, which, I would say, will be knowledge that is invaluable to the public. A chapter on the success of family planning in major Muslim countries is also eye-opening, showing that Islam is not an obstacle to family planning programme anywhere.

Dr Quraishi's conclusion that the problem at hand be not viewed as a 'Hindus versus Muslims' one but one that is common to both communities must be taken seriously. Finally, his bold appeal to Muslims to adopt family planning undeterred by provocative right-wing propaganda is an extremely positive initiative. He also suggests

---

16 National Family Health Survey (NFHS-4), 2015-16. Mumbai: IIPS.

17 Devendra Kothari, 'Managing Unwanted Fertility in India: Way Forward', in , *National Rural Health Mission: An Unfinished Agenda*, ed. Suresh Sharma and Joe William (New Delhi: Book Well, 2014).

a complete communication strategy to promote family planning among Muslims for which not only the Ministry of Health and Family Welfare but the country should feel grateful. I would not hesitate to add that *The Population Myth: Islam, Family Planning and Politics in India* is of great significance during these times, for, while in the process of shedding light on the issues of population and family planning, it also promotes national harmony and understanding among communities – a much needed service to the nation.

Devendra Kothari
Population and Development Analyst

Foreword

THIS well-documented book is a valuable addition to the literature presently available on Muslim thought and practice in respect of planned parenthood, viewed against the broad canvas of the general population-control situation in the country. S.Y. Quraishi has indeed done a commendable job.

Islamic tenets on family planning have always been a polemical subject. There are in abundance, in all parts of the world, proponents and opponents of its permissibility, both citing basic Islamic sources and offering their respective intertextual interpretations. It is their comprehension of the seventh-century wellsprings of Islamic theology and law that has shaped popular trends and dictated official policies concerning population control in Muslim societies across the globe.

In the galaxy of religions prevailing on the globe, it is Islam that provides meticulous guidance with regard to planned parenthood. Its teachings in this context are amazingly humane. This revolutionary religion was, in its origin, an unprecedented social-reform movement which had not left untouched any aspect of human life and welfare. Pre-Islamic Arabia was quite familiar with the so-called *azl* (coitus interruptus) and *isqat* (abortion) as preconception and post-conception techniques of birth control. The stand of the newly emerging Islamic code of conduct on these pre-existing practices was anxiously sought and authoritatively clarified in the heyday of Islam.

There are two foundational sources of Islamic theology and law: The Holy Quran, which is believed to be divine in its letter and spirit; and the *Hadith* and *Sunnah*, which are supposed to be authentic collections of the sayings and doings of the founder of Islam. For further development of the religio-legal code of his religion, the far-sighted founder had approved the technique of *ijtihad* (framing of new rules in the light of the two basic sources) which, in the course of time, was employed both collectively and individually (known as *ijma* and *qiyas* respectively). This is how a massive Islamic code of life had come into existence containing, *inter alia*, answers to all possible questions regarding the concept and methods of birth control.

In contemporary Muslim world, finding population control as an unavoidable national imperative, jurists of the time have proclaimed its religious validity, on the basis of which the governments of the day have floated variform schemes and projects. On the International Human Rights Day in December 1966, the United Nations issued a Basic Policy Statement on Population Control, among the nineteen high-level signatories of which there were four Muslim heads of state. Today, population-control measures are at work in several Muslim-dominated countries – prominent ones being Egypt and Jordan among the West Asian, and Morocco and Tunisia among the North African, Arab nations. Outside the Arab world, Turkey and Malaysia have been at the forefront in promoting planned parenthood within the permissible limits identified by the local Islamic scholars.

The story in India has been different. The majority of Muslim theologians here – whose fatwas have been and remain the Islamic law in action – regard the dissenters' views on the permissibility of birth control as sacrosanct and hence indisputable. Moreover, the Catholic version of Christianity professed by the British imperialists who ruled the subcontinent for about four centuries, has been dead opposed to birth control which it regards as a sacrilegious interference with God's will. It was in this background that Lord Macaulay's Indian Penal Code of 1860 had laid down stringent punishments for all forms of foeticide and prevention of child birth, for whatever reasons employed.

After Independence, demands were made by social reformers of the day for a new law permitting abortion for the sake of the health of women and children. A Medical Termination of Pregnancy Act was then enacted in 1971. Since then the old IPC provisions are not attracted where a registered medical practitioner terminates a pregnancy if, in his opinion, its continuance involves risk to the mother's life or grave injury to her physical or mental health, or if there is a substantial risk of the child being born with physical or mental abnormalities. No abortion is, however, allowed under the Act after twenty weeks of pregnancy. For deviating from this norm in some critical cases, women had to seek a verdict from the apex court of the country. Till date, abortion in India is not a private or family matter but a part of the country's public law, and is hence seen by orthodox sections of several communities as interference with religion. Under a new proposal mooted in January 2020, the government intends to amend the Medical Termination of Pregnancy Act to raise the maximum duration of pregnancy for permissible termination from the present twenty to twenty-four weeks. This will, however, not change the status of birth control as a state-controlled activity.

In the majority community, existence of a male child is considered desirable, or even compulsory, for religious purposes. Although the trends are changing with the advancement of education, in numerous families the craze for a male child still exists. As with the advancement of technology, detection of the gender of foetus has become possible, female foeticide is widely practised – ostensibly for keeping the number of children restricted as a contribution to the nation's population-control policy. With a view to controlling this unscrupulous practice, the Pre-Natal Diagnostic Techniques (Regulation and Prevention of Misuse) Act, 1994, was enforced. To widen its scope and give it more teeth, the law was replaced in 2003 with a new Pre-Conception and Pre-Natal Diagnostic Techniques Act (PCPNDT). Yet, despite all these controlling measures, instances of female foeticide in the name of birth control remain unabated.

The book at hand, unfolding against the backdrop of the national scenario the role and responsibility of Muslim citizens in the matter of its subject, must be hailed. The author begins his work with a glance through India's family planning story in general, relates it to the issue of population growth in the country as a whole with supporting census records, looks into who in India adopt birth-control measures and under what motivations, inspects the practice among the Muslim denominations in this respect, and then enters the hazardous arena of Islamic tenets on the subject. This is followed by a look into the situation in Muslim-majority nations, a comparative view of what various other religions have to say about birth control, a critique of unwarranted politicization of this wholly apolitical issue, and suggestions to move ahead in the right direction.

On the whole, this educative and informative *multum in parvo* will be of immense value to interested readers, researchers on demography, and makers of official population policies.

Tahir Mahmood
Professor, Institute of Advanced Legal Studies Amity University
Former chairman, National Minorities Commission of India

Introduction

A widespread narrative in India suggests that Muslims produce too many children, skewing the national demographic balance. The right-wing propaganda alleges that this is all part of a deliberate plan by Muslims to capture political power in the country. The common belief that Islam is against family planning, which is why Indian Muslims practise polygamy, has for decades caused bitter acrimony between the Hindu and Muslim communities. The demand for a uniform civil code is also born out of this belief.

This book seeks to cover the facts, figures and myths about the prevalence of family planning practices among Muslims in India

A study of family planning practices in India throws up some of the following interesting facts.

Muslim acceptance of family planning has been increasing

The demographic ratio has indeed changed, with clear increase in the percentage of Muslims in India – from 9.8 in 1951 to 14.2 in

2011. There is a corresponding decline in the Hindu ratio – from 84 per cent to 79.8 per cent – during the same period. Chapter 2 analyses this in detail.

Muslims have indeed the lowest level (45.3 per cent) of family planning practice, but Hindus have the second-lowest level among all communities, with a practice prevalence of 54.4 per cent.

The Muslims are, however, taking to family planning fast – in fact, faster than the Hindus. This is why the family planning gap between the two communities is narrowing, despite many Muslims believing that Islam is against the concept of family planning. There is no evidence of organized resistance to family planning among the Muslims.

The high birth rates in India are dependent on purely non-religious factors, such as levels of literacy, income and access to health services, among other reasons, as explained in Chapter 3.

The reasons for high fertility among Muslims are an obvious result of the community's backwardness in these determining factors, as brought out in Chapter 4.

Wide regional variations in family planning practices across states also indicate that there is no 'Muslim' or 'Hindu' birth rate.

Islamic tenets nowhere come in the way of adoption of family planning by Muslims, as analysed in Chapter 5 and Chapter 6.

If acceptance of family planning is to be an index of nationalism/patriotism, as often projected by some sections in India, it is not only the performance of Muslims that needs improvement but that of other communities as well (including the Hindus.)

In terms of total fertility rate, both the Hindu and Muslim communities are actually at the same end of the spectrum, since both have large sections that are most backward socio-economically. Giving all this a political angle is not only wrong but counterproductive too. This is the theme of Chapter 8.

The exact Islamic position in the light of the Quran and Hadith

The book argues that the Holy Quran has nowhere prohibited family planning. There are only interpretations, both for and against, the concept. Nor are there any traditions of Prophet Muhammad (peace be upon him) opposing it. The interpretations by Islamic jurists seem to conclude that though *sterilization* is not permitted, family planning by means of birth-spacing methods is not only allowed, but encouraged. For example, the mandate of the Quran for compulsory breastfeeding of children for two years has been interpreted as a measure to ensure gaps between births, in the interest of the health of both mother and child. There are numerous verses of the Quran and citations from the Hadith (traditions of the Prophet) which emphasize proper conditions as requisite for the upbringing of children, possible only when the number of children is small. These verses stress quality over quantity – an extremely progressive idea.

Even in India, several ulama (scholars) have interpreted Islamic injunctions as being supportive of family planning other than through the means of sterilization. Chapter 5 deals with this issue in detail.

Family planning in major Islamic countries

The book describes family planning programmes being actively pursued as a development priority in several Islamic countries, including the most conservative ones, such as Iran, Egypt, Indonesia and Bangladesh, in spite of the fact that there are no political compulsions to do so, unlike in India. This obviously indicates that these countries, despite their powerful clergies, did not find Islam antagonistic to the concept. Chapter 6 exemplifies this point.

Why is only Islam singled out for scrutiny in the context of family planning? We must look at the family planning practices of all religions.

While the focus of the family planning debate has been on Muslims, many other religions that do not approve of family planning are left out of the narrative. For instance, Christianity's opposition to contraception of all kinds is well established. Many other religions also have a clear position on family planning, but very little of this seems to be public knowledge. This book explains the comparative position of major religions on the subject and argues that though the prevalence of family planning among Muslims varies across countries, especially in India, where it is the lowest, Islamic injunctions are not the reason. This is the subject of Chapter 7.

How a statistical analysis shows that polygamy (more accurately, polygyny) is just not possible in India. Nor can it contribute to population explosion.

In India, the gender ratio is skewed: in 2020, India has 924 females per 1,000 males.[1] In such a situation, polygyny is just not possible. Even if there are some polygynous marriages, their impact on population growth is negative, as then there would then be a corresponding number of unmarried men. Besides, the number of children from a second wife is always much lower than from an only wife.[2]

---

1   http://statisticstimes.com/demographics/country/india-sex-ratio.
      php#:~:text=Sex%20Ratio%20of%20India%20is,compare%20to%20
      51.96%25%20male%20population. Accessed on 14.12.2020

2   R. Lesthaeghe, *Reproduction and Social Organization in Sub-Saharan Africa* (Berkeley: University of California Press, 1989).

'It is also significant to note that the assertion that Muslims are predominantly polygamous is a myth.'[3] Reports show that all communities in India are polygamous and Muslims are indeed the least so![4] In Chapter 5, the book examines polygamy in considerable detail, including what Islam says on the subject.

Absence of effort to dispel myths about Muslims and family planning

Although the high fertility rate among Muslims has been referred to in all the policy and plan papers, no efforts especially addressing this issue have ever been made by the government. This comes out loud and clear in Chapter 1. Even health staff has not been trained or equipped to deal with any resistance among the community on this score.

The birth rate among Muslims has continued to be the highest among all communities in India, but surprisingly, it has been declining at a rate faster than that of Hindus for almost three decades.[5] There

---

3   M. Z. M. Nomani, review of *Vision 2025 Social Economic Inequalities: Why Does India's Economic Growth Need an Inclusive Agenda*, by Amir Ullah Khan Abdul Azim Akhtar, *Journal of Exclusion Studies* 9, no. 1(2019): 86–93.

4   Report of the Committee on the Status of Women in India, 1974 (New Delhi: Ministry of Education and Social Welfare, Government of India). https://pldindia.org/wp-content/uploads/2013/04/Towards-Equality-1974-Part-1.pdf

5   See Ali Mehdi, 'What the Data Tells Us: Are Muslims Responsible for India's "Population Explosion"? Not Quite', *The Times of India*, Blogs 27 August 2019, https://timesofindia.indiatimes.com/blogs/toi-edit-page/what-the-data-tells-us-are-muslims-responsible-for-indias-population-explosion-not-quite/, accessed on 5 October 2020; Kartik Kwatra, 'What a Narrowing Hindu-Muslim Fertility Gap Tells Us', *Mint*, 21 February 2019, https://www.livemint.com/news/india/what-a-narrowing-hindu-muslim-fertility-gap-tells-us-1550686404387.html, accessed on 5 October 2020.

has been a lack of effort on the part of the government, NGOs and scholars to communicate this truth and dispel the myths about Muslims. At the same time, the Hindu right wing has continued to provoke Hindus to produce a large number of children by creating the fear that Muslims will outnumber them soon to capture political power in India. Chapter 8 is dedicated to the politics around population issues in India.

The way forward

On the basis of what emerges from the detailed analysis of the subject in this book, there are enough facts around which a carefully planned strategy can be evolved to remove misconceptions among our communities so that they may coexist in harmony. We also have to address the fears – genuine or imagined – of those Hindus who actively oppose family planning among their community just to prevent Muslims from outnumbering them. The myth that there is organized resistance on the part of the Muslim community to family planning must be dispelled.

This book exhorts Muslims to disregard the right-wing call to Hindus to produce a large number of children, and instead encourages Muslims to adopt family planning as the wisest course of action. It suggests strategies to promote family planning among Muslims.

In India the population debate has political connotations, as it attempts to create unfounded hate and fear among Hindus about Muslim population growth. This book seeks to dispel those myths empirically rather than with political or emotional arguments.

If I succeed even in a small measure in persuading both communities to shed their mutual suspicion and adopt family planning with equal fervour, I would consider that as my humble contribution to nation building.

1

India's Family Planning Story

INDIA'S population grew from 361.1 million in the year 1951 to 1,210.2 million in 2011. As on 1 July 2020, it has been estimated at 1.38 billion.[1] India is currently in the third stage of demographic transition,[2] where birth rates are falling but the population continues to grow as there is a large number (53 per cent) of people in the reproductive age of 15–49 years.[3] An analysis of the Indian Census data confirms a declining trend in the population growth rate over the last few decades. The decadal growth rate during the year 2001–2011 was recorded at 17.7 per cent, against 21.5 per cent over the period 1991–2001.[4]

---

1 As per the worldometers.info, a population meter operating for twenty countries.

2 Demographic transition is a transition from high mortality and high fertility to low mortality and low fertility.

3 See http://www.censusindia.gov.in/2011census/C-series/C-14.html.

4 Poonam Muttreja, 'Population Explosion or Declining Fertility in India', *Deccan Herald*, https://www.deccanherald.com/specials/

While, on one hand, decadal growth rates are declining among all religious groups, on the other, interstate and interregional variations continue, depending on the level of education, health, nutrition, employment and empowerment of women in the states. It is noteworthy that the total fertility rate (the average number of live child births[5] a woman will have in her life), which was as high as 6 or more in the 1950s, came down to 2.2 in 2015–16.[6] Despite the fact that couples not only desire but also have fewer children than earlier, the overall growth in numbers still appears high because of the population momentum, which is very much a result of the demographic transition underway.[7]

India has a high proportion of young persons (about 30 per cent) – adolescents (10–19 years) and youth (15–24 years) – who are in their reproductive age group or will at least soon be. Even if this group produces fewer children, there will still be a quantum increase in numbers because the number of people in the reproductive age will be very high. This is why India, especially with its large proportion of young persons, will take some time to stabilize its population.

Needless to say, India has been acutely aware of the gigantic problem and, over the decades, has initiated elaborate population-control policies and programmes, which are briefly discussed and evaluated to set the context. The country began with the idea of 'population control'; however, the discourse shifted to 'population

sunday-spotlight/population-explosion-or-declining-fertility-in-india-756767.html, accessed on 19 October 2020.

5   Population Reference Bureau, 'Glossary of Demographic Terms', 14 August 2019, https://www.prb.org/glossary/, accessed on 5 October 2020.

6   National Family Health Survey (NFHS-4), 2015-16, Mumbai; International Institute of Population Studies (IIPS).

7   'Population Explosion or Declining Fertility in India', https://www.deccanherald.com/specials/sunday-spotlight/population-explosion-or-declining-fertility-in-india-756767.html. Accesed on 20.10.2020.

stabilization' especially after the International Conference on Population and Development (ICPD) in Cairo in 1994. Hence, it is population stabilization that the National Population Policy aims to achieve by 2045.

In the post-Independence period, India soon realized that a very large population would put a strain on the meagre resources of the country, negate the effect of development and bring down the quality of life of its citizens. This was especially true for rural, tribal and backward communities, including the Muslims. It was hardly surprising, then, that small-family norms and population control were made an integral part of India's social-reconstruction strategy.

The launch of family planning

India launched the National Family Planning Programme (NFPP) in 1952, becoming the first country to launch such a plan nationally. The objective of the policy was 'reducing birth rate to the extent necessary to stabilize the population at a level consistent with the requirement of the national economy'.[8]

The 1950s

At the time of Independence, healthcare services were predominantly urban, hospital-based and curative. Management of health problems was limited, and generally out of reach of the poor. A majority of India's population was (and still is) in the rural areas, which did not have access to healthcare services. This led to high morbidity and mortality rates. Conceptions that were too early, too close, too many, and lack of or delayed antenatal care to detect and treat problems

---

8 Ninth Five Year Plan (Vol. 2), Chapter 3.5, 'Family Welfare', Section 3.5.2, https://niti.gov.in/planningcommission.gov.in/docs/plans/planrel/fiveyr/default.html.

during pregnancy resulted in high maternal and infant mortality rates. Antenatal, intra-partum, postnatal and contraceptive care were not readily available to women who required these services desperately.[9]

Many couples in urban areas would opt for sterilization. To some extent, this would reduce maternal mortality rates, but it still had no impact on mortality or fertility growth rates in the country as a whole because of poor outreach, especially in the rural areas.[10] *Moreover, fewer Muslim couples were reported to be inclined towards family planning, mainly on account of tradition and cultural reasons.* Efforts made to improve this desperate situation were just not sufficient due to manpower and resource constraints.

The 1960s

During this decade, several programmes were initiated to make contraceptives available far and wide. To popularize immunization and family planning programmes, the camp approach was adopted where 'cases' (mostly women) were brought for sterilization and other services. However, these services did not make much headway as they were not available when and where they were needed.

Since the 1961 Census showed a disturbing rising decadal population growth, sterilization became the focus of the NFPP. *Although the overall growth rate of the Muslim community was comparatively higher, the community did not favour vasectomy or even tubectomy.* Moving health education out of hospitals and into the community through the extension-education approach was attempted – especially in localities where there was a large concentration of Muslims too – so as to improve awareness and increase acceptance of family planning methods. Attempts were considerably made to provide contraceptives and facilities to eligible rural couples through camps. However, without the infrastructure to provide follow-up services, this device fell into considerable disrepute. It became obvious that it would not be possible to achieve any appreciable improvement in maternal and child health indices or reduce birth rates without substantial investment in infrastructure and manpower to provide the much-needed follow-up services.[11]

The 1970s

The government gave top priority to the NFPP and provided substantial funds for several new initiatives. Sterilization, especially vasectomy services, were made widely available. Intra-uterine devices (IUD) and condoms were made available through primary health centres (PHCs). The hospital-based postpartum programme provided contraceptive care to women coming for delivery. Independent surveys, including those by Operations Research Group (ORG), Baroda (now Vadodara) conducted in 1970, 1980, and 1988, and published in condensed form in 1971, 1983, and 1990 showed that the *decadal increase in family planning acceptance among eligible Muslim couples had gone up significantly.*[12] Besides, the Medical Termination of Pregnancy (MTP) Act, 1972 enabled women with unwanted pregnancies to seek and obtain safe abortion services.

Increasing concern about the rapidly growing population led to the NFPP being declared as a priority-sector programme during

---

11 Ibid., 173.

12 P. Reddy, 'Religion, Population Growth, Fertility and Family Planning Practice in India', *Economic and Political Weekly* 38, no. 33 (2003): 3500–9. http://www.jstor.org/stable/441391, accessed on 4 September 2020.

the Fifth Five Year Plan. The massive sterilization drive of 1976 did result in 8 million persons[13] undergoing sterilization. However, it caused immense resentment and backlash. Ironically, this did not have any perceptible impact on birth rates as the candidates for sterilization were not appropriately chosen. The family planning programme was renamed as the National Family Welfare Programme (NFWP).

Not surprisingly, there was a steep fall in its acceptance in the very next year. In 1979, the Expanded Programme of Immunization was included in the NFWP, and an attempt was made to achieve increasing integration of family planning services with maternal and child health (MCH) services.[14]

The 1980s

The major thrust during this decade was on operationalization of WHO's Alma Ata 1978 declaration of Health for All by 2000, establishing a network of centres in urban and rural areas to provide essential primary healthcare. The network of post-partum centres was expanded to improve access to family-welfare services. In 1983, the National Health Policy (NHP) was formulated. It provided a comprehensive framework for planning, implementation and monitoring of healthcare services.[15]

It may be noted that though the Census of 1981 showed a marginal *increase in the share of the Muslim population (11.71 per cent) in the country, Muslim couples were also reported to be turning to family*

---

13 V.A. Pai Panandiker and P. Umashankar, 'Fertility Control and Politics in India', *Population and Development Review* 20 (1994): 89–104, doi:10.2307/2807941.

14 Tenth Five Year Plan, Chapter 2.10, 'Family Welfare', 174, https://niti. gov.in/planningcommission.gov.in/docs/plans/planrel/fiveyr/10th/volume2/v2_ch2_10.pdf.

15 Ibid., 174.

planning, particularly to birth spacing. ORG reported a 22.5 per cent decadal increase in family planning acceptance among Muslims. A little later, in 1989, ORG reported that 33.8 per cent of Muslim couples were using 'any family planning method', and 19.1 per cent had even opted for sterilization.

The 1990s

The report of the National Development Council (NDC) Sub-Committee on Population gave a renewed thrust and dynamism to the NWFP. In view of the massive interstate and intra-state differences in access to services and health indices, the Ministry of Health and Family Welfare abolished the practice of setting centrally defined, method-specific targets for contraception. It was replaced by a decentralized, area-specific community needs–assessment approach, and planning and implementing programmes aimed at fulfilling these needs. In 1992–93, the first National Family Health Survey (NFHS)[16] was conducted to gain universal knowledge about

---

16 The National Family Health Survey (NFHS) is a large-scale survey conducted in multiple rounds with a representative sample of households all throughout India. The first survey was conducted in 1992–93, and since then three rounds of surveys have been conducted which provide state and national information for India on fertility, infant and child mortality, the practice of family planning, maternal and child health, reproductive health, nutrition, anemia, utilization and quality of health and family planning services. Every successive round of NFHS has two specific goals. One is to provide essential information on health and family welfare needed by the Ministry of Health and Family Welfare (MoHFW) and other agencies for policy and programme formulation. Secondly, it provides information on emerging health and family welfare issues. The MoHFW, Government of India has designated the Indian Institute of Population Sciences (IIPS) as the nodal agency responsible for coordinating and technical guidance. IIPS collaborates with a number of Field Organizations (FOs) for the implementation process. Each FO is responsible for conducting the survey in one or

national- and state-level estimates of fertility, infant and child
mortality, family planning practices, maternal and child health, and
utilization of services available to mothers and children. *The survey
estimated that only 27.7 per cent of Muslim couples were on 'any family
planning method'.*

In 1997, the Ministry of Health and Family Welfare initiated the
Reproductive and Child Health (RCH) programme, which aimed
at providing integrated health and family welfare services to meet
the healthcare needs of women and children.[17] Reportedly, *Muslim
couples were more receptive to this RCH programme.* To a large extent,
this trend was supported by the findings of NFHS-2 (1998–99) that
over 37 per cent of Muslim couples were using 'any method'.

The 2000s

The main objective of the National Population Policy 2000 was to
meet all the unmet need for contraception and healthcare among
women and children, and the long-term objective was to achieve
population stabilization by 2045.[18] The policy set the goal of universal
access to quality contraceptive services in order to lower the TFR to
2.1 by adopting small-family norms. Towards this, it adopted the
following aims:

- To promote delayed marriage for girls, not earlier than the age
  of eighteen and preferably after age twenty.
- To contain sexually transmitted diseases (STDs).

---

more states covered by the NFHS. Technical assistance for NFHS is
provided mainly by ORC Macro (USA) and other organizations on
specific issues. Funding for the different rounds of NFHS has been
provided by USAID, DFID, the Bill and Melinda Gates Foundation,
UNICEF, UNFPA and the MoHFW, Government of India.

17 Tenth Five Year Plan, Chapter 2.10; 'Family Welfare', 174.

18 Ibid., 175.

- To reduce maternal mortality rate (MMR) to less than 100 per 100,000 live births.
- To universalize primary education and reduce dropout rates at the primary and secondary levels to below 20 per cent among both boys and girls.

An empowered action group associated with the ministry of health and family welfare was constituted in 2001 to facilitate capacity building in low-performing states/districts so that they attained the goals set in the policy.[19]

It would be relevant to point out that these policy formulations have seldom addressed the issue of ideological resistance to family planning. Though this ignoring of the issue may have been considered politically correct, it meant an ostrich-like approach towards solving a community-specific need.

To give a new impetus to population issues, the National Commission on Population (NCP) was constituted in the year 2000 under the chairmanship of the prime minister. The commission had the following mandate:

- To review, monitor and give directions for implementation of the National Population Policy with the view to achieving its goals.
- To promote inter-sectoral coordination in planning and implementation of the programmes through different agencies at the centre and in the states.
- To develop a vigorous people's programme to support this national effort.

Subsequently, nine working groups were created to look into specific aspects of implementation of the programmes aimed at achieving

---

19 Ibid., 175.

the targets set in the National Population Policy. *It is noteworthy that none of these was meant to specifically focus on more vulnerable groups like the Muslims.* The NCP allocated funds for action plans drawn up by district magistrates in poorly performing districts for implementation of programmes aimed at accelerating the pace of decline in fertility.[20]

Contemporary scenario

For achieving population stabilization as envisaged by the National Population Policy, the National Rural Health Mission (NRHM) was established in the year 2005 as a comprehensive integrated strategy. The main components of the NRHM are convergence of service delivery at the village level for basic healthcare, family planning, MCH services, empowerment of women so they may access health and nutrition services, and promotion of male participation in family planning. The following specific initiatives were undertaken in pursuance of the objectives of NPP/NRHM towards population stabilization:

- The National Family Planning Insurance Scheme to compensate sterilization acceptors for failures, complications and deaths, and indemnity insurance cover to doctors.
- The Prerna and Santushti strategies, under which delayed marriage (beyond the legal age for marriage) among girls, proper spacing between childbirths and public-private partnership for providing family planning services were to be encouraged.
- The Jansankhya Sthirata Kosh (JSK) call centre, to provide information on promotion of health and issues related to family planning, reproductive and child health.

---

20 Ibid., 176.

- Introduction of Accredited Social Health Activists (ASHA) under the mission for establishing a link between the community and the health system.

Impact of India's high-focus approach

The government of India has categorized states, based on their TFR levels, into very-high-focus (TFR more than or equal to 3.0), high-focus (TFR more than 2.1 and less than 3.0) and non-high-focus (TFR less than or equal to 2.1) categories. There are three states in the very-high-focus category – Bihar, Uttar Pradesh and Meghalaya.

Cumulatively, these programmes did certainly make an impact on the targeted population. For instance, NFHS-3 (2005–2006) found that *36.4 per cent of Muslim eligible couples were using 'any modern method'* and, NFHS-4 (2014–15) found that *37.9 per cent of Muslim couples were using 'any modern method' of contraception.* The trend is unmistakable: the idea and practice of family planning are catching fast among the target population, even though reduction of the decadal growth rate across religions and decrease in TFR have been slow.

Five–year plans

The country's resources being meagre at the time of Independence, the policymakers formulated a prospective policy to lower birth rates. The rapid increase in the population of India and the resulting pressure on the limited resources of the country brought to the forefront the urgency of the need for family planning and population control.

First Five Year Plan (1951–56): It was realized in the first Five Year Plan (outlay ₹0.65 crore) that progress in family planning depended on creating a strong motivation in its favour in the minds of the people and, secondly, on providing the necessary advice and services, based on acceptable, efficient, harmless and economic methods. The Plan aimed to (a) identify factors contributing to the rapid population growth; (b) evolve suitable techniques for family planning and devise methods to disseminate information on these techniques; and (c) integrate family planning with the range of services offered by government hospitals and other agencies.

It may be noted that NFPP was, at this stage, purely clinical in approach.

Second Five Year Plan (1956–61): A vigorous action-cum-research programme was undertaken during the second Five Year Plan. Special attention was given to basic training in the public health aspects of nursing, including family planning. It was proposed and expected that about 300 urban and 2,000 rural clinics would be established during the Plan (outlay, ₹5 crore). Sterilization operations became a standard procedure in hospitals and medical institutions, and contraceptive-testing units, demographic research centres and training centres for family planning workers were started. Here, the point may well be kept in mind that during this Plan period, the emphasis was largely on sterilization operations, which *Muslim couples were (and are) generally averse to because of their religious belief that it is inconsistent with Islamic principles.*

Third Five Year Plan (1961–66): The third Five Year Plan emphasized the importance of stabilizing the population growth over a reasonable period by planned development. Additional funds were allocated for the development of family planning programmes. The programmes were infused with the extension-education approach to bring the family planning message and services to people in the rural areas. Thus, extension workers were inducted into the network of primary health centres (PHC) and sub-centres. A 'cafeteria approach' was adopted, offering acceptors a choice of methods they could select from to restrict the size of their family.

The total proposed outlay for family planning in the third Five Year Plan was ₹25 crore.

As family planning work was growing, the Department of Family Planning was created in 1966 and an extended research programme was undertaken.

Fourth Five Year Plan (1969–74): It was during the fourth Plan that numerical targets were laid out. For reducing the crude birth rate (CBR), sterilization became the major plank of the family planning strategy. This received an impetus from the Medical Termination of Pregnancy Act of 1971. An outlay of ₹330 crore was made for the family planning programme, and the actual expenditure was ₹288.43 crore.

Fifth Five Year Plan (1974–78): The NFPP was further reoriented during the fifth Plan. The thrust was on providing minimum public health facilities, integrated with family planning and nutrition for children and expectant and lactating mothers. During 1974–78, a sum of ₹408.98 crore was spent on the NFPP, and it received an enormous boost from the government in 1976 with the announcement of the National Population Policy.

The main objectives of the National Population Policy 1976 were the following:

- Raising of the minimum legal age for marriage.
- Enhancement of monetary incentives to acceptors and motivators of sterilization.
- Central assistance to states for family planning work.
- Introduction of compulsory measures and disincentives, left to the discretion of state governments.

In 1977, however, after the traumatic phase of the Emergency, during which sterilization was forcibly and indiscriminately done among the population, family planning became a dirty word and these issues were reconsidered. The government reiterated the voluntary basis of family planning, and the NFPP was renamed as the National Family Welfare Planning Programme (NFWP), adding to family planning the important component of maternal and child health (MCH). Emphasis was also laid on women's education, population education, a multi-media motivational approach and involvement of voluntary agencies.

Sixth Five Year Plan (1980–85): It was observed that the high rates of mortality, in general, and the very high infant mortality rates (IMR), in particular, were inhibiting acceptance of family planning and creating a psychological barrier against the programme. The Working Group on Population Policy recommended reduction of the Net Reproduction Rate (NRR) to fulfil the country's long-term demographic goals. During the sixth Plan, the NFWP was closely linked with socio-economic development. The Working Group reported:

> Population policy and the general development strategy are two sides of the same coin. Uncontrolled growth of population has profound implications for the development plans and concomitant problem of food supply, nutrition, and employment and above all for the essential dimensions of quality of life ... All development activity which ensures fulfilment of a desirable quality of life including comprehensive and distributive health policy which in turn brings down fertility should be emphasized. (Government of India, 1980)[21]

---

21 Chapter 19, 'The Lineaments of Population Policy in India: Women and Family Planning' (2017). United Kingdom: Taylor & Francis.

During the sixth Five Year Plan, an allocation of ₹10 crore was made for the family welfare sector.

Seventh Five Year Plan (1985–90): The seventh Plan (outlay ₹32.56 crore) provided for more media publicity, interpersonal communication and designing of programmes with positive messages. More effective coordination at central, state, district, PHC and sub-centre levels was the other major concern. FWP was to be linked with other sectors such as MCH, health education, agriculture and poverty amelioration.

The Plan analysed the shortfall in achievements during the sixth Plan. Some of the reasons identified for the shortfall were as follows:

- Lack of infrastructure facilities.
- Relatively high targets.
- Less than optimal use of available resources.
- Political, social, economic and cultural constraints.

To achieve the objectives of family welfare planning as stipulated under the sixth Plan, some specific strategies were evolved, that different plans were drawn up and adopted according to the requirement of states, the sterilization levels to be achieved by special drives and camps, the efforts required to mobilize and improve implementation relating to IUDs and oral pill and conventional contraceptive users, and especially the need to educate people on the benefits of late marriage and its social enforcement.

Eighth Five Year Plan (1992–97): The fast rate of population growth required the economy to grow faster – and this was an important cornerstone of the eighth Plan. Containing the population growth was accepted by the national planners as one of the six most important objectives of the eighth Plan, with the aim of reducing the birth rate from 29.9 per thousand in 1990 to 26 per thousand by 1997.

A committee of the National Development Council (NDC) on Population was set up in 1992, and it provided strategies for achievement of the goals of the Eighth Plan. One of the most important inputs of NDC was to make the family welfare plan successful with greater involvement of the people in population control and family planning programmes through the panchayati raj system, as envisaged in the Constitution (Seventy-Second Amendment) Bill 1991. The programme would become one of 'people's operation with government cooperation'[22]. It also emphasized the involvement of voluntary organizations and the community in improving the family planning programme. Greater use of the mass media was to be made, to disseminate the message of family planning to the remotest corners of the country. To fulfil the objectives underlying family welfare planning, the eighth Plan provided for an outlay of ₹6,500 crore.

Ninth Five Year Plan (1998–2002): Provisions were made in the Ninth Plan for a three-tier system consisting of primary, secondary and tertiary care facilities with adequate referral linkages[23] to essential health and family welfare services for the entire population (outlay, ₹15.12 crore). The objectives of the ninth Plan were: reduction in the population growth rate by meeting all the felt need for contraception, and reduction of infant and maternal morbidity and mortality.

Initiatives were taken under this Plan to improve access to family planning services, reduce the number of unwanted pregnancies, to cater to the demand for medical termination of pregnancy and improve access to safe abortion services by trained physicians. Other

---

22 Eighth Five Year Plan (Vol-2), Chapter 12, 'Health and Family Welfare', Section 12.5.3 point no (iv), https://niti.gov.in/planningcommission.gov.in/docs/plans/planrel/fiveyr/default.html.

23 Ninth Five Year Plan (Vol. 2), niti.gov.in, https://niti.gov.in/planningcommission.gov.in/docs/plans/planrel/fiveyr/9th/vol2/v2c3-4.htm

initiatives included increasing awareness about institutional delivery. The Ministry of Health and Family Welfare initiated steps to re-popularize vasectomy by addressing the concerns and perceived convenience/inconvenience among men and by introducing newer techniques.[24] The involving of men in planned parenthood was given much consideration. The Department abolished the system of centrally determined method-specific targets for family planning; the states were asked to undertake PHC-based need assessment and to attempt to meet all the felt need for contraception. *However, it is doubtful that this terminal method gained any substantial popularity among men, particularly among Muslim men.*

Tenth Five Year Plan (2002–07): The tenth Plan clearly articulated that 20 per cent of the current population growth was due to the unmet need for contraception and a further 20 per cent due to high fertility demand caused by high under-five mortality. Thus, reduction in the IMR was likely to contribute to a lower desire for fertility.

During this Plan, funds were provided by the central government to state governments for initiation of programmes for family welfare. New initiatives, like the 'centrally sponsored schemes' and Centre Sector Scheme (outlay ₹27.13 crore), were made.

The NDC Sub-Committee on Population recommended that there should be a paradigm shift in the NFWP, and in some major areas of the country the focus was predominantly on women-centred programmes to meeting the healthcare needs of the family, with an emphasis on involving men in planned parenthood.[25] The NFWP was to cater to a wider spectrum of healthcare needs of the

---

24 Ninth Five Year Plan (Vol. 2), Chapter 3, 'Family Welfare', Section 3.5.39, https://niti.gov.in/planningcommission.gov.in/docs/plans/planrel/fiveyr/default.html .

25 Tenth Five Year Plan, Chapter 2.10, 'Family Welfare', 166, 167, https://niti.gov.in/planningcommission.gov.in/docs/plans/planrel/fiveyr/10th/volume2/v2_ch2_10.pdf.

population – including MCH care, contraceptive care, management of gynaecological problems, and improved quality of services.[26]

The involvement of panchayati raj institutions and NGOs was one of the major initiatives taken during this time. This was to infuse and raise awareness about contraceptives and their benefits among the people. Apparently, *these schemes did manage to find their way among eligible couples, including Muslim couples.*

Eleventh Five Year Plan (2007–12): The eleventh Plan envisaged integration of health and family welfare programmes at the national, state and district levels. During the eleventh Plan, renewed efforts were made to provide need-based and integrated health and family welfare services, improvement of service coverage, and promotion of community participation. There was an urgent need to increase the involvement of civil society organizations (CSOs), voluntary organizations (VOs), non-governmental organizations (NGOs) and the private sector in the delivery of family planning services, especially in areas where the public sector was weak. An NGO, Janani, set up a network of more than 21,000 'Titli (butterfly) Centres' for this purpose. The Titli Centres were situated in villages and run by rural health practitioners (RHPs) trained to provide family planning counselling and sell non-clinical contraceptives.[27]

At this stage, it is worth noting that while calculated efforts were made to involve CSOs, VOs and NGOs to achieve the country's family planning goals, *no deliberate attempts were made to rope in the Muslim clergy for this important programme, even in Muslim-concentration areas.*

---

26 Tenth Five Year Plan, Chapter 2.10, 'Family Welfare', 172, https://niti.gov.in/planningcommission.gov.in/docs/plans/planrel/fiveyr/10th/volume2/v2_ch2_10.pdf.

27 Eleventh Five Year Plan, Chapter 3, 'Health and Family Welfare and Ayush', 95, https://niti.gov.in/planningcommission.gov.in/docs/plans/planrel/fiveyr/11th/11_v2/11v2_ch3.pdf.

Twelfth Five Year Plan (2012–17): The twelfth Plan strategies for population stabilization were to push up the age of marriage, to increase availability of a menu of contraceptives, to delay the first child and increase the gap between children. Availability of temporary contraceptives – both condoms and oral pills – is best made through social marketing, supplemented by easy availability of the products at public facilities. The ASHA programme as the main vehicle of social marketing was rolled out in a major way for the sale of sanitary pads and contraceptives.

Under the twelfth Plan, meeting the unmet need for contraception and reduction in under-five mortality were accorded high priority. Under this Plan, National Urban Health Mission (NUHM) and NRHM were to be separate programmes, with their possible merger in the thirteenth Plan period or later. The budget allocation for NUHM under the twelfth Plan period was envisaged at approximately ₹15,143 crore.

An appraisal of NRHM and NUHM reveals that they make for a well-thought-out health service programme. *However, they hardly paid the much-needed selective attention required by the educationally and economically backward segments of the population who were less inclined towards small-family norms and family planning.*

The delivery system

As early as in 1946, the Health Survey and Development Committee of Government of India, headed by Sir Joseph Bhore, recommended the establishment of a structured and comprehensive health service in the country with sound primary healthcare infrastructure.[28] However,

---

28 Ninth Five Year Plan (Vol. 2), Chapter 3, 'Human and Social Development', Section 3.4.1, https://niti.gov.in/planningcommission. gov.in/docs/plans/planrel/fiveyr/default.html.

on account of several political and administrative reasons, no action on the report took place – until 1952. Ever since, both state and central governments have pressed hard to extend and intensify the family welfare planning delivery system. Over the years, it has been continuously evolving, and one important initiative in this direction is the Pradhan Mantri Swasthya Suraksha Yojana (PMSSY, 2003)

Have the target population groups, especially Muslim eligible couples, been adequately exposed to these policies and programme initiatives? No effort seems to have been made to address this critical matter, despite a lot of verbal discourse on it.

The PMSSY was launched with the main objective of correcting the imbalances in the availability of affordable and reliable tertiary-level healthcare in the country, in general, and to augment facilities for quality medical education in the under-served states in particular. The Twelfth Five Year Plan recommended strengthening the existing infrastructure at the district level to ensure access to quality healthcare for all, and to streamline the referral system. In this regard, public-private partnership (PPP) was recommended as one of the instrumentalities with which to improve or reform the health of the population.[29]

It is estimated that presently public funding accounts for only 22 per cent of the total expenses towards healthcare in India.[30] Most of the remaining 78 per cent of private expenditure consists of out-of-pocket expenses. The total public expenditure on health has been around 1.28 per cent of the GDP in 2017–18.[31] This is leading to a high health-cost burden on the people, especially in the lower

---

29 'Report of the Working Group on Tertiary Care Institutions for 12th Five Year Plan (2012–2017)', http://www.pmssy-mohfw.nic.in/files/ WG_2tertiary.pdf.

30 http://www.pmssy-mohfw.nic.in/

31 Himani Chandna, 'At 1.28% of GDP, India's expenditure on health is still low although higher than before', The Print, 31 October 2019,, https://theprint.in/health/at-1-28-gdp-india-expenditure-on-

economic strata. It is estimated that 11.88 million households fall below the poverty line every year because of health-related expenses, as healthcare costs have been spiralling upwards.[32]

Under the ninth Plan, a healthcare delivery system aimed at providing basic health and family welfare services to the population within 1 km to 3 kms of their residence was to be made available by establishing Urban Health and Family Welfare Centres manned by medical and para-medical persons.[33]

Again, under the Plan, the Janani Shishu Suraksha Karyakaram (JSSK) was to be further strengthened and would guarantee free services, with no out-of-pocket expenditures, for all pregnant women admitted for delivery in public institutions and all sick newborns. This would include referral services, and transport from and drop back home. Complications in the antenatal and postnatal periods were also to be covered. The emphasis on promoting institutional delivery would continue, but in areas where home delivery could not be avoided due to the difficult terrain or for cultural reasons, the facility of Auxiliary Nurse and Midwife (ANM)-assisted home delivery was also to be developed. Safety and quality in abortion services would be included as part of the standards for provision of Reproductive Child Health (RCH) services.[34]

The success of the family planning programme would be largely dependent on these services, as rightly envisaged. However, there is

---

health-still-low-although-higher-than-before/313702/, accessed on 9 October 2020.

32 (India Health Report 2008) 'Report of the Working Group on Tertiary Care Institutions for 12 Five Year Plan (2012–2017)'.

33 Ninth Five-Year Plan (Vol. 2), Chapter 3, 'Human and Social Development', Section 3.4.34.

34 'Report of the Working Group on National Rural Health Mission (NRHM) for Twelfth Five Year Plan (2012–2017)', https://niti.gov.in/planningcommission.gov.in/docs/aboutus/committee/wrkgrp12/health/WG_1NRHM.pdf.

no evidence to suggest that efforts were made to find out whether these services were adequately reaching those who needed them most, the ones who were lagging behind in the family planning programme – notably, the Muslims.

It is important to note that the health and family planning policies in the country *have seldom focused on districts with high Muslim populations – which obviously needed more attention – apparently because it is a politically sensitive matter.* On the contrary, media and survey reports are aplenty that *family planning functionaries at the grassroots level in Muslim-concentration localities use the reluctance of Muslim couples to adopt family planning methods as an excuse for their own under-performance or even non-performance. They are, however, all too ready to put the burden of population explosion entirely on the Muslims. They have also unquestioningly believed the Muslims when they mentioned Islam as the reason for their reluctance to practise family planning.*

It is clear that the staff have not been trained and oriented to deal with difficult groups. A specific problem needs a specific solution. Unless the staff are trained to identify this particular *problem of Muslim reluctance to adopt family planning methods,* the reasons thereof, and the possible strategies to convert Muslim resistance into acceptance, they cannot deal with the problem effectively.

It may be restated that India has had a population policy and population-control strategies for a long time now. While there was no national two-child policy as of early 2020, there were local laws and laws specific to states.[35] The two-child norm is one of India's target-oriented family-size control policies that encouraged parents to limit their families to two children and created disadvantages for families with more than two children. The disadvantages included

---

35   Vanessa Page, 'Child Policy in India: One-Child Policy, Two-Child Policy, or No Policy?', 6 February 2020, https://www.investopedia.com/articles/personal-finance/051415/indias-twochild-policy.asp, accessed 1 October 2020.

disqualification from panchayat council positions and denial of certain public services and government welfare programmes, including maternal and child health programmes.[36]

There is no such evidence to vouch for the effectiveness of the two-child norm. Few states such as Bihar have failed to reduce fertility rates to the desired level even after implementing similar policies. A study, by Nirmala Buch[37], involving five states, that Madhya Pradesh, Andhra Pradesh, Haryana, Odisha and Rajasthan, found that there was an increase in sex-selective and unsafe abortion as a consequence of such policies. Men divorced their wives to contest for local-body elections and families gave up children for adoption to avoid disqualification. There is also no evidence whatsoever to show that larger family sizes are due to reasons other than those determined by economic and social circumstances, including poverty, lack of basic services and governance.

Various combinations of factors, including higher levels of female education, greater employment opportunities and access to a bigger basket of contraceptive choices are, therefore, the primary drivers of population stabilization, health and well-being. While there is compelling evidence from within India, including from states like Kerala, Tamil Nadu and Andhra Pradesh, analysis of global case studies from countries like Indonesia and Bangladesh indicate the importance of investing in education, especially women's education and access to healthcare, to advance family planning and population stabilization.

China, which enforced a one-child policy, had to abort it after finding itself in the midst of a population crisis. In Sri Lanka, the

---

36 'Nine Facts about "Two Child Norm"', 12 July 2017, https://pinkwhalehealthcare.com/blog/9-facts-about-two-child-norm/, accessed on 16 October 2020.

37 Nirmala Buch, 'Law of Two-Child Norm in Panchayats: Implications, Consequences and Experiences', *Economic and Political Weekly* 40, no. 24 (2005): 2421–29.

fertility rates stabilized by simply increasing the age of marriage, a move made more effective by ensuring education of girls. Increased access to education, economic and other development opportunities results in a natural fertility decline.[38]

With the changing demographic scenario, these policies have from time to time undergone changes and modifications. However, the gut issue is this: have all these policy initiatives and augmentation of institutional services made healthcare accessible to the common man, to rural and tribal population groups, and to educationally and economically backward communities, including the second largest community in India, the Muslims? These and other similar issues are proposed to be analysed in the sections that follow.

---

38 'Towards Population Stabilization in India: Why Stringent Control Measures Do Not Work, #PeopleBeforeNumbers', https://kractivist. org/towards-population-stabilisation-in-india-why-stringent-control-measures-do-not-work-peoplebeforenumbers/, accessed on 2 October 2020.

2
Population Growth and Family Planning

COMPARATIVE fertility levels and contraceptive use among Muslims and non-Muslims are a topic highly debated among academicians, policymakers and politicians in India. On occasion, when religion is politicized, the growth differentials between religious communities are highlighted. Debates on Muslim and Hindu population growth or on family planning by individual communities are mostly driven by ideological bias and are wanting in strong supporting empirical evidence. Most of the cited evidence is often based on small illustrations and non-representative data.

This chapter seeks to present evidence on the current use of family planning among different religious communities in India. Data from various sources are used here as evidence to understand population growth in different communities. This chapter has used data from the Census of India, ORG Surveys, National Family Health Surveys and other research studies. Differentials in population growth among religious communities are the most critical indicator for analysis of population dynamics. An effort is made in this chapter to analyse the trends in family planning practices, both nationally and among different communities.

It is imperative to assess the underlying factors in the current situation of population growth and low practice of contraception among different communities with objectivity and a microscopic lens. Here, the endeavour is not to defend a particular scenario but to bring out the factual situation with respect to current levels of fertility, practice of contraception among different communities, and the reasons thereof.

While the National Health Policy (1983)[1] targeted a replacement level of 2.1 in TFR by the year 2000, the National Population Policy 2000 aimed to achieve replacement level TFR of 2.1 by 2010 (as we have seen in Chapter 1). This policy states that 'the long-term objective is to achieve a stable population by 2045, at a level consistent with the requirements of sustainable economic growth, social development, and environment protection'. The International Conference on Population and Development (ICPD) held in Cairo in 1994 was a landmark event. It marked a 'quantum leap' for population and development policies as it involved a paradigm shift from the earlier emphasis on population control and demography to sustainable development. At the same time, the conference introduced a 'life cycle approach' and underscored the importance of reproductive health and reproductive rights. Asserting that people mattered more than numbers, the conference urged the world to agree that population is not just about counting people, but about making sure that every person counts.[2]

---

1   https://nhm.gov.in/images/pdf/guidelines/nrhm-guidelines/national_population_policy_2000.pdf. Accessed on 14 December 2020, 'http://www.iapsmgc.org/userfiles/NationalPopulation-Policy2000-2.pdf%20 Accessed%20on%2014.12.2020" http://www.iapsmgc.org/userfiles/NationalPopulation-Policy2000-2.pdf Accessed on 14.12.2020 Accessed on 14.12.2020

2   United Nations, 'Program of Action: Report from the International Conference on Population and Development' (New York, NY: United Nations, 1994).

This shift in thinking led to national-level changes in the policies, approaches and strategies. India announced its first National Population Policy (NPP) in 2000 where NPP adopted the basic philosophy of the ICPD-Programme of Action and focused on improving quality of life as a means to achieve population stabilization. The policy called for a comprehensive approach to population stabilization and called for addressing the social determinants of health, promotion of women's empowerment and education, adoption of a target-free approach, encouragement of community participation and ensuring convergence of service delivery at the community level. Social factors such as age at marriage, age of mother at first birth and education of girls for maternal and infant well-being find prominent place in the policy, along with promotion of a basket of contraceptive choices.

India's population-related policies and family planning programmes have been evolving over time in accordance with the nation's priority. It has also evolved from a population-control centric approach to a reproductive rights-based approach. The latest phase of India's family planning programme is guided by the commitment made by the government of India in London in 2012, and is known as India's 'VISION FP 2020'. Subsequent to the London Summit on Family Planning, India launched its call to action for child survival and development in February 2013, with the comprehensive Reproductive, Maternal, Newborn, Child and Adolescent Health (RMNCH+A) strategy. The major transition in approach is that family planning goes beyond being a simple strategy for achieving population stabilization and is now integrated as a critical intervention to reduce maternal and child mortality. However, under India's national FP 2020 goals, the current policy has increased focus on spacing contraceptive services without disturbing the sterilization pie. The emphasis is on voluntary adoption of family planning, based on the felt need of the community, and on ensuring that couples have children by choice, not by chance[3].

---

3   India's 'VISION FP 2020', 2014.

**Key features of the National Population Policy
2000 framework[4]**

- Client-centric approach and a focus on equitable healthcare.
- Accessible, affordable and quality healthcare for the rural population, especially the vulnerable groups.
- Establishing a fully functional, community-owned, decentralized health delivery system with inter-sectoral convergence at all levels.
- 'Continuum of care' approach, which includes integrated service delivery at various life stages of the citizen.
- Informed choice and voluntarism, wherein eligible couples may select contraceptive methods of their choice.
- Continuation of the target-free approach in administering family planning services.

Population Growth and Transition

Changes in the religion-wise break-up of the population from one census to the next have emerged as a prominent concern among certain sections who have been arguing that the Muslim population will supersede the current majority status of Hindus in India within a short time period in the future. There has been propaganda saying that Muslims will outnumber Hindus by 2035 or so and become the majority in India.[5]

How a country's population changes over time is termed as demographic transition. It helps to understand and analyse the changes in the size of the population and its segments. In the current context, let us analyse here the long-term changes in the size and

---

4   National Population Policy, Ministry of Health and Family Welfare. New Delhi: GOI; 2000.

5   Qamar Waheed Naqvi, 'The Myth of the Muslim Population Bomb', *Tehelka*, 13 February 2015, http://old.tehelka.com/the-myth-of-the-muslim-population-bomb/, accessed on 5 October 2020.

age composition of the population by religious community. The most suitable indicator would be to analyse Census of India data to study the decadal growth rate of the population in India. It gives an overview of the percentage of population growth in a particular decade. The Census collects population figures at an interval of a decade in India to obtain the decadal population growth.

Figure 2.1 demonstrates the demographic transition of a country and shows the typical path of population growth over a long period of time. According to the principle of demographic transition, no country will have its population growing forever, and so too it is for India. With socio-economic advancement, a country's birth and death rates decline continuously, reaching a point where growth becomes stable. To summarize it all, every country will reach a situation of population stability though the pace of stabilization may differ from country to country.

Figure 2.1: Diagram showing a typical demographic transition

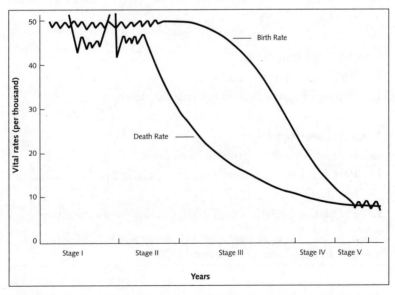

Source: http://papp.iussp.org/sessions/papp101_s01/PAPP101_s01_090_010. html. Accessed on 14 December 2020.

Demographic Transition: A transition from high birth and death rates to low birth and death rates. Decline in birth rates is usually preceded by decline in death rates, resulting in population growth during the transition period.

There are four stages in the classical demographic transition model:

Stage 1: Pre-transition
A. Characterized by high birth rates and high fluctuating death rates.
B. Population growth kept low by Malthusian 'preventative' (late age at marriage) and 'positive' (famine, war, pestilence) checks.

Stage 2: Early transition
C. During the early stages of the transition, the death rate begins to fall.
D. As birth rates remain high, the population starts to grow rapidly.

Stage 3: Late transition
E. Birth rates start to decline.
F. Population growth is set towards deceleration.

Stage 4: Post-transition
G. Rate of population growth decelerates.
H. Post-transitional societies are characterized by low birth and low death rates.
I. Population growth is negligible, or even enters a decline.

Source: http://papp.iussp.org/sessions/papp101_s01/PAPP101_ s01_090_010.html, accessed on 22 April 2020.

Figure 2.2: Demographic transition in India, 1901–2012

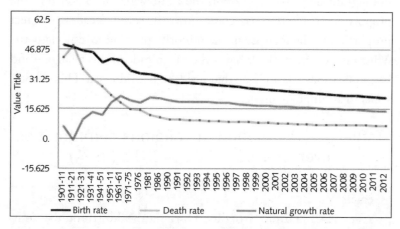

Source: Office of the Registrar General, India; Ministry of Home Affairs, Government of India

In terms of religious composition, Hindus constituted 79.8 per cent, Muslims 14.2 per cent, Christians 2.3 per cent, and others (such as Sikhs, Jains and Buddhists) 2.08 per cent of the population in the latest India Census of 2011. A shift is observed from the previous Census figures in the proportion of Hindus and Muslims, which has led to the controversy that Muslims are growing at much faster pace than Hindus in India. In 1951, the religious composition was different in the country; Hindus were at 84.1 per cent, Muslims at 9.8 per cent, Christians at 2 per cent, and others at 1.74 per cent.

The minorities together constituted 20.2 per cent of the population in 2011, up from 15 per cent in 1951.

Table 2.1 indicates that the share of Hindus in India's population has come down gradually, from 84.1 per cent in 1951 to 79.8 per cent in 2011 – a decline of about 4.3 percentage points in last six decades. The proportion of Muslims has gone up to 14.2 per cent in 2011 from 9.9 per cent in 1951 – an increase of about 4 percentage points.

The share of Sikhs has gone up too. Among the minorities, it is only the Buddhists whose share in the population has gone down, though not significantly. To this extent, the right-wing allegation that the proportion of Hindus has come down in seven decades in direct proportion to the increase in the minority population, especially the Muslims, is correct. But what is the magnitude of this change – and its implications – is an issue that needs to be addressed. This chapter seeks to attempt an answer.

Table 2.1: Population of religious communities over Censuses 1951–2011 (in %)

Census Year	All	Hindu	Muslim	Christian	Sikh	Buddhist	Jain
1951	100	84.1	9.8	2	1	0.74	0
1961	100	83.4	10.7	2.4	1.8	0.5	0.4
1971	100	82.7	11.2	2.6	1.9	0.5	0.4
1981	100	82.3	11.7	2.4	1.9	0.5	0.4
1991	100	81.5	12.6	2.3	1.9	0.4	0.4
2001	100	80.5	13.4	2.3	1.9	0.4	0.7
2011	100	79.8	14.2	2.3	1.7	0.7	0.4

Source: Census of India, 2011.

The decadal population growth narrative of India in Table 2.1 is fairly in tune with the classical theory of demographic transition, with a late beginning and slower pace.

Muslims in India number about 172.2 million, that 14.2 per cent of the total population of India (Table 2.2). According to Census 2011, the population growth rate of various religious groups has come down in the last decade (2001–2011). The Hindu population growth rate slowed, from 19.92 per cent (1991–2001) to 16.76 per cent (2001–2011), while the decline in the Muslim population growth rate was even sharper, from 29.52 per cent to 24.6 per cent (Table 2.2).

Through most of the nineteenth century, India witnessed a fluctuating but, ultimately, a more or less stagnant growth of population, and this trend continued into the twentieth century until 1921. Thereafter, the country passed through all the successive phases of demographic transition. The third phase of rapid growth of population transition is considered to be from 1951 to 1981. The office of the registrar general has predicted that India is ready to enter the fourth phase, usually characterized by rapidly declining fertility, by around 2026. Since 1951, the country's total population has grown from 361 million to 1,210 million, a growth of nearly three and a half times, cutting across all communities.

The inter-Census data show that population growth for Muslims has been consistently higher than for Hindus. Significantly, the percentage decadal growth since 1981 has registered a decline for the Hindu population (Figure 2.3). A similar declining trend in Muslim growth has also begun since 1991, a decade later. With the growth rate for both Hindus and Muslims continuing to slow, population growth for both communities will stabilize to the replacement level of fertility in the near future. This, in fact, is already happening (Figure 2.4). From 1991 to 2001, the Indian Muslim population grew by 29.3 per cent, however, in the subsequent decade it grew by 24.4 per cent – a fall, therefore, of almost 5 percentage points in comparison to the corresponding 1.5 percentage point fall in the Hindu population. The decadal growth data of the last decade indicate that Muslim population growth has started on a trajectory of gradual decline, as it did for the Hindus.

The crucial question is – how long will this phase extend and when will India achieve a stable population for all its communities? But it is important to note that even if a population attains replacement level fertility, it does not mean that the size of population will stabilize immediately. The acceleration in population growth will persist because of the large number of couples still in the reproductive age bracket in that population.

Table 2.2: Hindu and Muslim decadal population growth since 1951

Year	Muslim population (in 000s)	Absolute increase in Muslim Population (in 000s)	% Increase in Muslim Population	Hindu population (in 000s)	Absolute increase in Hindu population (in 000s)	% Increase in Hindu population	Difference in increase in PP
1951	35,856			3,03,676			
1961	46,941	11,085	30.9%	3,66,528	3,66,528	20.7%	10.2%
1971	61,418	14,477	30.8%	4,53,292	86,764	23.7%	7.2%
1981*	80,286	18,868	30.7%	5,62,389	1,09,097	24.1%	6.7%
1991**	1,06,715	26,429	32.9%	6,90,060	1,27,671	22.7%	10.2%
2001	1,38,188	31,473	29.5%	8,27,579	1,37,519	19.9%	9.6%
2011	1,72,245	34,057	24.6%	9,80,378	1,52,799	18.5%	6.2%

Source: Census of India
1981 Census: *Parts of Assam were not included in the 1981 Census data due to violence in some districts
1991 Census: **Jammu and Kashmir was not included in the 1991 Census data because of militant activity in the state

Figure 2.3: Decadal growth rate of Hindus since 1961 (in millions)

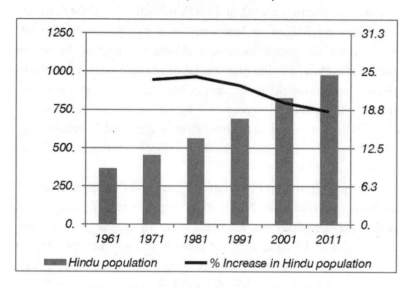

Figure 2.4: Decadal growth rate of Muslims since 1961 (in millions)

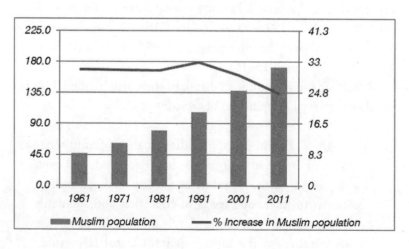

Signs of change in fertility

Population growth is a result of three factors – fertility, child mortality and migration. Migration, however, does not play an important role in changing the population size of Muslims except in the border states. Therefore, fertility and mortality are the major contributors to population growth. Technically, when mortality is at a low level then fertility plays a primary role in impacting population growth.

TFR is a standard demographic indicator used internationally. It is the most widely used fertility measure in programme-impact evaluations.

Data for Hindus and Muslims for the period 1992–93 to 2015–16 from four rounds of NFHS show that the total fertility rate is decreasing across all the religions, more so among the Muslims (Figure 2.4 and Figure 2.5). As a result, the gap between Hindu and Muslim fertility has narrowed during the period, dropping from 1.1 percentage points in 1992–93 to 0.5 percentage points in 2015–16 (Figure 2.6). It may be further observed from Figure 2.5 that fertility decline among Muslims was relatively higher than among Hindus during the period. Fertility among Muslims fell by 40.8 per cent (from 4.41 in 1992–93 to 2.61 in 2015–16). The drop in TFR among Hindus over the same period was 35.5 per cent (from 3.3 in 1992–93 to 2.13 in 2015–16).

R.B. Bhagat and Purujit Praharaj, in their article titled 'Hindu-Muslim Fertility Differentials', observed:

> Although a Hindu–Muslim differential in fertility has persisted in India, it is no more than one child, and even this gap is not likely to endure as fertility among Muslims declines with increasing levels of education and standards of living. While the lower level of contraceptive use among Muslims is the most important factor responsible

for the fertility differentials, the use of contraceptives has increased faster among Muslims in recent times. However, the relatively higher fertility among Muslims cannot be understood independent of its socio-economic and political contexts.[6]

Replacement Level Fertility

The level of fertility where a couple is replaced by their offspring. The total fertility rate of level 2.1 children per woman in a population is generally taken as replacement level fertility. Replacement level fertility is the precondition for population stabilization (zero growth of population). However, a population attaining replacement level fertility does not mean that the size of population stabilizes immediately. This takes quite some time, and the reason is because of population momentum. In other words, acceleration in population growth persists because of a larger proportion of existing couples in the reproductive age range in that population.

The trend in the last four rounds of NFHS data (Figure 2.5) clearly shows that the process of fertility transition is in progress steadily, as fertility for all religious groups is much lower than the replacement level fertility (TFR – 2.1). It is also important to recognize that Muslim fertility is falling in line with Hindu fertility and that the difference is narrowing. This would lead to a convergence in fertility levels for all religious communities in the long run, resulting in population stabilization in every community and in the country as a whole.

---

6   R.B. Bhagat and Purujit Praharaj, 'Hindu-Muslim Fertility Differentials', *Economic and Political Weekly*, 40 no. 5 (2005): 417; 411–18.

Figure 2.5: Trends in total fertility rate by religion over four rounds of NFHS

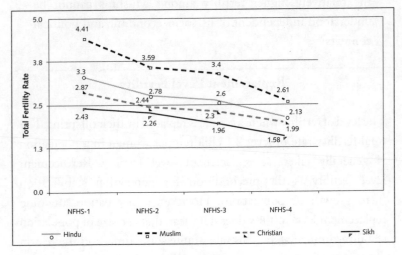

Source: NFHS-1, NFHS-2, NFHS-3, NFHS-4

Figure 2.6: Reducing gap in total fertility rate by religion over four rounds of NFHS

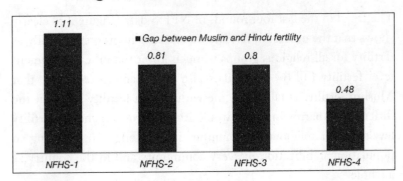

Source: NFHS-1, NFHS-2, NFHS-3, NFHS-4

Conditions influencing birth rate

Morgan et al, (2002)[7] found that Hindu-Muslim fertility differentials arise from localized conditions and thus vary widely from one area to the other. There is clear evidence that region rather than religion was more important in influencing fertility levels in India.

It is critical to note that fertility among a religious community varies substantially across states. Fertility among Hindus was much higher in Uttar Pradesh (2.67) than among Muslims in Tamil Nadu (1.74).

In general, India has large inter-state variations in fertility, ranging from the lowest TFR of 1.56 in Kerala to the highest TFR of 3.41 in Bihar, among the large states (Table 3). Similarly, TFR among Muslims varied from 1.74 in Tamil Nadu to nearly 4.15 in Haryana in 2015–16. Further, Muslim fertility in all the four southern states – Kerala (2.46), Karnataka (2.84), Tamil Nadu (2.57) and undivided Andhra Pradesh (2.53) – is much lower than Hindu fertility in any of the three largest states, namely, Uttar Pradesh (4.76, including Uttaranchal), Madhya Pradesh (3.39, including Chhattisgarh), and Bihar (4.44, including Jharkhand) in northern India.[8] Thus, it can be inferred that if populations of some religions were concentrated in high-fertility regions, they are likely to have high fertility on account of the region factor rather than the religion factor.[9] This suggests that there is no 'Hindu fertility', 'Muslim fertility' or 'Christian fertility' as such.

---

7   S.P. Morgan, S. Stash, H. Smith and K.O. Mason, 'Muslims and Non-Muslim Differences in Female Autonomy and Fertility, Evidence from Four Asian Countries', *Population and Development Review* 28, no. 3 (2002): 515–38.

8   P.M. Kulkarni and M. Alagarajan, 'Population Growth, Fertility, and Religion in India', *Economic and Political Weekly* 40, no. 5 (2005): 405; 403–10.

9   Ibid., 405.

The findings were similar in a study conducted using the 2011 Census data. In areas which have witnessed a considerable decline in fertility, there is hardly any district with very high fertility among Muslims. The notable exceptions are Assam and Haryana.

Besides, even in individual states, there is heterogeneity within a religion.[10] District-level analyses of TFR suggest that in all the districts of Andhra Pradesh and Tamil Nadu, TFR among Muslims has reached or is below the replacement level. Among the smaller states, TFR among Muslims has reached such a level in Sikkim. Besides, TFR among Muslims attained such a level in a significant proportion of districts in Odisha, West Bengal, Uttarakhand, Kerala and Chhattisgarh. In almost all the remaining districts in these states, TFR among Muslims is between 2 and 3, and approaching the replacement level.

In the north-central provinces, TFR is high both among Muslims and Hindus. Muslim TFR is low only in a few districts in these states. In Bihar, there is not a single district with low fertility among Muslims. Also, there are a substantial number of districts in these states where TFR among Muslims is between 2 and 3 and even more than 3. There are also a few pockets (eighteen districts) of very high fertility among Muslims (TFR>4) in Rajasthan, Bihar, Jharkhand and Meghalaya.[11]

In addition to the regional factor, socioeconomic conditions also influence fertility. For example, the literacy rate among Muslim women, which was seen to be quite low in NFHS-3, has improved by 30 per cent in the following ten years, as shown by NFHS-4, outpacing the corresponding rate for most other religions. A study

---

10 Ibid., 405.

11 S. Ghosh, 'Hindu–Muslim Fertility Differentials in India: Indirect Estimation at the District Level from Census 2011', *Indian Journal of Human Development* 12, no. 1 (2018): 37–51.

by Dyson and Moore[12] found that, like Hindus, Muslims are not a homogenous or monolithic group but differ widely in terms of their socioeconomic and demographic behaviour in different regions of the country. There is no such thing as 'Muslim (or for that matter, 'Hindu') family planning behaviour'. Regional factors outweigh religious factors, as Hindu and Muslims show more similarities with each other within regional demographic regimes than they do with co-religionists elsewhere in the subcontinent.[13] Many other studies also concluded that Muslims are closer to Hindus in their socioeconomic and demographic behaviour within each region in the country.[14]

The fertility data by religion in Table 2.3 shows that during the ten years from 2005–06 to 2015–16, fertility rates dipped across all states, among both Muslims and Hindus. During the same period, the Muslim community showed a larger decline in TFR, of 23 per cent (from 3.39 to 2.62) than the Hindus for whom the TFR decline was 18 per cent (from 2.59 to 2.13).

Table 2.3: TFR by religion for all states in 2005–06 and 2015–16

Sr. No.	State	NFHS-3		NFHS-4	
		Hindus	Muslims	Hindus	Muslims
1	Andhra Pradesh	1.79	1.89	1.80	2.00
2	Arunachal Pradesh	2.77	3.19	2.02	2.69

---

12 T. Dyson and M. Moore, 'On Kinship Structure, Female Autonomy, and Demographic Behaviour in India', *Population and Development Review* 9 (1983): 35–60.

13 Ibid.

14 R. Jeffery and P. Jeffery, 'Religion and Fertility in India', *Economic and Political Weekly* 35, no. 35 (2000): 3253–59; and P. Jeffery and R. Jeffery, 'A Population Out of Control? Myths about Muslim Fertility in Contemporary India', *World Development* 30, no. 10 (2002): 1805–22.

Sr. No.	State	NFHS-3		NFHS-4	
		Hindus	**Muslims**	**Hindus**	**Muslims**
3	Assam	1.95	3.63	1.84	2.92
4	Bihar	3.86	4.80	3.29	4.11
5	Chhattisgarh	2.64	2.58	1.60	2.11
6	Goa	1.66	2.44	1.47	2.73
7	Gujarat	2.38	2.72	1.98	2.61
8	Haryana	2.44	NA	1.92	4.15
9	Himachal Pradesh	1.93	2.33	1.87	2.45
10	Jammu & Kashmir	2.23	2.52	1.91	2.06
11	Jharkhand	2.96	4.16	2.49	2.92
12	Karnataka	2.08	2.16	1.74	2.11
13	Kerala	1.53	2.45	1.42	1.86
14	Madhya Pradesh	3.16	3.06	2.32	2.47
15	Maharashtra	2.00	2.85	1.82	2.33
16	Manipur	2.35	3.41	2.24	2.59
17	Meghalaya	1.95	3.33	1.49	3.56
18	Mizoram	2.06	Lf	1.43	1.93
19	Nagaland	2.35	7.11	1.71	3.86
20	Odisha	2.35	2.34	2.03	2.00
21	Punjab	2.04	3.22	1.65	2.11
22	Rajasthan	3.15	3.95	2.35	3.06
23	Sikkim	1.98	2.57	1.13	2.31
24	Tamil Nadu	1.78	2.19	1.69	1.74
25	Telangana	NA	NA	1.79	1.86
26	Tripura	2.07	3.48	1.65	1.92
27	Uttarakhand	2.47	3.36	1.92	3.02

Sr. No.	State	NFHS-3		NFHS-4	
		Hindus	Muslims	Hindus	Muslims
28	Uttar Pradesh	3.73	4.33	2.67	3.09
29	West Bengal	1.93	3.14	1.64	2.08
	All India	2.59	3.39	2.13	2.62

Lf indicates low frequency; NA indicates data unavailable.

Source: NFHS-3, NFHS-4

Level and trend of family planning

Some people attribute political motives to the high birth rate among Muslims, as mentioned in Chapter 8. The practice of family planning among the Muslims has been a subject of a lot of debate and speculation for decades, ever since the growth (or explosion) of the Indian population started getting public attention. It did not take very long for the debate to turn into a blame game among communities. In fact, in the absence of a serious and informed analysis, the debate got too distorted and murky.

It is, therefore, important that an objective analysis is made of the level of adoption of family planning among Muslims and how it compares with other religious groups in India. And what is very important is to look at the factors that influence fertility rather than the mere levels of fertility. Many studies have suggested that factors like age at marriage, education, better healthcare, acceptance of family planning measures and socioeconomic conditions are the main reasons behind progress in this regard. John Bongaarts analysed seven proximate determinants of fertility and concluded that four of them – marriage, induced abortion, post-partum infecundability, use and effectiveness of contraception – explain 96 per cent of the variance in fertility levels.[15] Contraceptive use is most commonly cited as the prime factor contributing to religious differentials in fertility.[16]

It is heartening to note that there is a jump of 16.5 percentage points between 1992–93 and 2015–16 (from 40.7 per cent to 57.2 per cent) in 'any contraceptive' use in India. During the same period, India's total fertility rate came down 18.7 per cent, from 2.68 to 2.18. What is particularly noteworthy is that this trend is seen across all religions.

Contraceptive Prevalence Rate

Percentage of women who use any contraceptive method among all women, currently married women, and sexually active unmarried women aged 15–49

Contraceptive prevalence among Muslims was estimated to be 37 per cent in 1998, which is not negligible.[17] In fact, this is higher than the overall prevalence levels in Uttar Pradesh and Bihar. Clearly, while contraceptive acceptance is lower among Muslims than among others, it is still substantial, and growing. Significantly, despite unanimity among Islamic scholars that sterilization is forbidden in Islam, it is quite high among Muslims (20.8 per cent in 2015–16).

The latest available information is the fourth National Family Health Survey 2015–16 (Table 2.4) in India.

---

15 J. Bongaarts, 'The Fertility-Inhibiting Effects of the Intermediate Fertility Variables', *Studies in Family Planning* 13, no. 6/7 (1982): 179–89.

16 Kulkarni and Alagarajan, 'Population Growth, Fertility, and Religion in India'

17 Ibid.

Table 2.4: Use of any method of contraception, NFHS-4 (2015–16)

	Hindu	Muslim	Christian	Sikh	Buddhist	Jain	Others
All India	54.4	45.3	51.2	73.9	67.7	62.0	42.0

Source: NFHS-4 (2015–16)

This table brings out the following scenario:

- Muslims have indeed the lowest level (45.3 per cent) of family planning practice.
- The proportion of Hindus using any kind of contraception (54.4) is lower than that of other minority groups, except Christians (51.2 per cent).
- Minorities other than Muslims have fared rather well.
- The most significant finding is that Hindus and Muslims are not on the opposite ends of the spectrum but are at the same end, with the lowest contraception prevalence, though the gap between the two is undoubtedly wide. This is explained in detail in Chapter 8.

While the population is counted by the Census every ten years, fertility practices are specifically studied by professional surveys. Since 1970, the Operations Research Group (ORG) conducted such surveys every ten years. This was replaced by the National Family Health Survey (NFHS), done by the International Institute of Population Studies (IIPS) from 1992–93 onwards. Both organizations have done three and four rounds of surveys, respectively. These surveys together throw light on the complex issue of fertility behaviour across all communities in all the states of the country over four decades.

Figure 2.7 shows that there was continuing increase in the practice of family planning (any modern method) from 1992-93 (NFHS-1) to 2005-06 (NFHS-3). Significantly, the increase in utilization was higher among Muslims in comparison to Hindus. However, in 2015-16 (NFHS-4) the utilization has decreased in both communities, the decrease being much higher among Hindus (-3.4 percentage points) than among Muslims (-0.4 percentage points).

The data of last five decades show that the trend is persistent. Three consecutive decadal surveys by ORG and, subsequently, four rounds of NFHSs underline the trend of growing acceptance of family planning among Muslims as well as among other religious groups. Between 1971 and 1981, it increased by 8.4 percentage points among Muslims and by 16.9 percentage points among Hindus.

Figure 2.7: Increasing trend of use of any modern method of contraception over last 50 years (in %)

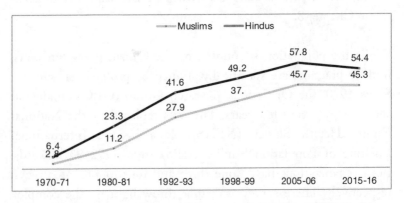

Source: Based on Family Planning Practices in India, Third All India Survey (1988) Vol. II, ORG, Baroda;

Source: NFHS-1, NHFS-2, NHFS-3, NHFS-4

Many recent studies have suggested that the progression of birth control in India follows a peculiar geographical pattern, starting from the coastal areas and moving towards the hinterland, regardless of socioeconomic differentials and religious affiliation.[18] It is noteworthy that adoption of family planning by different communities shows enormous inter-state variations across the country, which has important lessons, as analysed here (Table 2.5).

Table 2.5: Current use of any method of contraception by state, NFHS-4 (2015–16)

Sr. No.	State	Hindus	Muslims
1	Andhra Pradesh	70	61.9
2	Arunachal Pradesh	42.5	NA
3	Assam	53.6	50.1
4	Bihar	26.4	10.8
5	Chhattisgarh	58	54.8
6	Goa	25.1	39.3
7	Gujarat	47.4	40.5
8	Haryana	66.2	25.8
9	Himachal Pradesh	57.3	36.5
10	Jammu & Kashmir	60.4	55.8
11	Jharkhand	45.1	28.3
12	Karnataka	52.9	46.2

18 C.Z. Guilmoto and S. I. Rajan, 'Half a Century of Fertility Transition in Indian Districts, 1951–2001', *Population and Development Review* 27, no. 4 (2001): 713–38.

Sr. No.	State	Hindus	Muslims
13	Kerala	57.7	43.4
14	Madhya Pradesh	51.7	45.2
15	Maharashtra	65.2	58.5
16	Manipur	25.9	24.1
17	Meghalaya	34.7	43.2
18	Mizoram	18.4	NA
19	Nagaland	35.3	24
20	Odisha	57.2	51.6
21	Punjab	75.4	68.1
22	Rajasthan	60.9	46.4
23	Sikkim	46.1	NA
24	Tamil Nadu	53.5	49.3
25	Telangana	58.1	49.6
26	Tripura	64	66.3
27	Uttarakhand	56.2	35.1
28	Uttar Pradesh	46.9	38.3
29	West Bengal	73.6	63.9
	All India	54.4	45.3

Source: NFHS-4; state reports

About religious community-wise practice of contraception, this table reveals interesting pattern:

- No generalization can be made for the country as a whole, since there are wide variations among states – with the ratio of Muslim acceptors ranging from as low as 10 per cent in Bihar to as high as 68.1 per cent in Punjab, 66.3 per cent in Tripura and 63.9 per cent in West Bengal. Similarly, the range for the Hindus varies from 18.4 per cent in Mizoram to 75.4 per cent in Punjab.

- Acceptance of family planning among Muslims is higher in twenty-two states compared to acceptance among Hindus in Bihar. If religion were the factor, Muslims in all states would have been lagging Hindus anywhere.

- The table also shows that Muslims and Hindus in different states show a similar pattern of family planning acceptance. For instance, family planning is abysmally low among both communities in Bihar since their socioeconomic conditions are alike. Similar is the trend in Manipur.

A study by Sriya Iyer found that there is no statistically significant difference between Hindus and Muslims in the effect of religion on contraceptive adoption.[19] Another study of fourteen states for the overall population at the state level found that at the all-India level, this gap has been reduced by 0.4 children per woman between 2001 and 2011. The gap between the two major religions has further narrowed in most states. The reduction is found to be more than one child or very close to one child per woman in the eastern states of West Bengal and Assam, and in Kerala. However, the pace has remained slow in the central provinces, which have relatively higher fertility. The gap between the TFR of Muslims and that of Hindus remained the same in Madhya Pradesh and Gujarat.

---

19 Sriya Iyer, 'Religion and the Decision to Use Contraception in India', *Journal for the Scientific Study of Religion* 41, no. 4 (2002): 711–22, https://doi.org/10.1111/1468-5906.00156.

Thus, though overall convergence of fertility between Hindus and Muslims has been underway, significant regional variations persist since different states and religious groups are at different stages of transition.

In states which have achieved fertility transition during the last decade, reduction of the fertility gap was also faster compared with states in the middle or early stages of fertility transition.[20]

A similar trend can be observed in female sterilization (Table 2.6), which was increasing till the NFHS-3 round but saw a slight dip in NFHS-4 among both Hindus and Muslims. If we compare NFHS-1 to NFHS-4, a higher percentage point increase in female sterilization can be observed for Muslims (44 per cent) than for Hindus (32 per cent), despite the overwhelming religious opinion against it (as explained in detail in Chapter 5).

Table 2.6: Trend of female sterilization over NFHS-1, NHFS-2, NHFS-3, NHFS-4

Community	NFHS-1	NFHS-2	NFHS-3	NFHS-4	% Change NFHS-1 to NFHS-4
Hindu	29	36.2	39.9	38.2	32%
Muslim	14.4	19.6	21.3	20.8	44%

Source: NFHS-1, NHFS-2, NHFS-3, NHFS-4

Trend data of the spacing method shows a very interesting finding: over the twenty-five years between 1991–92, the first round of NFHS, to the fourth round of NFHS held in 2015–16, Muslims showed a much higher rate of acceptance of the spacing method

---

20 Ghosh, 'Hindu–Muslim Fertility Differentials in India', 44.

of contraception than Hindus (Figure 2.9). The level of use of the spacing method was slightly higher among Muslims (13.5 per cent) than among Hindus (12.6 per cent) in 1991–92. However, in 2015–16 use of the spacing method almost doubled, to 24.5 per cent, among Muslims, from 13.5 per cent in 1991–92, while increasing only marginally among Hindus, from 12.6 per cent in 1991–92 to 16.2 per cent in 2015–16.

Figure 2.8: Trend of limiting (sterilization) method by religion

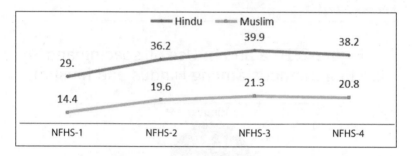

Figure 2.9: Trend of spacing method by religion

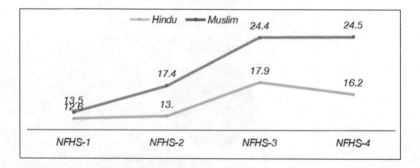

Use of spacing vs limiting method by community

It is by now clearly established that all religious communities in India are using contraceptives, though the rate of use among them varies. Contraceptive use data of NFHS-4 show that among Hindus, a little more than three fourth (78 per cent) were using the limiting method (female sterilization) while it was 55 per cent among Muslims.

Limiting methods: Male and female sterilization
Spacing methods: Injectables, intra-uterine devices (IUDs/PPIUDs), contraceptive pills, implants, female and male condoms, diaphragm, foam/jelly, the standard days method, the lactationalamenorrhoea method, and emergency contraception.

Source: NFHS-4

Figure 2.10 a and b: Use of spacing and limiting methods among Hindus and Muslims

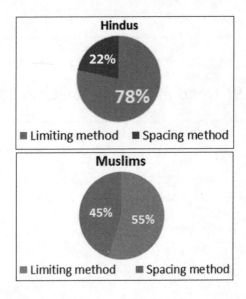

There are studies which have highlighted that Muslims prefer temporary methods to a greater degree than non-Muslims. Muslims who use contraception are more likely to use temporary spacing methods than sterilization.[21] It is noteworthy that the heavy reliance of India's family planning programme over the years on sterilization, considered forbidden in Islam by Muslims, who prefer non-terminal methods, may have contributed to lower acceptance of family planning among Muslims.

A 2004 working paper by Vinod Mishra[22] examines the differentials in fertility and contraceptive use by religion. The analysis reaffirms the finding that the heavy reliance of India's family planning programme on sterilization has discouraged Muslims from family planning since their preference is for temporary methods.

If the demand for spacing is higher among Muslims, efforts should be made to promote better accessibility and availability of spacing methods among the community. The spacing method also has religious sanction in Islam as explained elaborately in Chapter 5. It is interesting to note that the Islamic position coincides with India's current national FP 2020 which too has an increased focus on spacing services in preference to sterilization. This is consistent with the ideal of voluntary adoption of family planning, based on the felt need of the community, and ensuring that couples have children by choice, not by chance (India's 'VISION FP 2020', 2014).[23]

---

21 J. Caldwell and P. Caldwell, 'Is the Asian Family Planning Program Model Suited to Africa?', *Studies in Family Planning* 19, no. 1 (1988): 19–28. doi:10.2307/1966736.

22 Vinod Mishra, 'Muslim/Non-Muslim Differentials in Fertility and Family Planning in India', East-West Center Working Papers, Population and Health Series, No. 112, January 2004.

23 Family planning Division, Ministry of Health and Family Welfare, Government of India. November, 2014. http://www. familyplanning2020.org/sites/default/files/Indias-Vision-FP2020.pdf. Accessed on 14 December 2020.

Unmet need:

The most important factor in analysing family planning behaviour is the desire on the part of men and women to restrict the number of children they will have or, conversely, their resistance to the idea. Those who desire to restrict their family size should be promptly provided the means to do so.

> **Unmet need for family planning:** The proportion of women who (1) are not pregnant and not postpartum amenorrhoeic, are considered fecund, and want to postpone their next birth for two or more years or want to stop childbearing altogether, but are not using a contraceptive method, or (2) have a mistimed or unwanted current pregnancy, or (3) are postpartum amenorrhoeic and their last birth in the last two years was mistimed or unwanted.

Women with unmet need for family planning are those who are sexually active, do not want any more children or want to delay the next child, but are not using any method of contraception, presumably for lack of availability. Unmet need is the gap between women's reproductive intentions and their contraceptive behaviour.[24]

Unmet need is an important indicator for assessing the potential demand for family planning services. The prevailing unmet need for modern family planning services is high among all communities and, indeed, highest among the Muslims, at 16.4 per cent (Table 2.7).

The high demand for family planning generated among Muslims – a difficult task – is itself a great achievement. If we were to meet this demand immediately, the situation would change drastically. We need to analyse why the demand is not being met.

---

24 WHO, 2014, https://www.who.int/reproductivehealth/topics/family_planning/unmet_need_fp/en/

Is it because of lack of services in Muslim areas? Or the reluctance of doctors to go to Muslim areas? Or lack of Muslim staff?

Table 2.7: Current use of contraception and unmet need for contraception by religion, 2015–16

Religious group	% of couples (15–49 yrs) protected by any modern method	% of couples (15–49 yrs) protected by sterilization	% of couples (15–49 yrs) having unmet need for any modern method
Hindu	48.8	38.5	12.4
Muslim	37.9	20.9	16.4
Christian	47.9	40.4	12.9
Sikh	65.4	38.9	6.4
Buddhist	65.4	52.6	11.1
Jain	57.6	39.4	12.1
Total	47.8	36.3	12.9

Source: NFHS-4

Both total fertility and wanted fertility rates are declining continuously across all communities in India. Significantly, unwanted fertility rate has been the highest among Muslims (Table 2.8). NFHS-3 showed that wanted fertility was almost at the same level among Hindus (1.9), Muslims (2.0) and Christians (1.9). The situation has changed after a decade into NFHS-4 among Hindus, whose wanted fertility reduced to 1.7, while among Muslims it remained the same, at 2.0. However, it is logical to conclude that if unwanted fertility is addressed, TFR will reach replacement level for Muslims too. This underscores the need for better delivery of services.

Table 2.8: Total, wanted and unwanted fertility rates by religion

Community	NFHS 2			NFHS 3			NFHS 4		
	TFR	Wanted fertility rate	Unwanted fertility rate	TFR	Wanted fertility rate	Unwanted fertility rate	TFR	Wanted fertility rate	Unwanted fertility rate
Hindu	2.78	2.08	0.7	2.65	1.9	0.75	2.1	1.7	0.4
Muslim	3.59	2.54	1.05	3.09	2	1.09	2.6	2.0	0.6
Christian	2.44	2.07	0.37	2.35	1.9	0.45	2	1.7	0.3
Sikh	2.26	1.62	0.64	1.96	1.5	0.46	1.6	1.4	0.2
Neo/ Buddhist	2.13	1.57	0.56	1.96	1.5	0.46	1.7	1.5	0.2
Jain	1.9	1.7	0.2	2.02	1.7	0.32	1.2	1.0	0.2

Source: NFHS–2, NFHS–3, NFHS–4

The tables given here lead to the following conclusions:

- Muslims are lagging behind all other communities in family planning practices.
- They are, however, neither oblivious of nor averse to family planning and are trying to catch up – and fast.
- Religion does not seem to be a deterrent to acceptance of family planning among Muslims, as evident from the fact that their adoption of family planning is quite high in almost half of the states. If religion were the decisive factor, they would be shunning family planning in all parts of the country. Even opting for sterilization is fairly high in the community, despite the overwhelming religious opinion that it is un-Islamic.
- The fact that Hindus stand second shows that it is not religion holding back Muslims (as well as Hindus) from family planning but other important factors, such as literacy, income, service delivery, as analysed in detail later, in Chapter 3 and Chapter 4.

Justice Sachar's report (2006) on the Muslim community documented the substantial demand from the community for fertility regulation and modern contraceptive methods, and over 20 million couples had already used contraceptives. Figure 2.11 shows that practice of family planning (any method) increased from 41.6 per cent to 54.4 per cent for Hindus, and from 27.9 per cent to 45.3 per cent for Muslims, from 1992-93 to 2015-16. In fact, the pace of acceptance of contraception was faster among Muslims than Hindus. As a result, the gap in practice of family planning between the two communities has narrowed, from 13.7 percentage points in 1992-93 to 9.1 percentage points in 2015-16 (Figure 2.12).

Figure 2.11: Trend of use of any method of family planning by religion (in %)

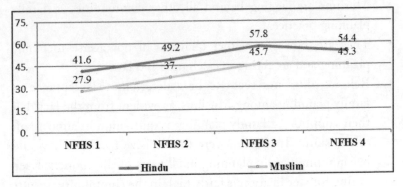

Source: NFHS-1, NFHS-2, NFHS-3, NFHS-4

Figure 2.12: Gap between Hindu and Muslim levels of family planning practice (%)

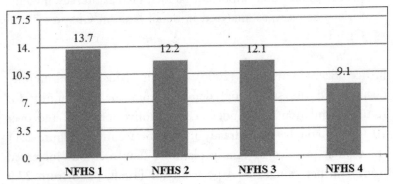

Source: NFHS-1, NFHS-2, NFHS-3, NFHS-4

Table 2.9: Percentage-point change in family planning acceptance (all methods) across NFHS surveys

Community	NFHS-2 to NFHS-1	NFHS-3 to NFHS-2	NHFS-3 to NHFS-4
Hindu	7.6	8.6	-3.4

Community	NFHS-2 to NFHS-1	NFHS-3 to NFHS-2	NHFS-3 to NHFS-4
Muslim	9.3	8.7	-0.4

Source: NFHS-1, NFHS-2, NFHS-3, NFHS-4

Rate of acceptance of sterilization, among both males and females, has increased in all communities (Table 2.9).

Table 2.10: Rate of change in family planning acceptance (sterilization)

Community	NFHS-1	NFHS-2	NFHS-3	NFHS-4	Percentage Point Change NFHS 2 to 1	Percentage Point Change NFHS 3 to 2	Percentage Point Change NFHS 4 to 3	Percentage Points Change NFHS 1 to 4
Hindus	32.7	38.3	32	38.5	5.6	-6.3	6.5	5.8
Muslims	16	20.4	17.5	20.9	4.4	-2.9	3.4	4.9
Christian	33.8	38.6	28	40.4	4.8	-10.6	12.4	6.6
Sikh	32.9	31.8	24.2	38.9	-1.1	-7.6	14.7	6.0
Buddhist	42.2	57.5	48.6	52.6	15.3	-8.9	4	10.4
Jain	36	43.7	34.2	39.4	7.7	-9.5	5.2	3.4
Other	29.1	27.1	13.6	15.1	-2	-13.5	1.5	-14

Source: NFHS-1, NFHS-2, NFHS-3, NFHS-4

Change in attitudes towards family planning

The increase in acceptance of family planning would not have been possible without a change in attitudes on the part of the people towards it. This change was noted among Muslims as much as in other communities, right from the decade of 1971–80.

Table 2.11: Attitude of eligible couples towards family planning: 1970 and 1980 (%)

	Hindus		Muslims		Others	
	1970	1980	1970	1980	1970	1980
Approving of FP	60	83	53	65	67	85
Disapproving of FP	40	16	47	33	33	15

Source: Operations Research Group, Baroda, 'Family Planning Practices in India - Second All India Survey' (1980)

Acceptance and practice of family planning among Muslims has increased sharply, keeping pace with that of their compatriots and, in fact, in many cases it has been much faster among the community than in others.

Reasons for non-adoption of modern contraceptive measures

There are many studies highlighting religious opposition as a frequently cited barrier to adoption of contraceptive measures among Muslims in India.[25] NFHS-2[26] and the subsequent rounds collected information on this aspect by asking people what their reasons for not currently using such measures were. The results presented in Table 2.12 show that only one-tenth of Muslim (12.5 per cent) women reported they did not use contraceptive measures because it was against their religion in 1998-99, and now only 4 per cent of women cited religious reasons for the same.

---

25 Caldwell and Caldwell, 'Is the Asian Family Planning Program Model Suited to Africa?'

26 National Family Health Survey (NFHS-2), 1998–99.

Table 2.12: Reasons for current non-use of contraceptive measures among Hindus and Muslims

Reasons	NFHS-2			NFHS-3			NFHS-4		
	Hindus	Muslim	All Religion	Hindus	Muslim	All Religion	Hindus	Muslim	All Religion
Not having sex	1.36	1.07	1.32	13.76	10.87	13.20	22.51	23.47	22.76
Infrequent sex / husband away	3.81	5.03	3.98	13.56	14.34	13.75	5.86	4.89	5.69
Menopausal/had hysterectomy	8.08	8.40	8.19	9.53	9.04	9.60	14.74	13.02	14.32
Sub-fecund/infecund	4.26	3.36	4.09	3.92	2.84	3.70	6.53	5.78	6.50
Post-partum/breast feeding	7.83	6.26	7.60	22.54	20.72	23.38	11.89	12.46	11.96
Wants as many children as possible/Fatalistic	46.27	35.74	44.64	10.87	11.09	10.79	6.61	8.84	6.99
Opposed to family planning	0.80	1.37	0.87	6.02	5.62	5.98	6.37	5.08	6.15

Reasons	NFHS-2			NFHS-3			NFHS-4		
	Hindus	Muslim	All Religion	Hindus	Muslim	All Religion	Hindus	Muslim	All Religion
Husband opposed	3.46	6.23	3.82	8.89	10.41	9.01	13.26	12.92	13.09
Other people opposed	0.77	0.61	0.72	1.37	0.93	1.27	0.84	0.83	0.83
Against religion	0.25	12.50	2.03	0.41	15.92	3.09	0.66	4.18	1.21
Knows no method	1.37	1.18	1.36	2.03	1.38	2.03	1.16	0.88	1.10
Knows no source	2.67	2.35	2.62	1.99	1.36	1.92	1.12	0.65	1.05
Health concerns	3.48	2.43	3.37	8.39	6.12	7.94	4.34	4.39	4.50
Worry about side effect	3.54	2.55	3.45	7.67	4.73	7.24	4.34	4.39	4.50
Hard to get method	0.45	0.36	0.44	0.58	0.43	0.55	0.74	0.39	0.71
Costs too much	0.94	1.46	1.01	2.53	3.05	2.56	2.67	3.23	2.77
Inconvenient	0.25	0.21	0.26	0.70	0.56	0.66	0.82	0.56	0.80
Afraid of sterilization/body processes	2.92	1.78	2.71	1.17	1.07	1.17	0.84	0.76	0.85

Reasons	Hindus	Muslim	All Religion	Hindus	Muslim	All Religion	Hindus	Muslim	All Religion
	NFHS-2			NFHS-3			NFHS-4		
Does not like the existing methods	3.12	3.19	3.15	3.59	2.00	3.31	4.42	4.90	4.48
Others	2.69	2.86	2.75	8.04	8.73	8.12	5.72	4.84	5.51
Don't know	1.70	1.05	1.62	1.16	1.43	1.23	1.89	2.24	1.93

Source: NFHS-2; NFHS-3; and NFHS-4

Are family planning services equally accessible to Muslims and Hindus?

Studies have claimed that there is a causal relationship between discrimination in access to healthcare and family planning services among religious groups and the differentials in fertility levels among them.[27] Communal tensions between Muslims and Hindus lead to a lower level of confidence and enhance mistrust between the religious groups. This also leads to ghettoization of Muslims. They are not allowed to buy or rent property in Hindu areas. The Muslim clusters are commonly and contemptuously referred to as mini-Pakistan. This prevents Hindu staff from going to these areas for health and other services, not to speak of their avoiding postings in these areas. Conversely, this also inhibits many Muslims, particularly women, from going to health centres where the bulk of staff are from the Hindu community. The only alternative left to the Muslims is to get these services from private healthcare providers.

To assess the situation of accessibility of family planning services across religious communities, the sources of modern contraceptive methods from NFHS-4 data were analysed as a proxy indicator. The data in Table 2.13 clearly indicate the disparity in the sources for different religious communities. More than seven of ten (75 per cent) modern-method contraceptive users obtained their means from the public health sector among Hindus, while only 56 per cent of Muslim users had accessed contraceptive means from the public sector. The rest of the users of modern methods obtained their facilities from the private health sector, including NGOs or trust hospitals/clinics. Only about one out four (24.9 per cent) Hindu users had accessed these services from private doctors, whereas 43 per cent of Muslim users had accessed contraceptive measures from the private sector.

---

27   Iyer, 'Religion and the Decision to Use Contraception in India'.

Table 2.13: Source of modern contraceptive methods by religious community, 2015-16

Religion	Public	Private
Hindu	75.06	24.94
Muslim	56.93	43.07
Sikh	70.62	29.38
Jain	37.69	62.31
Christian	67.82	32.18
Buddhist	78.13	21.87

Source: NFHS-4

Stabilization of the Muslim Population

Taking this falling growth rate into account, the Sachar Committee report has estimated that the Muslim proportion will stabilize at between 17 per cent and 21 per cent of the Indian population by 2100 – a far cry from Muslims becoming the majority in the country.

Professor Mari Bhat's projection of the Hindu-Muslim population by using the cohort component method before release of the Census 2001 data on religion was very close to the Census figures. According to this projection, the population of India will stabilize at about 1.7 billion with 1.27 Hindus and 320 million Muslims, by the year 2101. Also, the TFR of both Hindus and Muslims would converge to 2.1 in 2031–41. However, religion-specific data show that the Hindu population will stabilize four decades ahead of the Muslim population due to the lag in demographic transition. The proportion of Muslims in the total population would be 19 per cent in 2101, up from 13.5 per cent in 2001. It is important to understand that the Muslim population will increase by considerably less numbers than the Hindu population because of its lower base. The net addition up to 2101 is estimated to be 180 million for Muslims and 440 million for Hindus.

Table 2.14: Population projection by religion, all-India

Year	Population (in billions) Hindu	Population (in billions) Muslims	Muslims: Per cent in Total Population	Growth rate of Population (Per cent) Hindu	Growth rate of Population (Per cent) Muslims	Growth rate of Population (Per cent) Difference
1991	0.69	0.11	12.6			
2001	0.83	0.14	13.5	1.81	2.6	0.79
2011	0.95	0.17	14.4	1.41	2.22	0.81
2021	1.06	0.21	15.4	1.04	1.8	0.76
2031	1.14	0.24	16.1	0.76	1.33	0.58
2041	1.21	0.26	16.7	0.56	0.97	0.41
2051	1.25	0.28	17.3	0.34	0.78	0.44
2061	1.27	0.3	17.8	0.19	0.53	0.34
2071	1.28	0.31	18.2	0.06	0.35	0.29
2081	1.27	0.31	18.6	-0.03	0.2	0.23
2091	1.27	0.32	18.8	-0.04	0.1	0.14
2101	1.27	0.32	18.8	-0.01	0.04	0.05

Source: P.N. Bhat and A.F. Zavier (2005). Role of religion in fertility decline: The case of Indian Muslims. Economic and Political Weekly, p. 399.

Conclusions

- It is an absolute myth that Muslims will overtake Hindus in India. That can never happen, considering the trend of the last seven decades.

- The Indian population will stabilize at about 1.7 billion, with 1.27 billion Hindus and 320 million Muslims by the year 2101. Muslims will follow Hindus in population stabilization, but forty years later because of the existing lag.
- The empirical data clearly indicate that Muslims as a religious group in India are not averse to acceptance of family planning. In fact, they are the fastest accepting population segment. They are much ahead in acceptance of spacing methods of family planning than their Hindu counterparts.
- The large unmet need among Muslims clearly calls for policy and programme focus on better availability of and access to family planning services.
- Religion as a factor, though small, should also not be ignored. Religious leaders should be involved in advocacy and programme implementation. India has a great success story in its polio eradication programme among Muslims by engaging with community and religious leaders.

3

Who Chooses Family Planning and Why

IT will be unwise to discuss the issue of acceptance of family planning without reference to the socioeconomic conditions of the communities involved. Evidence is recurrent that the factors that have the maximum influence on family planning practices are socioeconomic and cultural – such as literacy, income, awareness and service delivery. To some extent, the religious factor is an influence too. There is an interplay of other factors too, like work participation by women, which adds to income on the one hand and delays marriage on the other. Both these happen with increase in literacy.

In 1994, the International Conference on Population and Development 1994 (ICPD) came up with the paradigm shift, giving a new and more realistic dimension to resolution of the global population problem in all circumstances. ICPD emphasized that the 'target' approach for controlling population growth has been ineffective and is to be rejected straightaway. In many countries, governments are drifting away from narrow demographic approaches to broader and inclusive population issues, including 'gender equality' and 'reproductive rights and choices' as sustainable solutions to population growth.[1]

The results of the consensus achieved at the ICPD acknowledged that a 'population policy' should reflect the broad consensus that women's education, empowerment and equality are paramount for better sexual reproductive health (SRH) outcomes. Actual access and use of contraceptives may also depend on a husband's willingness to let his wife go out of the house, the messages sent out by mass media, community standards around sex and fertility, or the words of religious or other personalities of authority and prominence.[2]

The cause-and-effect relationship between poverty and lack of access to reproductive health services is complex: whereas the financial costs of health services and supplies can be a barrier to access in some cases, income is linked to numerous social, institutional, political, geographical and economic forces that can also affect an individual's access to reproductive health. The close inter-relationship and two-way linkage between fertility and socioeconomic development was well recognized by the NPP 2000. It starts with the premise that 'the overriding objective of economic and social development is to improve the quality of life of people, to enhance their well-being and to provide them with opportunities and choices to become productive assets in society'. It also states in no uncertain terms that stabilizing the population is not merely a question of making reproductive health services available, accessible and affordable, but also one of increasing the coverage and outreach of primary and

---

1   Report of the International Conference on Population and Development, Cairo, 5-13 September, 1994. https://www.un.org/development/desa/pd/sites/www.un.org.development.desa.pd/files/icpd_en.pdf. Accessed on 14 December 2020.

2   UNFPA, 'Unfinished Business: The Pursuit of Rights and Choices for All', Chapter 8, pp. 124, State of World Population 2019, United Nations Population Fund, 2019 , https://www.unfpa.org/sites/default/files/pub-pdf/UNFPA_PUB_2019_EN_State_of_World_Population.pdf.

secondary education, extending basic amenities like sanitation, safe drinking water and housing, and empowering women with enhanced access to education and employment.

As D. Banerjee of Centre of Social Medicine and Community Health, Jawaharlal Nehru University, has pointed out,

> The decision-makers committed a very fundamental, and almost a fatal mistake in taking a very narrow view of the problem of rapidly rising population growth. They did not realise adequately that for containing population growth, a family planning programme forms merely a component of a wider spectrum which embraces a combination of programmes dealing with different social and economic problems of the country. Population control was considered, rather simplistically, to be a precursor of development in other social and economic fields.[3]

A study by India's ministry of health and family welfare of ninety districts with the highest birth rates also revealed that literacy, especially among women, infant mortality rate, income and age of marriage were the crucial factors influencing family planning acceptance. Religion as a factor for high birth rate was not found relevant, as quite a few of these districts had almost no Muslim population.[4]

There has been significant progress in extending access to services and information about the full range of sexual and reproductive

---

3   D. Banerjee, 1974, 'Family Planning in India – Some Inhibiting Factors', in *Population in India's Development 1947-2000*, ed., Ashish Bose, P.B. Desai, A. Mitra and J.N. Sharma (Delhi: Vikas Publishing House, 1974), 407.

4   Poonam Muttreja and Sanghamitra Singh, 'Family Planning in India: The Way Forward', *Indian Journal of Medical Research* 148, Suppl. 1 (2018): S1–S9, https://www.ncbi.nlm.nih.gov/pmc/articles/PMC6469373/, accessed on 12 June 2020.

health and rights in India. However, the progress has been uneven, and inequalities stick around at the level of communities, districts and states. These inequalities are severely influenced by education levels, income inequality, quality and reach of services and health systems, social and cultural norms, people's exposure to sexual education, and laws and policies. Let us, therefore, first look at these factors, starting with literacy, which is at the heart of family planning behaviour.

In the previous chapter, one saw that states like Kerala and Tamil Nadu have lower fertility rates, evidently because of better health facilities and higher female literacy than states with poor health facilities and lower female literacy. Kerala, for instance, had a literacy rate of 97.9 per cent, against 61 per cent in Uttar Pradesh in 2011. One hundred per cent of women in Kerala delivered in a health facility, against 68 per cent of women in Uttar Pradesh (NFHS-4). As much as 74.9 per cent of women were above the age of twenty-one in Kerala at marriage, against only 47.6 per cent in Uttar Pradesh. Thus, it is clear that fertility rates were more related to a state's level of development.[5]

Education and Literacy

Education has long been recognized as a crucial factor influencing fertility levels and patterns. There is extensive demographic literature devoted to the role of female education in promoting sustained fertility decline. According to United Nation's World Fertility Survey, there is compelling evidence to show that investment in education and elimination of institutional and cultural barriers to women's schooling promote development and fertility reduction.[6] This is

---

5   Census of India, 2011, Provisional Population Total, Government of India, https://censusindia.gov.in/2011census/population_enumeration.html.

6   United Nations, *Fertility Behaviour in the Context of Development: Evidence from the World Fertility Survey*, Population Studies No. 100 ST/ESA/SER.A/100 (New York, United Nations, 1987).

corroborated by numerous studies, including a United Nations study of twenty-six developing countries in 1995.[7] The study demonstrated that the main paths of influence by which women's education reduces fertility were its association with delayed age of marriage, desire for smaller families and increased use of contraception. Total fertility rates were found to be lower among women who had attained at least secondary education than among those with lower levels of education.[8]

Multi-country analyses of fertility data have shown a positive and significant association between change in fertility and socioeconomic development.[9] More highly educated women are more likely to use modern methods of contraception than less educated women. Education also tends to override the economic factor. There is less of a differential in modern contraceptive use between the rich and poor if the women are educated, as compared with the differential among women who are not educated, although the differential is not eradicated completely by education. Education can, therefore, be seen as 'levelling the playing field' between the rich and poor to a certain extent, with regard to modern contraceptive use As the level of education goes up, the TFR goes down. Women with no schooling have an average of 3.1 children, while women with twelve or more years of schooling have an average of 1.7 children (Figure 3.1).

---

7   United Nations, 'Women's Education and Fertility Behaviour', Department for Economic and Social Information and Policy Analysis, Population Division (New York: United Nations, 1995).

8   'Fertility Levels and Trends in Countries with Intermediate Levels of Fertility', Population Division, Department of Economic and Social Affairs, United Nations Secretariat, United Nations, 2001, https://www.un.org/en/development/desa/population/events/pdf/expert/4/population-fertilitylevels.pdf.

9   J. Bongaarts and S.C. Watkins, 'Social Interaction and Contemporary Fertility Transitions', *Population and Development Review* 22, no. 4 (1996): 639–682. doi:10.2307/ 2137804.

Figure 3.1: Fertility decreases with increase in educational levels

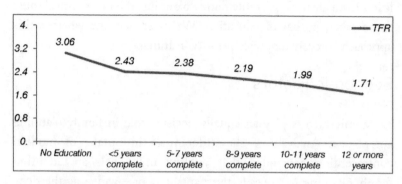

Source: NFHS-4, 2015-16

This phenomenon is equally evident in both rural and urban areas (Figure 3.2).

Figure 3.2: Nexus of literacy and fertility: TFR decreases with increase in literacy levels (urban and rural)

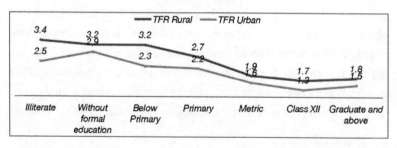

Source: Sample Registration System Report 2010, Registrar General, India

Literacy and Teenage Pregnancy

According to NFHS-4, the level of teenage pregnancy decreases with increasing levels of schooling. The survey said 20 per cent of women aged 15–19 with no schooling had already begun childbearing (during the period of the survey in 2015–16), against only 4 per cent of women who had twelve or more years of schooling. The message is loud and clear. To promote family planning, the most critical route to be taken is that of education. We must examine whether this approach is receiving policy priority in India.

Economic Factors

Economic factors play an equally decisive role in family planning acceptance. Analysis of the differentials in uptake of modern contraception concluded that wealthy individuals are adopting family planning practices faster than the poor – widening the rich-poor gap in service utilization and in the corresponding advantages of reduced fertility. Poor women in Indian states generally have poor access to education and healthcare. These women usually have little autonomy within and outside the household and have little control over their own reproductive and contraceptive choices.[10]

The World Health Organization has noted that poverty is related to poor sexual and reproductive health, as is clear at the country level. Poor investment in the required provisions to promote good sexual and reproductive health, such as hospitals and family planning clinics, has a great effect on a country's level of reproductive health.[11] Bongaarts also identified four variables that he held are mainly responsible for fertility variation among populations, most of which are closely related to poverty. A multi-country analysis of data by UNFPA shows that currently, in the majority of developing

---

10   S. Jeejeebhoy, *Women's Education, Autonomy and Reproductive Behaviour: Experience from Developing Countries* (Oxford: Clarendon Press, 1995), 328.

11   Shawn Malarcher (ed.), *Social Determinants of Sexual and Reproductive Health: Informing Future Research and Programme Implementation* (WHO, 2010), www.who.int › social_determinants › tools › 9789241599528_eng, accessed on 31 May 2020.

countries, access to critical sexual and reproductive healthcare is generally lowest among the poorest 20 per cent of households and highest among the richest 20 per cent. Women in the poorest households may find themselves with little or no access to sexual and reproductive healthcare, leading to unintended pregnancies, higher risk of illness or death from pregnancy or childbirth, and needing to give birth on their own, without the assistance of a doctor, nurse or midwife.[12]

Another study showed that rich-poor disparities in the health status of the population and utilization of health services among them are indicators of injustices in society, as well as markers of the capacity of the health system to meet the needs of the most vulnerable individuals in society. This should be of interest to those running public health programmes, political leaders and civil society members. This study of modern contraceptive use in fifty-five developing countries found a consistent gap between the rich and poor, both within and between countries, in the practice of contraception. Modern contraceptive use is lower in the poorest wealth quintile, and the differentials in usage between the rich and poor are widening as general use increases in the whole population, both of which factors further enhance inequality.[13]

The income and overall wealth of households do matter when it comes to reproductive health. As the wealth status of families improves, the total fertility rate decreases. For instance, the fertility rate among households in the lowest and second quintile of the wealth index was 3.2 and 2.6, respectively, whereas it was 2.1 in the

12 UNFPA, 'Worlds Apart: Reproductive Health and Rights in an Age of Inequality', State of World Population Report 2017, United Nations Population Fund, 2017.

13 E. Gakidou and E. Vayena, 'Use of Modern Contraception by the Poor is Falling Behind', *PLoS Medicine* 4, no.2 (2007): 381–89.

middle, and even lower in the fourth and fifth quintiles.[14] In other words, education and income matter—but not religion.[15]

For instance, in Bihar, women in the lowest wealth quintile have a total fertility rate of 5.08, while women in the highest quintile have a total fertility rate of 2.12. The same holds true for a richer state like Maharashtra, where the lowest wealth quintile has a total fertility rate of 2.78, and the richest a total fertility rate of 1.74. Women in the lowest wealth quintile have an average of 1.6 more children than women in the highest wealth quintile (TFR of 3.2 children versus 1.5 children). The income-fertility correlation is clearly evident. The data in Figure 3.3 show that as income grows, TFR goes down.

Figure 3.3: Fertility decreases with increase in household wealth

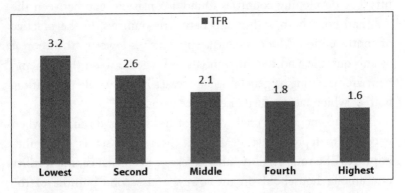

Source: NFHS-4, 2015–16

---

14 National Family Health Survey-4.

15 Poonam Muttreja, 'Human Development Is the Best Contraceptive— Why India Does Not Need a Two-Child Norm', *Think Global Health*, 11 February 2020, https://www.thinkglobalhealth.org/article/human-development-best-contraceptive-why-india-does-not-need-two-child-norm, accessed on 23 June 2020.

This nexus is re-emphasized by another set of statistics, which shows that the people who are employed have a lower fertility than those without work (Figure 3.4) both in terms of Total Fertility Rate (TFR) and Total Marital Fertility Rate (TMFR).

Figure 3.4: TFR higher among non-workers (rural and urban)

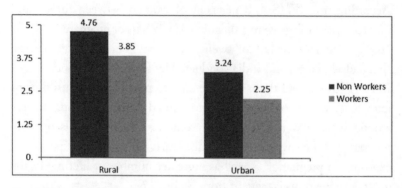

Source: Sample Registration System (SRS), 1990 Registrar General, India

Figure 3.5: TFMR higher among non-workers

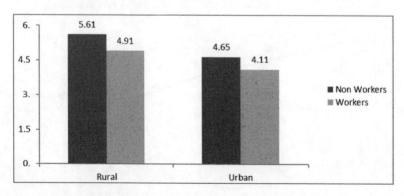

Source: SRS:1990

Age at Marriage

The next critical factor is age at marriage, as marriage and sexual activity determine the extent to which women are exposed to the risk of pregnancy. Thus, they are important determinants of fertility levels. Though fertility in the 15–19 age group is decreasing, still a substantial proportion of teenagers had begun childbearing, as of 2015–16. According to NFHS-4, 8 per cent of women between fifteen and nineteen years of age were either already mothers or pregnant in 2015–16. A systematic review of twenty-three programmes from Africa, Bangladesh, Nepal and India conducted by Population Foundation of India (PFI) showed that social pressure to prove fertility, insufficient knowledge about contraceptives and limited decision-making powers among women were the main reasons for the high levels of early pregnancy.[16] The women who marry early have a longer period of exposure to pregnancy as well as a greater number of lifetime births on an average. This is evident from Figure 3.6.

Figure 3.6: TFR decreases with increase in the age of marriage (rural and urban)

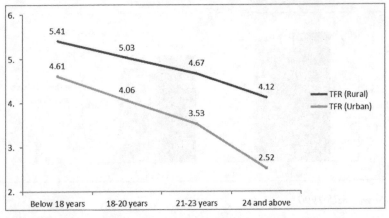

Source: NFHS-3

---

16 Population Foundation of India, 'Repositioning Family Planning: A Review on Evidence on Effective Interventions' (New Delhi: PFI, 2013).

The bitter reality is that despite the law prescribing eighteen years as the minimum age of marriage for women in India, an overwhelming proportion of them still marries below the legal minimum age. The median age at marriage is defined as the 'age by which half of women have been married at the time of survey' (NFHS).

As per Census 2011, 23 million girls had been minors at the time of their marriage, which means nearly half (47 per cent) of Indian girls were married before the legal age of 18 years. Imagine, one in every two marriages in India is illegal, and yet there is not a whimper about it. About 18 per cent of women are married even before they reach 15 years of age.

Age at marriage, in turn, is itself influenced by core factors such as education and economic status. There is ample evidence to show that an increase in the education level of women delays the age of marriage (Figure 3.7). Women with twelve or more years of schooling marry much later than women who do not. The median age at first marriage for women aged 25–49 at the time of NFHS-4, increases from 17.2 years for women with no schooling to 22.7 years for women with twelve or more years of schooling (Figure 3.7).

Figure 3.7: Median age at first marriage among women (currently aged 20–49) increases with increase in educational levels

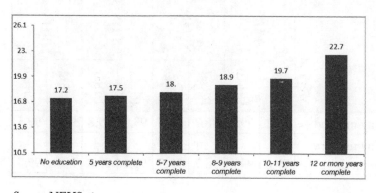

Source: NFHS-4

Informed Choice

To make an informed choice about contraceptive methods it is critical for men and women to have knowledge about them. National Family Health Surveys collect information from men and women about their knowledge of the methods of contraception available in India.

Table 3.1 shows that knowledge of contraception among women and men is universal, as at least 99 per cent of married women and men aged 15–49 know of one or more methods of contraception. The mean number of methods known is an indicator of the breadth of knowledge of family planning methods among the population. NFHS data show that on an average, more than six modern methods of family planning are known to men (6.8 methods in rural areas and 7.5 in urban areas) and women (6.5 methods in rural areas and 7.5 methods in urban areas) in India.

Table 3.1: Knowledge of contraceptive methods among married men and women (in %)

| Method | Currently married women | | | | Currently married men | | | |
| | NFHS-3 | | NFHS-4 | | NFHS-3 | | NFHS-4 | |
	Rural	Urban	Rural	Urban	Rural	Urban	Rural	Urban
Any method	99.1	99.6	98.7	99.6	99.1	99.8	98.5	99.5
Any modern method	99.0	99.6	98.7	99.5	99.1	99.8	98.4	99.5

Method	Currently married women				Currently married men			
	NFHS-3		NFHS-4		NFHS-3		NFHS-4	
	Rural	Urban	Rural	Urban	Rural	Urban	Rural	Urban
Female sterilization	98.1	99.1	97.3	98.6	97.2	98.7	93.5	95.8
Male sterilization	81.2	87.7	82.7	88.6	90.3	95.4	86.0	91.4
Pill	84.6	93.2	86.2	92.4	81.6	91.6	82.1	89.8
IUD	68.5	87.4	72.2	85.5	51.5	71.4	45.6	59.4
Injectables	49.3	60.1	70.0	80.0	43.7	56.4	61.9	74.8
Condom/ Nirodh	70.9	87.6	78.1	89.5	90.1	98.1	93.0	97.4
Female condom	5.8	13.9	17.7	29.1	13.7	23.5	29.7	44.5
Emergency contraceptives	8.9	18.8	36.6	52.3	18.9	30.1	43.5	55.0
Other modern method	0.1	0.3	0.3	0.3	0.0	0.1	0.2	0.2
Mean number of methods known	5.5	6.5	6.6	7.5	5.9	6.8	6.5	7.5

Source: NFHS-3, NFHS-4

Media exposure

Exposure to family planning messages, for obvious reasons, helps to bring about an understanding of contraceptive use, and hence contributes to achievement of the desired family size among citizens. Post ICPD, an informed choices model of service delivery was introduced in India in 1998, emphasizing individual reproductive and family planning needs and rights, and offering quality services without any form of coercion or discrimination. Although the impact of informed choices cannot be directly measured, evidence shows changes in the contraceptive method mix among recent users (NFHS-3, 2005–06).

Recognizing the importance of the role communication in promoting family welfare programmes, the Department of Family Welfare created the Mass Education Media (MEM) programme in 1968–69. Evidence of exposure of women and men to mass media is critical for development of educational programmes and dissemination of all types of information, particularly information about family planning, HIV/AIDS, and other important health topics.

Judith Bruce of the Population Council, an architect of the 1994 International Conference on Population and Development, developed a 'quality of care' framework, which contained six elements:

• Ensuring choice among a range of different contraceptive methods appropriate to the needs of clients.
• Exchange of information with clients to ensure informed choices.
• Technical competence of providers.
• Respectful and supportive interpersonal relations.
• Follow-up and continuity mechanisms to address discontinuation rates.

- An appropriate constellation of services to ensure that clients receive the range of services they need, to address both their health needs and their wider social setting.

Exposure to family planning messages has been seen as empowering women and men through providing information and understanding on issues related to contraceptive use.[17]

In NFHS-4, both women and men were asked if they had come across messages about family planning through radio/television/ newspapers/magazines/wall-paintings/hoardings in the few months prior to the survey. Exposure to mass media is defined in the NFHS as reading a newspaper or magazine, listening to the radio, watching television, or going to the cinema. Those who respond saying they do any of this at least once a week are considered to be regularly exposed to that form of media. Data on exposure to family planning messages by background characteristics like education, religion, caste and wealth show significant variation. Figure 3.8 shows that about three fourths (71.2 per cent) of women heard or saw a family planning message during the specified months before the survey (59 per cent on television, 53 per cent on a wall painting or hoarding, and only 18 per cent on the radio) while more than one fourth (28.8 per cent) of women did not have any exposure.

Women in rural areas are twice as likely to have had no exposure to family planning messages from these media sources – 34.6 per cent, against 16.4 per cent among their urban counterparts. About half of women with little or no schooling (49.1 per cent) had no exposure. Women from scheduled tribes (60.7 per cent) and Muslim women (65.6 per cent) have much lower exposure. Less than half of women in the lowest wealth quintiles (44.5 per cent) have exposure to family planning messages (NFHS-4).

---

17   Judith Bruce, 'Fundamental Elements of the Quality of Care: A Simple Framework', *Studies in Family Planning* 21, no.2 (1990): 61–91.

Figure 3.8: Exposure to family planning messages, women

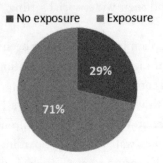

Source: NFHS-4, 2015–16

Exposure to family planning messages is slightly higher among men (76 per cent) than women (72 per cent) (Figure 3.9). About three fifths of men aged 15-49 heard or saw a family planning message on television (61 per cent) in the months before the survey or on a wall painting or hoarding (59 per cent) (NFHS-4).

Figure 3.9: Women (aged 15–49 years) have less exposure to family planning messages as compared to men (aged 15–49 years) at the national level

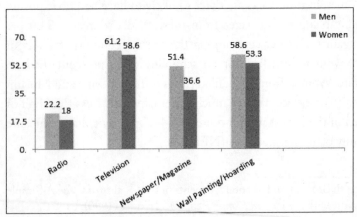

Source: NFHS-4, 2015–16

Figure 3.10: Women have less exposure to family planning messages through any media, by age

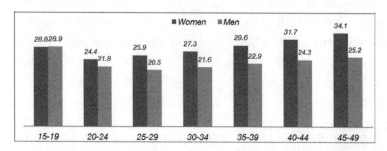

Source: NHFS-4, 2015-16

Figure 3.11: Rural women have less exposure to family planning messages through any media

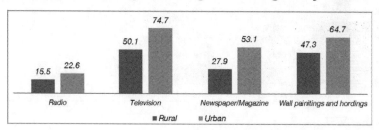

Figure 3.12: Lower levels of education result in higher rates of unawareness to family planning messages for both men and women

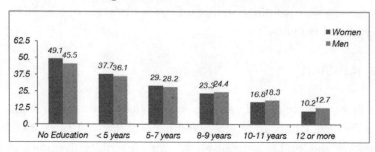

Source: NHFS-4, 2015-16

This clearly illustrates that as the level of education goes up, so does exposure to the media, and consequently to family planning messages.

Exposure to family planning messages is also influenced by the income factor. With prosperity, the level of exposure goes up. For instance, exposure of women to family planning messages among households in the lowest quintile of the wealth index was less than half (45.5 per cent), whereas it was highest among women in fifth quintile (90 per cent), as Figure 3.13 shows.

Figure 3.13: Lower wealth index is associated with higher rates of unawareness about family planning for both men and women

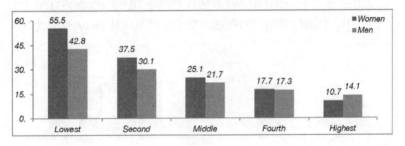

Source: NHFS-4

Lower exposure to electronic media could be due to lower ownership of radio and television which, in turn, could be the result of the subject's economic status. Further, lower exposure to newspapers, magazines, wall paintings and hoardings is obviously due to lower literacy and mobility.

Conclusion

Fertility is a complex and intricate issue to analyse and comprehend at individual, family, community and national levels. A plethora of literature and studies is available to explain fertility dynamics at these levels. Broadly, it is concluded that continuation of the trends in age at marriage, contraceptive prevalence, educational attainment and urbanization will ensure continuing fertility declines in long run. This is the finding of a study by the UN, which focused on fertility trends and associated factors in seventy-four countries with intermediate levels of fertility, that is, in those countries whose total fertility has been estimated at between 2.1 and 5 children per woman in 1995–2000. For the past three decades, fertility has been declining in all these countries, with the pace of decline varying according to their levels of fertility (Population Division, 2002).[18] Another interesting study of thirty-three predominantly Muslim countries conducted by using the dynamic panel data estimation method demonstrates that socioeconomic conditions are the primary reason for the high fertility rates seen in some of the countries studied. The study shows an inverse relationship between economic development and fertility rate.[19]

In their 2013 article 'The Impact of Freedom on Fertility Decline', Campbell et al.[20] also assert that in societies free from child marriage, wherever women have access to a range of contraceptive methods, along with correct information and backed up by safe abortion, family size will always fall. Education and wealth can make adoption of family planning easier, but they are not prerequisites

---

18 Fertility levels and trends in countries with intermediate levels of fertility, Population Division, 2002, Department of Economic and Social Affairs, United Nations Secretariat. file:///C:/Users/USER/Downloads/Population%20Myth_13th%20Dec.pdf. Accessed on 14 December 2020.

19 C. Yurtseven, 'The Socioeconomic Determinants of Fertility Rates in Muslim Countries: A Dynamic Panel Data Analysis', *Economics and Sociology* 8, no.4 (2015): 165–78, doi: 10.14254/2071-789X.2015/8-4/12.

20 M.M. Campbell, N. Prata and M. Potts, 'The Impact of Freedom on Fertility Decline', *Journal of Family Planning and Reproductive Health Care*, 39, no.1 (2013): 44–50.

for fertility decline. By contrast, access to family planning itself can accelerate economic development and the spread of education. The statement 'Development is the best contraceptive', made by Dr Karan Singh at the World Population Conference in Bucharest in 1974, highlighted a change in thinking and the need for a more balanced approach to population stabilization. Social development had a role in reducing the fertility rate at that time by creating a more conducive environment.[21]

We must now focus on the developmental factors, especially education, income and availability of family planning services at all levels and sections of society in the country so that fertility among all communities will achieve stability.

21　Mathai Matthews, 'The Global Family Planning Revolution: Three Decades of Population Policies and Programmes', *Bulletin of the World Health Organization* 86, no. 3 (March 2008): 161–240, https://www. who.int/bulletin/volumes/86/3/07-045658/en/, accessed on 23 June 2020.

4

Family Planning among India's Muslims

A S we have seen in the previous chapter, it is the socioeconomic factors that play the most crucial role in the adoption of family planning practices by any community. These factors include poverty, employment, education level, age of marriage, infrastructure and service delivery, unmet need for family planning, and the like. These factors in turn determine a family's acceptance and utilization of family planning initiatives. The role of religion at best is secondary and minimal. Let us take a look at how different religious groups fare in the context of these factors.

Education and Fertility

In Chapter 3 we have seen that education is the most important determinant of fertility behaviour. The total fertility rate goes down in direct proportion to increase in the level of education. In this context, Muslims fare most poorly.

Muslim men

Despite acquisition of knowledge being a sacred duty in Islam, it is indeed a strange paradox that the followers of a religion whose teachings begin with the first word 'iqra' (read/recite) are the most backward in education. Only 66.1 per cent of Muslim men have completed standard six or higher, and Muslim men account for the highest proportion of people who cannot read at all at – 19.1 per cent – among all religious groups. The percentage of literacy among the community is only 80.3, the lowest among all religious groups (see Table 4.1).

Table 4.1: Literacy levels lowest in Muslim men

Men	Completed standard 6 or higher	Cannot read at all	Percentage literate
Hindu	77.6	13.2	86.4
Muslim	66.1	19.1	80.3
Christian	80.8	10.2	89.4
Sikh	81.5	11.7	88.3
Buddhist/Neo-Buddhist	82.2	5.3	94.2
Jain	94.5	2.9	97.1

Source: NFHS-4; International Institute of Population Studies (Mumbai, IIPS)

Muslim women

The education level of Muslim women is even lower than that of men. Only 53.7 per cent of Muslim women have completed standard six or higher, and 34.6 per cent of Muslim women cannot read at all, which is the highest among all religious groups. The percentage literate is only 64.2, the lowest in the category (Table 4.2).

Table 4.2 Literacy levels lowest among Muslim women

Religion	Completed standard 6 or higher	Cannot read at all	Percentage literate
Hindu	60.4	31	68.3
Muslim	53.7	34.6	64.2
Christian	72.5	18.7	80.8
Sikh	71.8	18.8	81.1
Buddhist/Neo-Buddhist	72.8	18.1	81.1
Jain	95.4	2.3	97.5

Source: NFHS–4; Mumbai, IIPS

Enrolment of children in school

Enrolment of Muslim children, more so of girls, is the lowest among all religious communities, while the dropout rate is the highest at all levels, from primary, through middle school to secondary school. From Table 4.3 we can see that Muslims have the lowest net attendance ratio (NAR) of 77.1 per cent at the primary school level as well as lowest NAR of 56.2 per cent at middle, secondary, and higher secondary school levels (Table 4.3).

Table 4.3: Net attendance ratio (NAR) lowest in Muslims

Religion	Net Attendance Ratio (Primary School)			Net Attendance Ratio (Middle, Secondary and Higher Secondary School)		
	Male	Female	Total	Male	Female	Total
Hindu	78.5	77	77.8	71.4	68	69.8
Muslim	78	76.3	77.1	56.9	55.5	56.2
Christian	80.7	81.6	81.1	75	76.3	75.6
Sikh	78.5	75.7	77.2	77.5	77.9	77.7
Buddhist/ Neo- Buddhist	76.3	80.3	78.1	79.1	78.9	79
Jain	84.8	74.9	80	83.7	78.9	81.7

Source: NFHS–4; Mumbai, IIPS

The Sachar Committee report had identified poverty to be the major barrier to education among Muslims, as young children in the community are tasked with the responsibility of supporting their family instead of studying. Muslims have faced socioeconomic poverty for the past several generations, and this has blurred their vision of education. Muslim settlements are lacking in proper infrastructure, and most schools are traditional, not being linked appropriately with employment opportunities. One interesting thing to note here is that Muslims do not see attaining education as a means to formal employment because of the low representation of their community in the private and public sectors and the perceived discrimination when it comes to securing salaried jobs. The community, especially members of the educated middle class, feels alienated as a result of the lack of opportunities in the administrative and political space.

The extent of reality of this perception of discrimination is examined later in the chapter.

There are but a few good-quality schools, especially government schools, to be found in Muslim areas. Schools beyond the primary level are much fewer in Muslim areas. These schools also have very high teacher-pupil ratios, which is sometimes the reason why Muslim children attend private schools if they can afford it, or otherwise drop out of school. According to the Sachar Committee report, 66 per cent of Muslim children in the age group of 7–16 years attend government school, while only 30 per cent enroll in private schools. The remaining 4 per cent attend madrasas. Schools that do exist in Muslim neighbourhoods are merely centres of low-quality education for the poor and the marginalized. The poor quality of learning that results necessitates private tuitions, especially for first-generation learners, which involves high costs. Once again, we come across the causal link between poverty and education.

Another disturbing factor for school-going Muslim children is the lack of representation or negative representation of their community in the school texts,[1] which often results in a culturally hostile atmosphere of marginalization and discrimination. The history books portray Indian Muslims as foreign aggressors, a discourse that was furthered during the Partition of India.[2] Even though many Indian Muslims preferred to stay in India, following the unfortunate terrorist attacks during the last couple of decades, a well-orchestrated propaganda dubbed the entire Muslim community as terrorists. When confronted, those driving the

---

1   Noor Fatima Noor, 'Minority Education: A Study of Indian Muslims', *Socrates* 4, no. 1 (2016): 52–60.

2   Ghazala Jamil, 'Nothing like Equal Opportunities', Qantara.de, 16 December 2015, https://en.qantara.de/content/muslims-in-india-nothing-like-equal-opportunities, accessed 2 October 2020.

propaganda gave a new spin to the narrative – 'all Muslims are not terrorists, but all terrorists are Muslims'.[3] Later, when some Hindu terrorists were caught, the narrative was tweaked to say that terror has no religion.

A campaign specifically designed to create a rift between the two communities goes as far as polluting young minds with ideas of 'we and they'. Bharatiya Janata Party leader Kapil Mishra had tweeted, 'If you want pollution to come down, then you should reduce these firecrackers and not the ones burst on Diwali', along with a photo of a man with a skull-cap, a woman in burqah and several children standing next to them, thereby comparing Muslim children to pollution. Although the tweet was later taken down by Twitter on grounds of violation of its guidelines, Mishra maintained that he was trying to raise awareness about population control. However, the inappropriate use of the picture infuriated many, and consequently a complaint was filed against him,[4] to say that his tweet was nothing but propaganda that was 'demeaning, degrading and obscene, and would corrupt minds and hurt religious sentiments'.

One can see evidence of discrimination against Muslim teachers as well as Muslim students. The total share of Muslims in the Indian population is 14 per cent; however, the proportion of Muslim students in Indian colleges is 5.23 per cent, and in institutes of national importance only 2.19 per cent. Similarly, the percentage of

---

3   Siddharth Varadarajan (ed.), *Gujarat, the Making of a Tragedy* (New Delhi: Penguin Books, 2002), 7.

4   'Complaint Filed against BJP Leader Kapil Mishra for Allegedly Comparing Muslim Children to Pollution', Scroll.in, 29 October 2019, https://www.google.com/amp/s/amp.scroll.in/latest/941982/complaint-filed-against-bjp-leader-kapil-mishra-for-allegedly-comparing-muslim-children-to-pollution, accessed on 2 October 2020.

Muslim faculty in Indian colleges is 5.35 per cent, and in institutes of national importance, 2.88 per cent.[5]

Madrasas have become a symbol of Muslim identity in India; it is through them that the community ensures that its future generations acquire knowledge of Islam. They are, however, looked at with suspicion by the larger society. Often, madrasas are the only source of education available to Muslim children in areas that have no schools for the Muslim masses. These children attend the madrasas not out of choice but due to unavailability and inaccessibility of other options, especially the absence of alternative means of education in their mother-tongue. The issue, however, remains that the madrasas have a theological base of teaching and often miss out the association between development of skill-sets and capabilities and employment opportunities.[6]

In a rapidly changing and modernizing world, those with modern skills provided by schooling are favoured over those that do not have these skills. Schooling in the developing world encourages the self-confident and effective family planner that an educated woman can be.[7] Islam says 'a mother's lap is the first school for a child'.[8] Also,

Seeking knowledge is a duty of every Muslim, man or woman.

And

Whoever takes a path upon which to obtain knowledge, Allah makes the path to Paradise easy for him.[9]

---

5   See https://twitter.com/RajatDutta13/status/1253203548076048385

6   Tasneem Shazli and Sana Asma, 'Educational Vision of Muslims in India: Problems and Concerns', *International Journal of Humanities and Social Science Invention* 4, no. 3 (2015): 21–27.

7   Alaka Basu, 'Why Does Education Lead to Low Fertility? A Critical Review of Some of the Possibilities', *World Development* 30, no. 10 (2002): 1779–90, doi: 10.1016/S0305-750X(02)00072-4.

8   Al Tirmidhi Hadith 218.

9   Jami at Tirmidhi 2646, narrated by Abu Hurairah.

Together, the Quran and the Hadith promote education and acquisition of knowledge for all. Islam enjoins upon both men and women equally to acquire education, but the community fares very poorly compared with other religious communities on this front.

Effect of Poverty

In the previous chapter we have seen that poverty is a great determinant of fertility behaviour. Let's see where different communities stand in this respect. There is striking variation in the proportions of the poor among different religious groups. With about 25 per cent of their population falling in the 'poor' category, Muslims are the poorest religious group among all religious communities. Buddhists come close, with 24.4 per cent of their population falling in the 'poor' category, followed by the Hindus, at 22 per cent. The least poor religious groups in the country are the Sikhs and the Christians, with only 6 per cent and 16 per cent of their respective populations falling in the 'poor' category[10] (Table 4.4). Jains are the richest religious community, with more than 70 per cent of their population in the top wealth quintile.[11] On average, across India, Muslims are poorer than Hindus, with an average monthly per capita household expenditure of ₹833, compared with ₹888 for Hindus, ₹1,296 for

---

10 Sukhadeo Thorat and Mashkoor Ahmad, 'Minorities and Poverty: Why Some Minorities Are More Poor Than Others?', *Journal of Social Inclusion Studies* 1, no. 2 (2015): 126–42.

11 Roshan Kishore, 'Delhi and Punjab Richest States, Jain Wealthiest Community: National Survey', *Hindustan Times*, 13 January, 2018, https://www.hindustantimes.com/india-news/delhi-and-punjab-richest-states-jain-wealthiest-community-national-survey/story-sakdd3MBOfKhU2p5LrNVUM.html, accessed on 2 October 2020.

Christians and ₹1,498 for Sikhs, according to a National Sample Survey report based on data from 2009–10.[12]

Table 4.4: Incidence of poverty highest among Muslims

Religion	Rural	Urban	Total
Hindus	25.6	12.1	21.9
Muslims	26.9	22.7	25.4
Christians	22.2	5.5	16.4
Sikhs	6.2	5	5.9
Buddhists	24.2	24.8	24.4

Source: NSS Expenditure Survey, 68th round, 2011–12.

According to the United Nation's Development Programme (UNDP) and the Oxford Poverty and Human Development Initiative (OPHI) multi-dimensional index, every third person belonging to the Muslim community (and scheduled caste community) is multi-dimensionally poor. Scheduled tribes are worse off, with every second person being in this category.

The term multi-dimensional in this report defines poor not only on the basis of income but also by other indicators, like nutrition, health, education, living standards, assets and the like.[13] Malnutrition

---

12 'Employment and Unemployment Situation among Religious Groups in India 1999-2000', Report No. 468 (55/10/6), NSS 55th Round, 1999–2000, http://mospi.nic.in/sites/default/files/publication_reports/468_final.pdf.

13 Oxford Poverty and Human Development Initiative, *Global Multidimensional Poverty Index 2018: The Most Detailed Picture To Date of the World's Poorest People* (UK: Oxford Poverty and Human Development Initiative (OPHI), University of Oxford, 2018), https://ophi.org.uk/wp-content/uploads/G-MPI_2018_2ed_web.pdf, accessed on 16 October 2020.

is a condition that includes both under-nutrition and over-nutrition. It also includes deficiencies, excesses or imbalances in intake of protein and other nutrients, and is indicative of poverty and backwardness. 39.8 per cent of Muslim children below the age of five are chronically undernourished, and 38.5 per cent of Hindu children.

The quality of housing and access to basic amenities like potable drinking water determine the quality of life and standard of living, and work as a basis for analysing the differences in socioeconomic well-being across various socio-religious groups. One of the main features of urban settlements is the increasing presence of apartment complexes or 'flats'. NSS data show that only 35 per cent of Muslims lived in flats, while 40 per cent of Hindus lived in flats, in 2012. In this context, it is important to note that the percentage of Muslims with independent housing is 51, against 47 among Hindus, but this could be a consequence of the difficulties faced by Muslims, or their unwillingness, to join group housing schemes. Some exclusively Muslim neighbourhoods had sprung up in the past decade in northern and western cities like Delhi, Mumbai and Ahmedabad in the aftermath of the Hindu-Muslim riots, when Muslims came together for greater security or were removed from mixed neighbourhoods. Analysts say that Muslims face bias when buying or renting property. This deep-rooted bias erodes the multi-cultural nature of India, creating separate neighbourhoods that further perpetuate the communal divide that exists because of fear of violence.[14]

Muslims also occupy smaller homes. For this we go by average floor area, which indicates the size of a dwelling. In 2012, according to NSS data, the average floor area of Muslim houses was 387 sq. ft, which was considerably lower than the national average of 422 sq.

---

14 Rina Chandran, 'As Indian Cities Develop, Minorities Forced into Slums', *The Christian Science Monitor*, 17 January 2018, https://www.csmonitor.com/World/Asia-South-Central/2018/0117/As-Indian-cities-develop-minorities-forced-into-slums, accessed on 2 October 2020.

ft. Tap water is the main source of drinking water in urban India. However, the percentage of households using tap water in 2012 was lowest for Muslims, at 63.7 per cent; it was 69.7 per cent for Hindus. Also, a smaller proportion of Muslims had houses with proper modern drainage facilities. Only about 56 per cent of Muslim households had underground or covered drainage, against the national average of 60 per cent or 60.6 per cent for Hindu households. 29.4 per cent of Muslim households did not have adequate arrangements for garbage collection, while the national corresponding figure was 24.2 per cent.[15]

According to the Sachar Committee report, Muslims have poor access to bank credit, and the average size of credit they obtain is small compared with what other socio-religious groups obtain. Some banks have identified a number of Muslim areas as 'negative geographical zones', where bank credit and other facilities are not adequate.[16] All of this results in financial exclusion of Muslims, and consequently results in their increased economic vulnerability and educational backwardness. They lack access to capital assets and regular salaried jobs, especially in urban areas, and as a result pursue self-employed economic activities by setting up enterprises or businesses. However, their lower ownership of capital and lesser involvement in regular salaried jobs, vis-à-vis the rest of society, push them to undertake petty residual jobs that offer meagre earnings.

---

15 Post Sachar Evaluation Committee (Kundu Committee Report), 2014, https://sabrangindia.in/sites/default/files/audio_listing_images/kundu_commission_report_0.pdf?698, accessed on 15 October 2020.

16 Prime Minister's High Level Committee, Cabinet Secretariat, Government of India, 'Access to Bank Credit', in 'Social, Economic and Educational Status of the Muslim Community of India: A Report', The Sachar Committee Report, 2006, 126, http://www.minorityaffairs.gov.in/sites/default/files/sachar_comm.pdf, accessed on 15 October 2020.

Table 4.5: Bank credit (amount outstanding in per cent) lowest for Muslims

	Muslims	Other Minorities	Others
Private Sector Banks	6.6	7.9	85.5
PSUs	4.6	6.3	89.1

Source: Sachar Committee Report, 2005–2006

Muslims constitute about 12 per cent of all scheduled commercial bank (ASCB) account holders. This is quite close to their share of the population. However, the share of other minorities in this respect is slightly more than 8 per cent, which is considerably higher than their share in the population of 5.6 per cent. It is noteworthy here that the share of Muslims in the 'amount outstanding' is only 4.6 per cent, against 6.3 per cent for other minorities (Table 4.5). Advances from public sector banks (PuSBs) to Muslims are higher in magnitude compared with that of private sector banks (PrSBs), but the latter are performing better in extending advances to Muslims. For instance, the Muslims' share in 'amount outstanding' is only 4.6 per cent in PuSBs but 6.6 per cent in PrSBs (Table 4.5).[17]

Availability of health infrastructure and services

As we have seen in the previous chapter, family planning acceptance is also dependent on delivery of health services to the communities and individuals in question. Here, again, we find Muslims lagging. According to NFHS-4 data, only 77 per cent of Muslim women in the age group of 15-49 has received antenatal care from a skilled provider, which is the lowest among all religious groups (Table 4.6). They also lag behind in accessing delivery services at healthcare

---

17 Ibid.

facilities and receiving advice on family planning from community health workers, as is evident from Table 4.7 and Table 4.8. This results in lower acceptance of family planning practices by the community.

Table 4.6: Percentage of women in the age group 15–49 who received antenatal care from a skilled provider lowest for Muslims

Religion	Percentage receiving antenatal care from a skilled provider
Hindu	79.3
Muslim	77
Christian	84.2
Sikh	93.6
Buddhist/Neo-Buddhist	93.2
Jain	93.7

Source: NFHS–4; Mumbai: IIPS

Table 4.7: Percentage distribution of live births among women aged 15–49 delivered in a health facility lowest for Muslims

Religion	Percentage Delivered in a Healthcare Facility
Hindu	80.8
Muslim	69.2
Christian	78.5
Sikh	92.5
Buddhist/Neo-Buddhist	92.2
Jain	98.1

Source: NFHS–4; Mumbai, IIPS

Table 4.8: Percentage of women in the age group 15–49 who received advice on family planning lowest for Muslims

Religion	Percentage Who Received Advice On Family Planning
Hindu	69.7
Muslim	65.2
Christian	72.6
Sikh	77.1
Buddhist/Neo-Buddhist	81.6
Jain	70.4

Source: NFHS-4; Mumbai, IIPS

Reach of ICDS schemes

The government of India started the Integrated Child Development Services (ICDS) scheme in 1975 in order to ensure proper early childhood development. The underlying objective was to ensure child survival, the basic prerequisite for acceptance of family planning. Some of the ICDS objectives are:

- To improve the nutritional and health status of children in the age-group 0-6 years.
- To lay the foundation for proper psychological, physical and social development of the child.
- To reduce the incidence of mortality, morbidity, malnutrition and school dropout.
- To achieve effective coordination of policy and implementation among the various departments to promote child development.
- To enhance the capability of the mother to look after the normal health and nutritional needs of the child through proper nutrition and health education.[18]

---

18 ICDS scheme, http://wcd.nic.in/icds.htm, accessed on 16 July 2013.

The ICDS scheme provides essential care in terms of proper nutrition, immunization and pre-school education for expecting mothers and children. This is a measure to improve the health of the nation's children. ICDS schemes have the least coverage in Muslim areas. Table 4.9 shows the percentage of coverage of the scheme across India by religion. The coverage is 10.9 per cent for Hindus, 13.5 per cent for others and only 7.6 per cent for Muslims. As the outreach of ICDS schemes is poor in Muslim habitations, they receive less than the national average of healthcare for their children and expecting mothers, and it is not difficult to understand that they have less knowledge of family planning and its benefits[19] (see Table 4.9).

Table 4.9 : Percentage coverage of ICDS of population 0–6 years old, by state and Socio–religious Communities (SRCs), 2004–05, is least for Muslims

Percentage coverage of ICDS of population 0–6 years old, by state and SRC, 2004-05							
			Hindus				
Incidence	All	All Hindus	SC/STs	OBCs	General	All Muslims	All Others
India	10.5	10.9	10.2	12.5	9.9	7.6	13.5
West Bengal	16.6	17.9	16.3	18.8	21.5	13.8	24.5
Kerala	20.9	25.2	26.9	31.2	22.2	9.4	29.1
Uttar Pradesh	1.9	2	1.5	2.7	1.6	1.9	0
Bihar	2.7	3	1.8	2.3	3.5	1.7	0

19 'Social, Economic and Educational Status of the Muslim Community of India', The Sachar Committee Report, 2006.

Percentage coverage of ICDS of population 0–6 years old, by state and SRC, 2004-05						
		Hindus				
Incidence	All	All Hindus	SC/STs	OBCs	General	All Muslims	All Others
Assam	11.8	13.3	12	10.8	19.3	10.4	2.8
Jammu & Kashmir	6.6	1	1.3	0.6	0.9	10.1	0
Jharkhand	2	1.8	0	0.9	2.9	4	0.7
Karnataka	10.6	11.1	6.2	14.8	11.4	6.7	15.4
Uttaranchal	3.1	2.5	1.4	4.8	1.7	7.8	0
Delhi	0	0	0	0	0	0	0
Maharashtra	21.2	22.2	16.6	23.4	26.6	14	21.4
Andhra Pradesh	9.6	9.9	8	13.1	8.7	6.3	9.8
Gujarat	23.3	22.5	14.3	28	22.9	31.7	11.7
Rajasthan	2.4	2.5	5.6	2.4	1.6	2.2	0.2
Madhya Pradesh	5	4.8	2	6.1	4.6	8.1	0.9
Haryana	23.7	24.7	20.2	25.2	30.1	6.6	20.2
Tamil Nadu	17.6	18.3	8	22.7	17.1	15.1	8.8
Orissa	38.3	38.3	34.1	40.4	37.6	39.3	39.8
Himachal Pradesh	17.8	18.2	21.1	17.3	8.9	9	15.9
Chhattisgarh	22.5	22.7	12.1	25.2	21.4	2.6	17
Punjab	4.1	5.9	7.5	6.5	0.6	0	3.2
All Other States	20.1	10.5	4.3	16.8	9.5	12.4	32.4

Source: Sachar Committee report, 2006

Worker-population Ratio

A direct consequence of poor educational levels is a lower ratio of employment in the community. The 2011 Census shows that Muslims have the lowest share of working people among all communities, at 32.6.[20] Hindus have a worker-population ratio of 41, Christians 41.9, Buddhists 43.1, Sikhs 36.3 and Jains 35.5 (Figure 4.1).

Only 15 per cent of Muslim women are employed, while 27 per cent of Hindu women, 31 per cent of Christian women and 36 per cent of Buddhist women are employed (Figure 4.2). Employment is lowest among Jains, at only 12 per cent.[21] This low rate of female workforce participation among Jains could be attributed to their having the highest share of voluntary non-workers as a consequence of higher education and prosperity. Therefore, in the context of Jains, the low rate of workforce participation is due to high household income, which reduces the need for women to take up work.[22] A study of the bidi-makers of Allahabad underscores the widely held belief that purdah results in the exclusion of Muslim women from the labour force and they are, therefore, restricted to home-based work.[23] However, there can be a reverse causal link between purdah and poverty, in the sense that poverty and unemployment are responsible for the continuation of the purdah system rather than the other way

20 Abantika Ghosh, 'Muslim Working Proportion Lowest among Communities,' *The Indian Express*, 26 February 2016, https://indianexpress.com/article/india/india-news-india/muslim-working-proportion-lowest-among-communities/, accessed on 2 October 2020.

21 Subodh Varma, 'Only 33% of Muslims work, lowest among all religions', *The Times of India*, 4 January 2016, https://timesofindia.indiatimes.com/india/Only-33-of-Muslims-work-lowest-among-all-religions/articleshow/50433358.cms, accessed on 2 October 2020.

22 Rohan Kishore, 'Religions with Most Educated Women Have the Most Non-working Women in India', *Live Mint*, 21 September 2016, https://www.livemint.com/Politics/ePCoqgRAn0PNuDTb3vL9XI/Religions-with-most-educated-women-have-the-most-nonworking.html, accessed on 2 October 2020.

23 Zarina Bhatty, 'Economic Contribution of Women to the Household Budget: A Case Study of the Beedi Industry', in *Invisible Hands: Women in Home-based Production*, ed. Andrea Menefee Singh and Anita Kelles Viitanen (London: Sage Publications, 1987), 35–50.

round. The role of purdah in limiting a women's capability is rather debatable, as purdah is no handicap when it comes to employment of home-based skills such as weaving, embroidery, zardozi and chikankari in which women excel.

Figure 4.1: Worker-population ratio in India lowest among Muslims

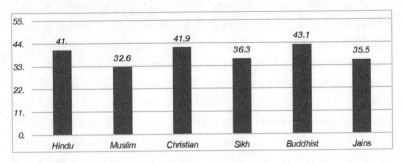

Source: Census 2011

Figure 4.2: Per cent distribution of female workforce participation in India low among Muslims and Sikhs

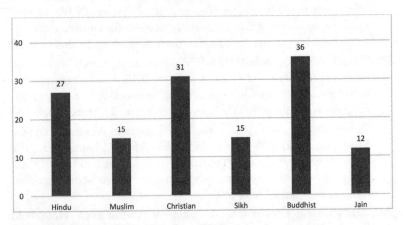

Source: The Times of India, 4 January 2016

High illiteracy/low education among Muslims ensures that they are trapped in a vicious cycle of poverty. It adversely affects their job opportunities and quality of employment. This reflects in their low consumption expenditure and poor labour force participation rate (LFPR), employment status and worker-population ratio. Among the various religious groups, Muslims have the lowest living standard, with their average per-capita expenditure at just ₹32.66 a day, according to a National Sample Survey Organization (NSSO) report titled 'Employment and Unemployment situation Among Major Religious Groups in India' (2011-12). At the other end of the spectrum, the Sikh community enjoys a much better lifestyle, as the average per capita spending among them is ₹55.30 per day; for Hindus this figure is ₹37.50, and for Christians ₹51.43.

Another factor is that Muslim communities are increasingly being shunted out of Hindu-dominated areas in Indian cities, leading to their 'ghettoization'. Urban ethnic conflicts and the threat of violence result in the confinement of Muslims to 'community-bound' enclaves, especially for women, as the security of women and children is better ensured within the ghettos. This further restricts work opportunities for women. What aggravates this situation is the poor social mobility of Muslims among all communities. This has increased their reliance on the family trade or craftsmanship, without much opportunities of upward mobility.[24]

Age of Marriage

We had earlier seen that the level of literacy also influences knowledge of and compliance with the legal age for marriage across all communities. The median age at first marriage is lowest among

---

24 Asim Ali, 'COVID as an Excuse to Push Indian Muslims out of Informal Sector Jobs. Apartheid the Next Step', The Print, 9 April 2020, https://theprint.in/opinion/covid-an-excuse-to-push-indian-muslims-out-of-informal-sector-jobs-apartheid-the-next-step/398236/, accessed on 2 October 2020.

Muslims – a position they share with their Hindu counterparts. NFHS-4 showed that both Hindu and Muslim women in the age group of 20–49 years had the lowest median age at first marriage, of 18.9 years and 19 years, respectively. For women in the age group of 25–49 years, the median age at first marriage for Muslims was 18.6 years, and for Hindus 18.5 years (Table 4.11). Teenage pregnancies and motherhood are, therefore, 16 per cent higher among Hindus and Muslims than among other religious groups, highlighting the relationship between early marriage and teenage pregnancy.[25]

Table 4.10: Median age at first marriage for men and women in the age group 25–49 by background characteristics, 2015–2016, similar for Hindus and Muslims

Religion	Men age 25–49	Women age 25–49
Hindu	24.3	18.5
Muslim	24.6	18.6
Christian	A	21.6
Sikh	A	20.9
Buddhist/Neo-Buddhist	A	19.2
Jain	A	21.2
a= Omitted because less than 50% of the men were married before reaching the beginning of the age group.		

Source: NFHS-4; Mumbai, IIPS

The percentage of women aged 15–19 who have begun child-bearing is highest among Muslims, as is the percentage of women

25 Khabar Lahariya and Prachi Salve, IndiaSpend.com, 'Hindu and Muslim Girls Marry Earliest, Jains and Christians Later', Scroll.in, 7 May 2015, https://scroll.in/article/725562/hindu-and-muslim-girls-marry-earliest-jains-and-christians-later, accessed on 2 October 2020.

pregnant with their first child. The proportion of women in this age
bracket who have had a live birth is highest among Buddhists. But
Muslims are not very far behind. In fact, the proportion is almost the
same for both these religious groups. More importantly, Muslims
have the highest percentage of women in the age group of 15–19 in
all the three categories of 'have had a live birth', 'are pregnant with
first child' and 'who have begun childbearing' (Table 4.11).

Table 4.11: Percentage of women aged 15–19 who have had a live birth or who are pregnant with their first child, and percentage who have begun child-bearing highest for Muslims

Religion	Percentage of Woman aged 15–19		
	Have had a live birth	Are pregnant with first child	Who have begun childbearing
Hindu	5.1	2.7	7.8
Muslim	5.9	3.1	9
Christian	4.6	1.8	6.4
Sikh	1.8	0.9	2.6
Buddhist/ Neo-Buddhist	6.0	1.4	7.4
Jain	1.2	0	1.2

Source: NFHS-4; Mumbai, IIPS

Exposure to mass media

Exposure to family planning messages is essential for adoption of
desirable practices by the people. This exposure is lowest among the
Muslim community. This can be viewed from the perspective of a
causal link between poverty, education and exposure to mass media.
Because of their poverty, fewer Muslims have access to television

or radio. Gaining information from newspapers or wall-paintings/hoardings is possible only when the receiver has the appropriate education level to read and understand the messages. Here too Muslims are handicapped (Table 4.14 and Table 4.15).

Table 4.12: Percentage of women aged 15–49 who heard or saw a family planning message on radio, television, in a newspaper or magazine, or on a wall painting or hoarding, lowest among Muslims

Religion	Radio	Television	Newspaper/ Magazine	Wall-painting/ hoarding	None of these
Hindu	18.5	59.5	37.1	54	27.7
Muslim	15.9	50.8	30.5	46.9	34.4
Christian	19.2	58.1	45.1	60.1	25.3
Sikh	5.5	81.2	48.3	60.6	12.4
Buddhist/ Neo- Buddhist	22.6	69.9	44.7	60.8	20.2
Jain	29.7	84.3	73	73.9	10.9

Source: NFHS–4; Mumbai, IIPS

Table 4.13: Percentage of men aged 15–49 who heard or saw a family planning message on radio, television, in a newspaper or magazine, or on a wall painting or hoarding lowest among Muslims

Religion	Radio	Television	Newspaper/ Magazine	Wall-painting/ Hoarding	None of these
Hindu	22.5	62	52.8	59.8	23

Religion	Radio	Television	Newspaper/ Magazine	Wall-painting/ Hoarding	None of these
Muslim	20.4	53.7	42.2	51.1	28.5
Christian	25.7	57.2	50.4	55.1	26.7
Sikh	7.2	77.9	57.1	66.1	12.1
Buddhist/ Neo-Buddhist	27.7	69.2	56.2	57	19.3
Jain	24.4	78.2	65.5	59.1	16.6

Source: NFHS-4; Mumbai, IIPS

Initiatives to address the communities at large often fall short in appreciating the simple fact that the needs of all households are not similar, and neither is their understanding and operational capacity. A family planning message that is not customized to the needs of the target community will always fall short of reaching its audience. Then, even if information is available, the willingness of the recipients to actually utilize the information depends, to a large extent, on the level of education of the target community. As discussed above, Muslims lag behind in educational status compared with other religious communities. Taking information to the community is, therefore, not enough. It needs to be assured that, along with exposure to mass media carrying family planning messages, the community also has the appropriate means and motivation to utilize that information effectively.

Unmet need for family planning

Addressing the unmet need for contraception was one of the immediate objectives of India's National Population Policy 2000. However, evidence suggests that there is still a considerable unmet need for family planning services, which has been consistently high over several decades. For Muslims, in particular, unmet need has been the highest, which too has contributed to their lower adoption of family planning. In general, when unmet need is high, prevalence of contraceptive practice is low. Unmet need for contraception and unwanted pregnancy constitute a major public health problem in India.

One of the most important ways to meet the unmet need for family planning is to increase the number and diversity of contraceptive methods and to encourage individual choice of contraception, based on individual needs and family characteristics. Availability of more options can help meet the needs of family planning and contraception and lead to increased practice of contraception. Making available a wider range of contraceptive options not only addresses the unmet need for family planning but also prevents transmission of sexual diseases.[26] The unmet need for family planning is highest among Muslims in comparison with all other religious groups. (Table 4.14)

Table 4.14: Unmet need for family planning highest among Muslims

| Religion | Unmet Need For Family Planning | | |
	For Spacing	For Limiting	Total
Hindu	5.4	7	12.4
Muslim	7.1	9.4	16.5
Christian	6.9	6	12.9
Sikh	2.4	4	6.4

26 Heather Clark, Saumya RamaRao, Catherine Unthank, Kazuyo Machiyama and Nandita Thatte, 'Family Planning Evidence Brief Expanding Contraceptive Choice', WHO/RHR/17.14:1-4, 2018, https://apps.who.int/iris/bitstream/handle/10665/255865/WHO-RHR-17.14-eng.pdf;jsessionid=04FD68BFD6D8126D498E1E71B332AACB?sequence=1, accessed on 16 October 2020.

Religion	Unmet Need For Family Planning		
	For Spacing	For Limiting	Total
Buddhist/ Neo-Buddhist	4.9	6.2	11.1
Jain	4	8	12

Source: NFHS-4; Mumbai, IIPS

Practice of polygamy

Polygamy is the practice of having more than one spouse at the same time. This practice is outlawed in India, except for Muslims and some tribal communities, as their customary laws permit it. At the very top of the misinformation campaign is the propaganda that Muslims have multiple wives to have more children. Muslims in the country are subject to the terms of the Muslim Personal Law (Shariat) Application Act of 1937 which is interpreted by the All India Muslim Personal Law Board. But in a judgement of February 2015, the Supreme Court of India stated that 'Polygamy was not an integral or fundamental part of the Muslim religion and monogamy was a reform within the power of the state under article 25.' This meant that although their personal law permits Muslim men to have as many as four wives, the Supreme Court has ruled that a Muslim's fundamental right to profess Islam does not include the practice of polygamy.

At the very centre of the debate around polygamy lies the belief that Islam encourages polygamy, which eventually leads to population growth. The reality, however, is different. There is only one verse in the Quran (Surah An-Nisa [4:3]).

The only study on the subject of polygamy ever done was by the Committee on the Status of Women in India, 1974, which showed that polygamy as a practice was not just exclusive to Muslims but was prevalent among all communities of India. In fact, it was found that Muslims were the least polygamous among all the groups (Figure 4.3).

Figure 4.3: Incidence of polygamous marriages lowest among Muslims

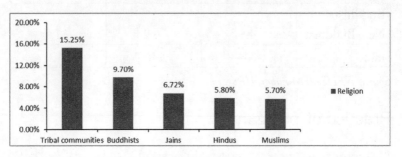

Source: Towards Equality: Report of the Committee on the Status of Women in India, 1974, Ministry of Social Welfare

Trends through three decadal Censuses, from 1931 to 1960, confirm that polygamy cuts across all communities, is declining among all of them, and, most importantly, is least among the Muslims (Table 4.15). The Hindu Marriage Act of 1955 imposed a ban on polygamy for Hindus, Sikhs, Buddhists and Jains so it is quite possible that the numbers have changed in the years and generations hence. However, the Report of the Committee on the Status of Women in India, 1974, Ministry of Social Welfare was the last to look at polygamous marriages in India.

Table 4.15: Polygamous marriages in India lowest among Muslims

Incidence of Polygamous Marriages in India			
Community	1931-40	1941-50	1951-60
Tribal	9.53	17.53	17.93
Hindus	6.79	7.15	5.06
Muslims	7.29	7.06	4.31

There is an interesting dimension missed by everyone. Polygamy is not even possible in India, as the number of women has been significantly lower than the number of men throughout the seven decades under study, as shown in Table 4.16.

Table 4.16: Sex ratio (females per 1000 males) since 1951

Year	Sex Ratio (Females Per 1000 Males)
1951	946
1961	941
1971	930
1981	934
1991	927
2001	933
2011	943

Source: Census data from above mentioned years

Statistically, therefore, no Indian man has even one full wife! Each has 0.9 of a wife. Experts, in any case, are of the opinion that polygamy cannot lead to a high birth rate as the number of polygamous men, however few, would result in an equal number of unmarried men (who will not find wives).[27] Another Indian study shows that the average number of children from the second wife of Muslim men was only 1.78 as compared with 4.67 from the first wife.[28] Thus, it is clear that the presumption of a high polygamy rate among Muslims

---

27 S.Y. Quraishi, 'The Polygamy Myth', *The Indian Express*, updated 6 July 2017, https://indianexpress.com/article/opinion/columns/the-polygamy-myth-pakistan-muslims-family-planning-4737608/, accessed on 2 October 2020.

28 Kamala Gopal Rao, *Studies in Family Planning: India* (New Delhi, Abhinav Publications, 1974).

is unfounded and that polygamy is not a factor leading to high birth rate among Muslims.

Infant mortality rate

There is, however, one area in which Muslims fare better than all other religious communities. In India, Muslim children are more likely than their Hindu counterparts to survive to their fifth birthday, despite Muslim parents being poorer and less educated on average than Hindu parents. By age five, mortality among Muslims is about 18 per cent less than among Hindus.[29] In their 2010 article titled 'The Puzzle of Muslim Advantage in Child Survival in India', Bhalotra et al. described this consistent pattern as the 'puzzle of Muslim advantage in child survival in India'.[30] It was demonstrated that no factor – education, wealth, family demographics, state trends, cohort effects, development expenditure, village-level health services and health infrastructure – could explain the Muslim mortality advantage that has existed since the 1960s. Health behaviours like breastfeeding, antenatal care or even place of delivery had very little role to play in explaining this disparity.

The only plausible explanation for the highest child sex ratio among Muslims could be the emphasis of Islam on gender equality.[31] The sacred text of the glorious Quran bears witness to the fact that in

---

29 Michael Geruso, 'Muslim Mortality Paradox and the Importance of Sanitation for Children', *Mint*, 18 August 2014, https://www.livemint. com/Opinion/vkvuknMxLInXEs3lXN1LDM/Muslim-mortality-paradox-and-the-importance-of-sanitation-fo.html, accessed on 10 October 2020.

30 S. Bhalotra, C. Valente and A. Van Soest, 'The Puzzle of Muslim Advantage in Child Survival in India', *Journal of Health Economics* 29, no. 2 (2010): 191–204.

31 'Social, Economic and Educational Status of the Muslim Community of India', The Sachar Committee Report, 33–38.

Islam women are considered as vital to life as men. Men and women are equal and therefore have similar rights and duties, as given in the Quran and the Hadith:

> *'Never will I waste the work of a worker among you, whether male or female, the one of you being from the other.'*
>
> (Al-Quran 3:195)
>
> *'Observe your duty to Allah in respect to the women, and treat them well.'*
>
> (Prophet Muhammed's last sermon)
>
> *'Verily, women are the twin halves of men.'*
>
> (Abu Dawud, Tirmidhi)
>
> *'And for women are rights over men similar to those of men over women.'*
>
> (Quran, 2: 228)

CONCLUSION

It is true that a Hindu-Muslim fertility differential persists in the demographic reality of India. However, this is due to the relative backwardness of the Muslims in almost all the factors that determine fertility behaviour, namely, literacy, income, access to services, etc. Nor will this gap in fertility persist for a very long duration, as the fertility level of Indian Muslims is steadily declining with improvement in literacy and living standards among them. Religion is not as important in determining fertility levels as it is made out to be, but factors like literacy level, age of marriage, exposure to mass media and economic factors come together to determine the fertility levels of Indian Muslims.

If religion were the only factor, then it would become rather difficult to explain the high unmet need for family planning among the Muslim community. The truth is, a combination of these factors and their inter-relatedness is the cause behind the relatively high fertility levels among Muslims. Lack of such an understanding could result in religion bashing and even communal violence, given the existing conflicts between competing religious groups like the Hindus and Muslims.[32] It is, therefore, imperative to understand that the presumption that Muslims' relatively higher fertility levels have their roots in Islamic theology, as well as the 'anti-nationalist' propaganda against them, is completely baseless. They are merely a means to vilify the community and a part of communal propaganda by some vested interests.

---

32 Bhagat and Praharaj, 'Hindu-Muslim Fertility Differentials', 417.

5

Tenets of Islam and Family Planning

HAVING seen that prevalence of family planning among Muslims is lowest among all communities in India on account of their being at the bottom of the ladder in education, economic status and the access to health services – the main determinants – let us see if religion has been a contributor too.

Are Islamic tenets opposed to family planning, as widely believed by non-Muslims and Muslims alike?

To find the answer to this, we need to focus on the following questions:

- What is the stance of Islamic principles on women?
- What does Islamic law prescribe with regard to family planning?
- What is the opinion of the ulama or religious scholars in India and other (Islamic) countries about family planning, in general, and about different family planning methods, in particular?

- We must begin with the basic premise that Islam is not confined to theology and is meant for all mankind and for all times.

As Abder Rahim Omran, Professor at University of Al-Azhar, Cairo and the founding father of the World Association of Muslim Scholars for Population, Health and Development, observed, Islamic legislation is most comprehensive and does not deal exclusively with questions of faith and worship. It also regulates moral behaviour, social interaction and business dealings as well as systems of legislation, taxation, family formation, community development, societal structure and international relations.[1]

Muslims constitute the second largest population in the world, numbering 1.9 billion, or 24 per cent of the global population.[2] The image projected by international media often shows Islam as a religion that cages women and treats them as nothing more than a tool for men to derive pleasure and beget children from. These perceptions ignore, or are unaware, of the Islamic tenet of respect to women, as specified in the holy Quran, and the traditions of Prophet Muhammad (PBUH).

This chapter attempts to shed light on Islamic tenets dealing with such fundamental issues as gender equality and family planning. At the outset, it must be pointed out that the Indian situation represents a unique culture resulting from interactions among various religious groups and intermixing of different communities. So many cultural predispositions come into play too, which very often transcend the boundaries of religion. These cultural factors sometimes even distort the real thrust of religions.

For instance, polygamy has been practised in India for centuries, regardless of religious beliefs. It has been more a cultural than religious practice. However, while Muslims are projected as

---

1   Abdel Rahim Omran (with UNFPA), *Family Planning in the Legacy of Islam* (London: Routledge, 1992).

2   Muslim Population by Country 2020 - World Population Review, https://worldpopulationreview.com/country-rankings/muslim-population-by-country, accessed on 16 October 2020.

polygamous, many non-Muslims are polygamous too, and several of them practise polygamy by 'converting' to Islam to avoid legal hurdles. Ironically, Muslims, irrespective of the fact that they have been found to be the least polygamous, accept this and take refuge under Islam for justifying a phenomenon which is more cultural than religious. Therefore, those cultural practices against which Islam has issued injunctions (e.g., polygamy), with the passage of time, are sought to be defended, strangely, in the name of Islam.

Conversion as a ploy to remarry

Conversion to Islam by Hindus as a ploy to get rid of the first wife and take a second has been exposed by several high courts, by the Supreme Court, and by the Law Commission of India headed by Justice Lakshmanan[3]

Here are some key observations from the Law Commission report: For a very long time, the Law Commission observed, married men, whose personal law does not allow bigamy, have been resorting to the unhealthy and immoral practice of converting to Islam for the sake of contracting a second bigamous marriage under a belief that such religious conversion enables them to marry again without getting their first marriage dissolved.

The Supreme Court of India outlawed this practice in the case of *Sarla Mudgal* v. *Union of India*, AIR 1995, SC 1531.

The ruling was reaffirmed five years later, in *Lily Thomas* v. *Union of India* (2000) 6 SCC 224.[4] There is also a trend in society to use devices, supposedly legal, 'to escape application of IPC provisions'. Some of these devices are: deliberately incomplete and 'defective' (sic) marriage ceremonies; non-marital cohabitation with a woman by a married man; or a fake change of religion.

---

3   227th Report of the Law Commission of India, 2009, https://lawcommissionofindia.nic.in/reports/report227.pdf.

4   Lily Thomas v. Union of India, (2000) 6 SCC 224.

Hindu Marriage Act, 1955

Since time immemorial, it was believed – rightly or wrongly – that Hindu religious law allowed unrestricted polygamy and imposed no specific conditions on the polygamist. The Muslim rulers of India had left the Hindu law on polygamy – whatever it was – untouched. The British rulers did the same. Finally, in 1955, the Indian parliament enacted the Hindu Marriage Act, putting a blanket ban on bigamy for Hindus, Buddhists, Jains and Sikhs.

Bigamy under Muslim Personal Law

It is generally believed that under Muslim law a husband has the unfettered right to marry again, even with his earlier marriage subsisting. On close examination of the relevant provisions of the Quran and the other sources of Islamic law, this does not seem to be the truth.

The rule of Muslim law conditionally permitting bigamy in fact visualized two or more women happily living with a common husband. Taking a second wife after forsaking or deserting the first was not Islam's concept of bigamy.

Bigamy with no restrictions or discipline whatsoever was rampant in the society where Islam made its first appearance, and also in many other societies across the globe. The Holy Quran put restrictions on it.

To this Quranic reform, the Prophet added a highly deterrent warning: 'A bigamist unable to treat his wives equally will be torn apart on the Day of Judgement.'

In India, bigamy is not very common among Muslims. In fact, the Muslim society of India, in general, looks at polygamy with great disfavour. A bigamist is looked down upon as an outsider in his family.

Despite this, unfortunately, the religious leaders are not prepared for any legislative reform in this matter. And even where religious conversion seems to be genuine, it cannot be a licence for a man's indulging in bigamy by deserting the first wife, in violation of Islam's insistence on treating co-wives with unexceptional equality and equal justice.

The fact, of course, is that conversion in such cases is invariably insincere, and is generally followed by formal or informal reconversion.

What Hindu men indulging in such practices do, and are helped by ill-educated religious functionaries and misinformed lawyers to do, is a fraud on Hinduism, a disgrace to Islam, a cruel joke on the freedom-of-conscience clause in the constitution of the country, and criminal scheming against the law of the land.

Polygamy and Islam

At the centre of the debate that Muslims produce too many children is the belief that Islam encourages polygamy, which leads to a spurt in population growth. The reality is that Islam permits polygamy subject to two conditions: marrying orphans and giving them equal treatment. Even this permission has to be understood in the historical context. It is mentioned only in the context of treatment of the orphans.

وَءَاتُوا الْيَتَٰمَىٰٓ أَمْوَٰلَهُمْ ۖ وَلَا تَتَبَدَّلُوا الْخَبِيثَ بِالطَّيِّبِ ۖ وَلَا تَأْكُلُوٓا أَمْوَٰلَهُمْ إِلَىٰٓ أَمْوَٰلِكُمْ ۚ إِنَّهُۥ كَانَ حُوبًا كَبِيرًا

'And give to the orphans their property and do not substitute worthless (things) for (their) good (things) and do not devour their property, this is surely a great crime.' (Surah An-Nisa – The Women 4:2)

The next verse goes on to secure the position of the orphans even further:

وَإِنْ خِفْتُمْ أَلَّا تُقْسِطُوا فِي الْيَتَمَى فَانكِحُوا مَا طَابَ لَكُم مِّنَ النِّسَاءِ مَثْنَى وَثُلَثَ وَرُبَعَ ۖ فَإِنْ خِفْتُمْ أَلَّا تَعْدِلُوا فَوَاحِدَةً

'And if you fear that you cannot act equitably towards orphans, then marry such women as seem good to you, two and three and four; but if you fear that you cannot act equitably (towards them) then (marry) only one.' (Surah An-Nisa – The Women 4:3)

In fact, the Holy Quran itself warns,

وَلَن تَسْتَطِيعُوا أَن تَعْدِلُوا بَيْنَ النِّسَاءِ وَلَوْ حَرَصْتُمْ

'You will never be able to do perfect justice between wives even if it is your ardent desire.' (Surah An-Nisa – The Women 4:129)

It is obvious that the permission to have more than one wife has often been abused by some Muslims, who do not realize that it is a conditional permission. In fact, it is subject to not one but two conditions: marrying orphans and equal treatment of them. It is pertinent to note that these are the only two verses in the Quran touching on polygamy, one 'permitting' polygamy conditionally, the other cautioning against it.

The emphasis of the Holy Quran is very clearly on having one wife. The permission for polygamy has to be understood in the twin context in which it was ordained, that the Arab custom of marrying an unlimited number of women on the one hand and the presence of a large number of orphaned girls and widows as a result of the constant tribal wars in the pre-Islamic and early Islamic years on the other hand.

The permission for a man to have more than one wife was given with a view to rehabilitating these orphans and widows – as wives enjoying perfect equality and not as sex slaves. Scholars are also of the view that in an age when men of means used to have multiple marriages, the Quranic injunction ('permission') had actually put a ceiling on the number of wives. In his highly respected English commentary on the Quran, Abdullah Yusuf Ali, a British barrister and scholar, whose commentary on the Holy Quran is highly regarded, has clarified that 'the number of wives of Jahiliyya (the age of ignorance) was now strictly limited to a maximum of four, provided you could feed them with perfect equity in material things as well as in affection and immaterial things. As these conditions are more difficult to fulfil, I understand the recommendation to be towards monogamy.'[5]

View from the Shariah

'Shariah' in Arabic means the path to be followed by Muslims. It can be described as Islamic law. The original sources of Shariah are three: the Quran, Sunnah ('habitual practices' of the Prophet [PBUH]) and Ahaadith (recorded sayings of the Prophet [PBUH]).

Based on these, and subservient to them, are two more sources:

Ijma (The Consensus of Jurists), and Qiyas (Analogy).

The Hadith consists of the actions and sayings of the Prophet (PBUH) as reported by his companions (sahaaba), who were witness to them, or by their successors (tabi'un) who learned about these acts or sayings directly from their predecessors.

The Ahaadith (plural of Hadith) were compiled mostly in the second and third centuries AH (After Hijrah – the Islamic calendar commemorating the migration of the Prophet [PBUH] from Mecca to Medina) by devoted compilers after decades of painstaking

---

5   All translations of the Qurani verses have been taken from Omran who had them authenticated by a three-member theological committee. The certificate of the same is published as the Preface in Omran, *Family Planning in the Legacy of Islam*, XVIII.

research. The two most respected and authentic compilations are Al-Bukhari and Al-Muslim.

Over a period of time, several schools of thought (jurisprudence) were born, both among the Sunnis and Shias. There are four Sunni schools named after their Imams (founders): Hanafi, Maliki, Shafei, and Hanbali. The Sunnis believe in the democratic succession of the Khalifas after the Prophet (PBUH) and recognize all four immediate Khalifas, namely Abu Bakr, Omar, Usman and Ali as legitimate successors.

The Shiites (meaning the inclined, or partisans) are devoted to Imam Ali (a cousin and son-in-law of the Prophet). They believe that Imamism[6] should be confined to Ali's descendants from Fatima, the Prophet's daughter, and consider the first three Caliphs (Khalifas) as usurpers. They call the fourth Caliph as Imam and the only rightful successor to the Prophet (PBUH). Several Shiite schools developed over time, some of which have disappeared. The leading contemporary schools are the Zaydis, the Imamis and the Ismailis.

The Quran and Hadith are replete with verses and traditions supportive of the concept of family planning. *It is extremely important to note that nowhere has the Quran prohibited family planning! There are only interpretations, for or against it.*

It is relevant to point out that the Holy Quran has made it clear that what Allah wanted to prohibit, He had done specifically, as evident from the following verse:

$$\text{وَقَدْ فَصَّلَ لَكُم مَّا حَرَّمَ عَلَيْكُمْ إِلَّا مَا اضْطُرِرْتُمْ إِلَيْهِ}$$

... And He (Allah) has specified to you in detail that which is forbidden (haraam) to you ... except when compelled by necessity. [Surah al-Anam – The Cattle 6:119]

There is no text prohibiting birth control in the Quran. According to the rules of jurisprudence, the silence of the Quran on some issues

6   Also known as *Ithnā'ashari.*

is not a matter of omission on the part of the Lawgiver for He is All Knowing; neither can it be because there was no population problem during those times, for Islam is meant for all times.[7]

The anti-family planning interpretation of Islamic regulations is based on the following concepts:

Tawakkul (Reliance on Allah),
Qadr (Predestination – everything is predestined), and
Rizq (Provision – Allah has created you and will provide for you)

وَمَا مِن دَآبَّةٍ فِي ٱلْأَرْضِ إِلَّا عَلَى ٱللَّهِ رِزْقُهَا وَيَعْلَمُ مُسْتَقَرَّهَا وَمُسْتَوْدَعَهَا

And there is not a creature on earth, but its sustenance depends on Allah. He knows its habitation and its depository. (Surah Hud[8] – 11:6)

It, however, does not mean the man should become lazy and should not strive for it, as the following verse has clarified:

وَأَن لَّيْسَ لِلْإِنسَٰنِ إِلَّا مَا سَعَىٰ

And that man can have nothing but what he strives for. [Surah An Najm – The Star 53:39]

The following are some other verses interpreted as being against family planning:

وَلَا تَقْتُلُوٓا۟ أَوْلَٰدَكُم مِّنْ إِمْلَٰقٍ ۖ نَّحْنُ نَرْزُقُكُمْ وَإِيَّاهُمْ

---

7   Omran, *Family Planning in the Legacy of Islam.*
8   All Prophets with Arabic names have an English version of their names; for instance, Nuh is Noah, Ibrahim is Abraham, Isha is Jesus. Contrarily, Hud is a prophet whose name has no English equivalent.

And do not kill your children (for fear of poverty); We make provisions for you, and for them too. (Surah Al Anam – The Cattle 6:151)

وَلَا تَقْتُلُوٓا أَوْلَٰدَكُمْ خَشْيَةَ إِمْلَٰقٍ ۖ نَّحْنُ نَرْزُقُهُمْ وَإِيَّاكُمْ ۚ إِنَّ قَتْلَهُمْ كَانَ خِطْئًا كَبِيرًا

And do not kill your children for fear of poverty. We provide for them and for you. Indeed, their killing is ever a great sin. (Surah Al Isra – The Night Journey 17:31)

وَٱللَّهُ جَعَلَ لَكُم مِّنْ أَنفُسِكُمْ أَزْوَٰجًا وَجَعَلَ لَكُم مِّنْ أَزْوَٰجِكُم بَنِينَ وَحَفَدَةً

And Allah has made for you your mates for yourselves, and made for you, out of them, children and grandchildren . . . (Surah An Nahl – The Bee 16:72)

نِسَآؤُكُمْ حَرْثٌ لَّكُمْ فَأْتُوا۟ حَرْثَكُمْ أَنَّىٰ شِئْتُمْ ۖ وَقَدِّمُوا۟ لِأَنفُسِكُمْ

Your wives are a place of sowing of seed for you, so come to your place of cultivation however you wish... (Surah Al Baqarah – The Cow 2:223)

Besides the Quranic verses above, the Ahaadith cited against family planning are as follows:

The Prophet (PBUH) said, 'Marry and multiply, for I will make a display of you on the Day of Judgement.' (Abu Dawoud)

The pro-family planning interpretations of the Quran

The pro-family planning interpretations of the Quran are many more, and these are based on the following concepts:

Tranquility as the purpose of conjugal life;
Emphasis on ease and convenience;
Injunction on breastfeeding;
Preference for quality over quantity; and
Permission for al-azl (coitus interruptus), etc.

Clinching verse of the Quran

The following injunction of the Quran, in my view, is absolutely
clinching in this matter:

وَلْيَسْتَعْفِفِ ٱلَّذِينَ لَا يَجِدُونَ نِكَاحًا حَتَّىٰ يُغْنِيَهُمُ ٱللَّهُ مِن فَضْلِهِ

Let those who find not the wherewithal for marriage keep themselves
chaste, until Allah gives them means out of His grace. (Surah an Nur
– The Light 24:33)

This is explained and amplified by the Prophet: 'O young
men! Those of you who can support a wife and household should
marry. For, marriage keeps you from looking with lust at women
and preserves you from promiscuity. But those who cannot, should
take to fasting, which is a means of tampering sexual desires. (Al
Bukhari)[9]

Importantly enough, even a method to prevent conception is
suggested. Abu Sa'ad, a companion of the Prophet, reported, 'A man
came to the Prophet to ask about the practice of al-azl (withdrawal
method) with his mate. He added, "I do not like her to get pregnant
and I am a man who wants what other men want. But the Jews claim
that al-azl is minor infanticide."

The Prophet said, "The Jews lied, the Jews lied."'

---

9   Mohammad Al- Bukhari is the Persian scholar and researcher, who
     compiled the most authentic collection of the Ahaadith (traditions of
     the Prophet [PBUH]). The collection itself is called *Al-Bukhari*.

(This has been authenticated by Abu Dawoud, Ibn Hanbal and al-Tahawi.)

(There are a number of other Ahaadith on the same theme.)

I consider the above-mentioned verse of the Quran and the two Ahaadith above as a *complete prescription for family planning*.

The first line of prescription is the Quranic injunction to delay marriage until one has the means; the second is elaboration on the same injunction by the Prophet, and the third prescribes the method of birth control.

The following Quranic verses and traditions of the Prophet reinforce this interpretation.

Islam as a religion of ease

يُرِيدُ ٱللَّهُ بِكُمُ ٱلۡيُسۡرَ وَلَا يُرِيدُ بِكُمُ ٱلۡعُسۡرَ

Allah desires for you ease (yusr); He desires not hardship (usr) for you. (Surah Al Baqarah – The Cow 2:185)

وَٱعۡلَمُوٓاْ أَنَّمَآ أَمۡوَٰلُكُمۡ وَأَوۡلَٰدُكُمۡ فِتۡنَةٌ

And know that your wealth and your children are a persecution (or trial) (Fitna). (Surah Al Anfal – The spoils of war 8:28 and Surah At Taghabun – The mutual loss and gain 64:15)

لَا تُكَلَّفُ نَفۡسٌ إِلَّا وُسۡعَهَا ۚ لَا تُضَآرَّ وَٰلِدَةٌ بِوَلَدِهَا وَلَا مَوۡلُودٌ لَّهُۥ بِوَلَدِهِۦ

No soul shall impose (upon itself) a duty but to its capacity; neither shall a mother be made to suffer injury on account of her child, nor shall he to whom the child is born (be made to suffer) on account of his child. (Surah Al Baqarah - The Cow 2:233)

The most gruelling trial is to have plenty of children with no adequate means. (al-Hakim)

A multitude of children is one of the two poverties (or cases of penury), while a small number is one of the two cases of ease. (Musnad al- Shahab)

Purpose of marriage conjugal tranquillity

هُوَ ٱلَّذِى خَلَقَكُم مِّن نَّفْسٍ وَٰحِدَةٍ وَجَعَلَ مِنْهَا زَوْجَهَا لِيَسْكُنَ إِلَيْهَا

It is He who created you from a single soul (nafs) and therefrom did make his mate, that he might dwell in tranquility with her . . . (Surah Al Araf – The Heights 7:189)

وَمِنْ ءَايَٰتِهِۦٓ أَنْ خَلَقَ لَكُم مِّنْ أَنفُسِكُمْ أَزْوَٰجًا لِّتَسْكُنُوٓا إِلَيْهَا وَجَعَلَ بَيْنَكُم مَّوَدَّةً وَرَحْمَةً

And one of His signs is this: He created for you mates from yourself that you might find tranquillity in them, and He ordained between you love and mercy . . . (Surah Ar Rum – The Romans 30:21)

It is significant that neither verse mentions children or procreation. This suggests that 'tranquility' is the overall purpose of marriage, which is more attainable, since all couples can achieve tranquillity but not all couples are fertile.[10]

Islam as a religion for quality

كَم مِّن فِئَةٍ قَلِيلَةٍ غَلَبَتْ فِئَةً كَثِيرَةً بِإِذْنِ ٱللَّهِ

How often, by Allah's will, has a small force vanquished a numerous force. (Surah Al Baqarah – The Cow 2:249)

لَقَدْ نَصَرَكُمُ ٱللَّهُ فِى مَوَاطِنَ كَثِيرَةٍ وَيَوْمَ حُنَيْنٍ إِذْ أَعْجَبَتْكُمْ كَثْرَتُكُمْ فَلَمْ تُغْنِ عَنكُمْ شَيْئًا وَضَاقَتْ عَلَيْكُمُ ٱلْأَرْضُ بِمَا رَحُبَتْ ثُمَّ وَلَّيْتُم مُّدْبِرِينَ

---

10 Omran, *Family Planning in the Legacy of Islam*, 14.

Allah has given you victory in many battles; but on the day of
Hunayn, when you exalted in your multitude, it availed you naught.
And the earth, vast as it is, became tight for you, then you turned
back in retreat. (Surah At Tawbah – The Repentance 9:25)

Ahaadith about the rights of the children

The right of a child on his parent is to be given good breeding and
good name. (al-Baihaqi)

To leave your heirs rich is better than leaving them dependent
upon people's charity (al Bukhari).

Children are considered a joy, an adornment, as well as a way to
continue one's descent. Islam enjoins us to have children, but it insists
at the same time that they should be good and righteous, which
requires an intensive effort to raise them correctly. The ability to raise
children correctly is an inherent requirement of marriage in Islam.[11]

Breastfeeding to help spacing

وَٱلْوَٰلِدَٰتُ يُرْضِعْنَ أَوْلَٰدَهُنَّ حَوْلَيْنِ كَامِلَيْنِ

And mothers shall suckle their children two full years to complete
breastfeeding (Surah Al Baqarah – The Cow 2:233)

حَمَلَتْهُ أُمُّهُ وَهْنًا عَلَىٰ وَهْنٍ وَفِصَٰلُهُ فِي عَامَيْنِ

... His mother bears him in weakness upon weakness, and his
weaning is in two years ... (Surah Luqman – Luqman the Wise
31:14)

Islam encourages Planning

---

11 Ibid., 30.

This is clear from Joseph's interpretation of the Pharaoh's dream and the seven-year plan he devised to help cope during the anticipated bad years of famine, as can be gathered from the passages of Surah Yusuf.[12] (12: 47-48)

His plan for the 'future' was not considered to be mistrust of Allah, or antagonistic to tawakkul, but farsightedness.

Islam emphasizes moderation

Prof. Omran has rightly observed that Islam stands for moderation and discourages excesses, extremism, rigidity and undue restrictions. Moderation is also coupled with the stamping out of extremism, even in worship. Jurists have reported the Prophet's angry rejection of extremism even in the form of prayers day and night, continuous fasting, self-imposed celibacy and choice of an isolated and harsh way of life.

Gender equality

There is a lot of misinformation that Islam treats women badly. Nothing can be farther from the truth. As early as fourteen centuries ago, Islam recognized women as equal partners to men in all possible ways. They participated in business, in war, and in all activities, shoulder to shoulder with men. Islam was also the first religion to recognize property and inheritance rights for women, which many other religions granted only in the twentieth century.

The Holy Quran and Hadith are replete with injunctions to recognize equality of the two genders. Here is a sample of them:

$$\text{وَلَهُنَّ مِثْلُ ٱلَّذِى عَلَيْهِنَّ بِٱلْمَعْرُوفِ}$$

And for women are rights over men similar to those of men over women ... [Surah Al Baqarah – The Cow 2:228]

---

12 Ibid., 63.

هُنَّ لِبَاسٌ لَكُمْ وَأَنْتُمْ لِبَاسٌ لَهُنَّ

They (your wives) are your garment and you are a garment for them.
(Surah Baqarah 2: 187)

فَاسْتَجَابَ لَهُمْ رَبُّهُمْ أَنِّي لَا أُضِيعُ عَمَلَ عَامِلٍ مِنْكُمْ مِنْ ذَكَرٍ أَوْ أُنْثَى ۖ بَعْضُكُمْ مِنْ بَعْضٍ

Their Lord responded to them: 'I never fail to reward any worker
among you for any work you do, be you male or female – you are
equal to one another.' (Surah Al e Imran – The Family of Imran
3:195)

وَالْمُؤْمِنُونَ وَالْمُؤْمِنَاتُ بَعْضُهُمْ أَوْلِيَاءُ بَعْضٍ

And the believers, men and women, are helpers, supporters,
friends and protectors of one another . . . (Surah At Tawbah – The
Repentance Quran, 9: 71)

Ahaadith supplement the verses of the Quran with explanations
and elaboration.

The most complete believer in faith is the best in morals, and the
best among you is the best to their wives. (Tirmidhi)

A man asks the Prophet (PBUH), 'Who deserves my
companionship most?' The Prophet said, 'Your mother.' The man
asked, 'Who next'? The Prophet said, 'Your mother.' The man asked,
'Who next?' Prophet said, 'Your mother.' He asked, 'Who next?'
The Prophet said, 'Then your father.' (Narrated by Abu Hurairah–
Bukhari and Muslim)

Observe your duty to Allah in respect to the women, and treat
them well. (Prophet Muhammed's, PBUH, Last Sermon)

Verily, women are the twin halves of men. (Abu Dawud, Tirmidhi)

Men and women are equal halves. (Abu Dawoud)

Virtue of having daughters

It is well known that many Indians, driven by the traditional preference for sons, continue to have children until they get a male child and end up with a large family. Lately, with the invention of sex determination tests, female foeticide has become rampant, despite stringent laws against it. The Quran forbade female infanticide fourteen centuries ago.

وَإِذَا بُشِّرَ أَحَدُهُم بِٱلْأُنثَىٰ ظَلَّ وَجْهُهُ مُسْوَدًّا وَهُوَ كَظِيمٌ

يَتَوَٰرَىٰ مِنَ ٱلْقَوْمِ مِن سُوٓءِ مَا بُشِّرَ بِهِۦٓ أَيُمْسِكُهُۥ عَلَىٰ هُونٍ أَمْ يَدُسُّهُۥ فِى ٱلتُّرَابِ أَلَا سَآءَ مَا يَحْكُمُونَ

And when one of them gets a baby girl, his face becomes darkened with overwhelming grief. Ashamed, he hides from the people, because of the bad news given to him. He even ponders: should he keep the baby grudgingly, or bury her in the dust. Miserable indeed is their judgement. (Surah An Nahl – The Bee 16:58-59)

Do not hate having daughters, for they are the comforting dears. (Al-Tabarani)

It is a woman's blessing to have a girl as her first child. (Mardaweih)

Whoever has three daughters and he cares for them, he is merciful to them, and he clothes them, then Paradise is certain for him. (Jabir ibn Abdullah)

There are 939 females for every one thousand males among Hindus; the corresponding number among Muslims is 951. This difference in figures could be attributed to lower number of female foeticide among Muslims, due to religious injunctions.

Prof. Omran has comprehensively summed up the position of women in Islam as enunciated in Surah An Nisa (The Women 4:11,12).[13] Islam championed equality for women in all matters – religious, social, economic and familial. A woman cannot be forced

13 Ibid.

into marriage by her family or guardian – she has to give her consent. Islam endorses a woman's consent to such an extent that a marriage could be annulled when it has been forced on a woman by her guardian.

In marriage, a woman can keep her maiden name. In fact, it is the preferred way. She is completely independent financially and can do with her money as she pleases, while her husband (or the father or brother) is responsible for providing for her and her children. She has complete and total control of her possessions. As a mother, she is placed ahead of her husband in regard to the children's loyalty and affection. She is free to choose her marital partner and has a right to demand, at the time of the marriage contract, the power of divorce and also the power to disallow polygyny by her husband.

Islam gives women equal legal status with men. This means she has the right to enter into all kinds of contractual arrangements and to conduct business on her own without the need of her husband's consent. In terms of inheritance, she, as a daughter, gets half of her brother's share. But under other circumstances, she gets as much, or even more than other men in the family.

Opinion of Renowned Imams

The founders of the four Islamic schools of jurisprudence approve the practice of birth control. Interestingly enough, there are competing reasons for and against birth control expounded by the learned. For instance, the Prophet's companions, like Ibn Mas'ud and 'Abd Allah bin 'Abbas, advocated prohibition of birth control. On the other hand, these traditions have been rejected by another companion of the Prophet, Abu Sa'id Khudri, whose Hadith on al-azl (coitus interruptus) was categorical about the Prophet's approval of it.

Opinions of the ulama down the ages

Ijma, or Consensus of jurists

Having taken into account the provisions of the Quran and the Hadith, one could turn attention to the Ijma (consensus), the fourth important source of Islamic Law. Quite a few fatwas by the leading ulama from different Islamic countries are available on the issues under discussion. Some of the important among them, whose explicit approval of family planning in Islam is very clear, have been cited below.

Imam Shafei, the first contributor to the principles of Islamic jurisprudence, said that more children should not be produced if they cannot be properly supported.

Imam Raghib, the eleventh-century Muslim scholar, interpreting surah 17 verse 31 of the Quran, says it is not only the physical killing of children which is prohibited in Islam, but also their spiritual and intellectual killing. Denial of education to children, for example, amounts to killing them intellectually.

'Those few (qalil),' records a Hadith, 'who are virtuous are superior to those many who are undesirable.' It implies that the number of children should be restricted to the capacity of the parents to make them virtuous.

Imam Ghazali, a sufi of great eminence, mentions a tradition from the Prophet:

Smallness of the family (qillat al'ayal) is a facility (yusur) and its largeness (kathrat) results in faqr (indigence, poverty).

Opinion of Haji Nasiruddin Latif (Indonesia, 1974):

He says there is no verse in the Quran forbidding the wife or husband from practising family planning. 'I, for one, do not feel that Islam interdicts family planning to ward off hardship in Muslim married life.'

Opinion of Sheikh Abdel Aziz (Jordan, 1985):

Family planning in Islam starts with the choice of the wife and lays great emphasis on raising children physically, educationally and spiritually; that is why quality is favoured over quantity.

Fatwa of Sheikh Mahmoud Shaltout, Great Imam of Al-Azhar (1959):

• Strong endorsement of the use of contraceptives on an individual basis for health, social or economic reasons.
• Under certain conditions, contraception becomes mandatory.

Fatwa of Advisory Council on Religious Matters (Turkey, 1960):

• Contraception allowed with the wife's consent; even without the wife's consent in case of war, turmoil or conditions where bringing up children becomes difficult.

Opinion of Sheikh Sayyid Sabiq (Saudi Arabia, 1968):

The use of contraception is allowed, especially if the husband already has a large family, if he cannot bring up his children correctly, if his wife is weak or sick or has repeated pregnancies, or if the husband is poor.

Opinions of the Indian ulama

The opinions of the Indian ulama are on the same lines.

Bahs o Nazar, a quarterly magazine from Patna (editor: Maulana Mujahidul Islam Qasmi) has documented the first fiqhi (Islamic jurisprudence) seminar held in New Delhi in 1989 in its special issue of September 1989.[14] It contains a great debate on the issue of family planning in Islam. Some of the views expressed by the participating scholars are given below:

The great Indian scholar Shah Abdul Aziz (1864) states in his monumental Tafsir (commentary) of the Quran: '*Al-azl is lawful on the basis of authentic and well-known traditions of the Prophet. The use*

---

14 All Bahs e Nazar quotes have been translated by the author.

of medicines before or after coitus for preventing conception is as lawful as al-azl.'[15]

- Islam acknowledges change as a reality and has ample scope for change – natural and bonafide change.
- Religion (Islam), while it supports fast movement of life, also acts an overseer, guardian and teacher.

Maulana Masood Ahmad Qasmi Nazim-e-Deeniyat, Aligarh Muslim University, Aligarh:

Family planning can be adopted for the following reasons:

- To provide for appropriate spacing between two children.
- To provide for (proper) upbringing, education and training of children.
- In the event of a large family.[16]

Allama Shah Zaid Abul Hasan Farooqi, Delhi:

- All the four (Sunni) Imams – Imam Abu Hanifa, Imam Maalik, Imam Shafei, Imam Ahmad ibn Hanbal – regard azl as permissible. However, in one Hadith, a condition has been prescribed, that it should be done only with the wife's consent.
- Scholars Ibn Abidin, Tahtawi and Abus Saud opine that even a woman has the right to shut off the mouth of her uterus without the permission of the husband to avoid pregnancy.
- Anti-pregnancy pills and medicines are also permissible. However, for using any contraceptive medicine, it is advisable to consult an experienced doctor.

---

15 *Bahs o Nazar*, Quarterly Journal, special issue on the first *fiqhi* (Islamic jurisprudence) seminar held at New Delhi (September 1989).

16 Ibid.

Maulana Masood Ahmad Qasmi, Nazim-e-Deeniyat, Aligarh Muslim University:

- When permissibility of azl is proven, the use of other comparable measures (like condoms) stands automatically endorsed.

Maulana Jamil Ahmed Naziri, Jamia Arabia, Ahya-ul-uloom, Mubarakpur, Azamgarh:

- To prevent short spacing between children, which will make them naturally weak, use of temporary contraceptive methods like the loop (intra-uterine device), nirodh (condoms), medicine or ointment is valid.

Mufti Zafir-ud-din Miftahi, Mufti, Darul-Uloom, Deoband:

- If there is a valid reason or disease because of which a woman cannot bear the hardship of pregnancy, in such a situation, Shariah allows temporary birth control measures.

Islam and Sterilization

It is amply clear that Islam is fully supportive of temporary methods of family planning. However, sterilization or other irreversible methods are disallowed by almost all sections of the ulama, though some ulama have a positive Islamic interpretation of sterilization too.

Opinions of the Indian Ulama

Maulana Abul Hasan Ali Nadvi, 1989, President, All India Muslim Personal Law Board, Lucknow:[17]

- Birth control is valid under certain conditions.
- If someone who has full faith in Allah as the Absolute Provider adopts family planning in view of his special circumstances, there is no bar in the light of the Quran.[18]

Maulana Khalid Saifullah Rahmani, Sadar Mudarris, Dar-ul-Uloom Sabeel-ul-Islam, Hyderabad:[19]

- Any device which does not permanently stop conception but prevents it temporarily is not forbidden in Islam.
- Practice of contraception for reasons of proper upbringing and education of children is not forbidden.[20]
- If the husband or wife is suffering from a disease which can be transmitted to the child, birth prevention is permissible.[21]
- Preventing conception temporarily, which does not lead to permanently impairing the capability (to procreate), is legal.[22]
- Use of the loop (IUDs) and nirodh (condoms) is like the practice of azl.[23]

Maulana Mumtaz Ahmad Qasmi, Imam Jama Masjid, Shimla:

---

17 *Bahs o Nazr*, 64.
18 *Bahs o Nazar*, First Fiqhi Seminar Special Issue, Patna, 302.
19 Ibid.
20 Ibid., 304.
21 Ibid.
22 Ibid., 313.
23 Ibid.

- Family planning should not be linked with religion at all, but with the social conditions of the country.
- So long as our faith in Allah as the Absolute Provider is firm, family planning will not only be permissible, but in certain conditions essential as, after all, using all valid means is also His mandate.

Maulana Abdul Jaleel Chaudhary, Amir-e-Shariat, Assam:

- If, in the opinion of an experienced doctor, a woman is not in a position to bear the pregnancy, she can use those valid contraception methods which are necessary to save her life and health.[24]

Maulana Mohammad Mian, Sheikhul Hadith, Madrasa Ameenia, Delhi and Secretary Jamiat-ul-Ulema-i-Hind:

- If contraception is practised because a woman's health is not good and pregnancy will aggravate it, appropriate measures can be adopted as an individual choice, since it is more important to protect a present life than a life yet to be born.
- Birth control as a government movement is not justified.

Dr Fazl-ur-Rahman Ganauri, Aligarh Muslim University, Aligarh:

- Birth control is not against the basic objectives of marriage.[25]

Reversible Methods

Several Hadiths listed by Imam Ghazali underline the benefits of al-azl:

---

24 Ibid., 343.
25 Ibid., 383.

- Preservation of wife's beauty and charm.
- Protection of her health and life.
- Shielding her from hardship (kathrat al-haral) on account of childbirth.
- Saving the family from financial hardship.

The Imam goes to the extent of saying:

'If a man practises azl with this intention that the woman retains her beauty and his love for her endures, then azl is permissible.' (Ahya-ul-uloom 23/2, Tehdid-e-Nasl, p.135).[26]

There cannot be a more progressive interpretation.

Shah Abdul Aziz (1864):

In his tafsir (commentary) of the Quran, Shah Abdul Aziz (1864) remarks: 'Al-azl is lawful on the basis of authentic and well-known traditions of the Prophet. The use of medicines before or after coitus for preventing conception is as lawful as Al-azl.'

Sheikh Abdel Aziz (Jordan, 1985):

- Family Planning in Islam starts with the choice of the wife and puts a great emphasis on raising children physically, educationally and spiritually, that is why quality is favoured over quantity.
- Use of pills is sanctioned because, like al-azl, it is not murder or crime against a being.
- Decision (to practise family planning) must be individual rather than national.

Fatwa of Sheikh Mahmoud Shaltout, Great Imam of Al-Azhar (1959):

---

26 Ibid., 355.

- Strong endorsement of use of contraceptives on an individual basis for health, social or economic reasons.
- Under certain conditions contraception becomes mandatory.

Fatwa of Advisory Council on Religious Matters (Turkey, 1960):

- Contraception allowed with the wife's consent.
- Allowed even without wife's consent, in case of war, turmoil or conditions where bringing up children becomes difficult.

Fatwa by Sheikh Abdullah Al-Qilqili (Jordan, 1964):
Contraception definitely allowed by the Hadith.

Opinion of Sheikh Sayyid Sabiq (Saudi Arabia, 1968):
The use of contraception is allowed, especially if the husband already has a large family, if he cannot bring up his children correctly, if his wife is weak or sick or has repeated pregnancies, or if the husband is poor.

Centuries-old consensus in India

About 500 religious scholars who codified Islamic law in 1670, during the time of the Mughal ruler Aurangzeb, unanimously allowed contraception with the mutual consent of the partners.[27]

Turning to the contemporary scene, the opinion of leading ulama and other scholars from the Indian subcontinent are equally pertinent. Allama Shah Zaid Abul Hasan Farooqi, Delhi:

---

27 *Fatawa-e-Alamgiri* is a compilation of various fatwas in the era of Aurangzeb's rule. Five hundred scholars were gathered to interpret various Islamic injunctions, including birth control which were listed in the book called *Fatawa-e-Alamgiri*. It was translated in Urdu by Maulana Syed Amir Ali, in 1931 (Lahore: Maktaba Rahmania).

- All the four Imams regard azl as permissible. However, because of one Hadith, a condition has been prescribed that it should be done only with the wife's consent.[28]
- It is wrong to assume that the honour and glory of the Muslims lies in their numbers, even if they are dirty and wicked. Often, small numbers triumph over large numbers, as had happened in the Battle of Badr.[29]
- A man seeking vasectomy is not working under the influence of Satan. He is doing it because of his own constraints. He says, 'The children granted to me by Allah are enough for me. I will arrange for their sustenance, upbringing and education with great difficulty. More children will become a greater problem for me, and I will start resorting to illegal means (to support them). This will anger Allah and please the Satan.' This is entirely in accordance with the spirit of the Quranic verse, 'We do not put any one under weight he cannot bear.'

However, Allama Ibn-i-Hamam states that if a man fears that the child to be born would be unworthy, then the wife's consent is not necessary and he can do azl without her consent.

Anti-pregnancy pills and medicines are also permissible. However, for using any contraceptive medicine, it is advisable to consult an experienced doctor.

Maulana Masood Ahmad Qasmi, Nazim-e-Deeniyat, Aligarh Muslim University:

- There is no reason for azl to be forbidden. It is proven that sahaaba (companions of the Prophet) would practise it.[30]

---

28 *Bahs o nazar*, 10.
29 Ibid., 28.
30 Ibid., 288.

- When permissibility of azl is proven, the use of other comparable measures (like condoms) stands automatically endorsed.

Maulana Khalid Saifullah Rahmani, Sadar Mudarris, Dar-ul-Uloom, Sabeel-ul-Islam, Hyderabad:

- Preventing conception temporarily, which does not lead to permanently impairing the capability (to procreate), is legal.[31]
- Use of the loop (IUDs) and nirodh (condoms) is equivalent to the practice of azl.[32]

Maulana Jamil Ahmed Naziri, Jamia Arabia, Ahya-ul-uloom, Mubarakpur, Azamgarh:

- To prevent short spacing between children, which will make them naturally weak, use of temporary contraceptive methods like the loop (IUD), nirodh (condoms), medicine or ointment is valid.[33]
- When there is strong apprehension of children going astray because of degeneration and degradation of the environment, several Islamic jurists permit azl.
- When a woman is disobedient and the husband intends to divorce her, and there is an apprehension that childbirth will increase her disobedience and rude behaviour (since the woman could think that the husband cannot divorce her any longer because of the child), jurists allow azl.[34]

Mufti Zafir-ud-din Miftahi, Mufti, Darul-Uloom, Deoband:

---

31 Ibid., 313.
32 Ibid.
33 Ibid., 317.
34 Ibid., 318.

If there is a valid reason or disease because of which a woman cannot bear the hardship of pregnancy, in such a situation, Shariah allows temporary birth control measures.[35]

Maulana Sultan Ahmed Islahi, Aligarh:

Imam Ghazali regards Azl as permissible. Azl, according to Imam Ghazali, is not like killing a child or burying him alive.[36]

Maulana Mohammad Mian, Sheikhul Hadith, Madrasa Ameenia, Delhi and Secretary Jamiat-ul-Ulema-i-Hind:

- If contraception is practised because a woman's health is not good and pregnancy will aggravate it, appropriate measures can be adopted as an individual choice, since it is more important to protect a present life than a life yet to be born.
- Birth control as a government movement is not justified.

Maulana Mufti Mohammed Zaid, Jamia Arabia, Hathora, Banda:
- When a specialist doctor opines that a woman is permanently unfit to bear a child, or for whom pregnancy will endanger her life, there is scope for permanent sterilization.[37]
- The Prophet has disallowed azl with a woman without her permission.
- Azl is permitted by a majority of the sahaaba (companions of the Prophet) and by jurists, and all the four Imams.[38]
- Azl and modern methods of contraception are legally on the same footing, and both are permitted as individual choice.[39]
- If a man's nature is such that the wife's beauty is the only way for his love (for her) to continue, contraception may be allowed.[40]

---

35 Ibid., 336.
36 Ibid., 260.
37 Ibid., 347.
38 Ibid., 349.
39 Ibid., 350.
40 Ibid., 354.

Islam and irreversible family planning methods

While there is overwhelming opinion in favour of contraception, permanent sterilization is disallowed by most sections of the ulama.

Fatwa from the Fatwa Committee of Al Azhar (1953):

The committee has permitted contraception or reversible family planning methods, on health and other grounds, but has disallowed permanent sterilization.

Fatwa of Haji Abdel Jalil Hassan (Malaysia, 1964):

Contraception is permitted but sterilization is disallowed.

Maulana Zubair Ahmed Qasmi, Shaikh-ul-Hadith, Darul-Uloom Sabil-ul-Islam, Hyderabad:

Those methods of contraception which permanently impair the fertility of the male or the female are illegal and forbidden.[41]

Mufti Shamsuddin, Delhi:

- It is wrong to regard vasectomy as castration.[42]
- Vasectomy and tubectomy do not amount to terminating the birth cycle but to keeping it limited.[43]

Islam on abortion

Hadith

The Prophet's companion, Hazrat Ali, about whom the Prophet said, 'I am the City of Knowledge and Ali is its gate', has even permitted abortion before the ensoulment of the foetus, which happens after four months of conception, according to Islamic belief.

---

41 Ibid., 325.
42 Ibid., 255.
43 Ibid.

Fatwas and opinions of scholars on abortion – international

Fatwa by Sheikh Abdullah Al-Qilqili (Jordan, 1964):
Allowable is taking of drugs to cause abortion before quickening (ensoulment of the foetus).

Opinion of Sheikh Sayyid Sabiq (Saudi Arabia, 1968):
Abortion is disallowed after ensoulment (after 120 days of conception).

Fatwa by Sheikh Jadel Haq, Grand Imam, Al-Azhar (1979–80):
All schools of jurisprudence disallow abortion after four months except to save the mother's life.

Fatwas and opinions of Indian ulama on abortion:

Maulana Khalid Saifullah Rahmani, Sadar Mudarris, Dar-ul-Uloom Sabeel-ul-Islam, Hyderabad:

*   If pregnancy occurs during the breastfeeding of an infant leading to stopping of milk, abortion can be resorted to, before four months.[44]
*   Abortion after four months of conception is forbidden.[45]

Qazi Mujahidul Islam, Imarat-e-Shariah, Bihar, Patna:
Before ensoulment of the foetus, abortion can be allowed under certain circumstances.[46]

Maulana Mufti Mohammed Zaid, Jamia Arabia, Hathora, Banda:

---

44 Ibid., 306.
45 Ibid.
46 Ibid., 388.

Some ulama permit abortion even after ensoulment of the foetus if the woman's life is in danger.[47]

Maulana Jamil Ahmed Naziri, Jamia Arabia, Ahya-ul-uloom, Mubarakpur, Azamgarh:

Abortion is not allowed even within 120 days, if it is on the basis of medical determination of the female sex of the foetus.[48]

The evidence is recurrent that Islam does not at all oppose family planning. On the contrary, it emphasizes birth-spacing, the health of the mother and the rights of the child to health and quality upbringing.

To be specific, there is no evidence to show that the Holy Quran has even implicitly prohibited birth control. In fact, several verses seem supportive of the concept, as shown earlier. Many interpretations, however, suggest that Islam is opposed to the terminal methods of family planning, especially abortion after four months of conception (the Medical Termination of Pregnancy Act 1971 forbids it too), but provided for permission for termination of certain pregnancies within twelve weeks.

The MTP Act is now proposed to be modified to allow for abortion up to five months (twenty weeks) of pregnancy, on the advice of a medical board, by the Medical Termination of Pregnancy (Amendment) Bill 2020, which has been introduced in the Lok Sabha in March 2020.

On reversible or temporary methods of family planning, the position of Islam is positive. That Prophet Muhammad (PBUH) allowed his companions to practise al-azl to ward off social and economic hardship and risk to the health of the mother and child is well established. And, by implication, there is no bar on the use of other temporary methods. In short, in Islam, all temporary methods are allowed, mostly with the wife's knowledge and consent.

---

47 Ibid., 347.
48 Ibid., 322.

It may be finally remarked that a large number of the ulama have not only allowed Muslims to practise family planning but some of them have also recommended it. Several among them permit even abortion, with the wife's concurrence and so long as it is within four months of pregnancy. However, most of them appear to have reservations about permitting any permanent method of contraception.

Role of Indian Imams

As we have seen, there are many enlightened and liberal ulama in India who are concerned about the educational backwardness of Muslims in the country, although these ulama are currently confined to certain isolated pockets, particularly in the south. In this context, the lead taken by the Punjab Wakf Board to organize a seminar on Rights of Children in Islam in 1994 was commendable, and showed promising results.

The seminar was jointly organized by the Punjab Wakf Board (a board for the four states of Punjab, Haryana, Himachal Pradesh and the union territory of Chandigarh), the Organization of Imams of Punjab Wakf Board and Jamiat-Ul-Ulama-i-Hind (Organization of Ulama of India). Among the notable participants were Justice Sardar Ali Khan, chairman of the Minorities Commission of India, Maulana Mujibullah Nadvi, member of the Muslim Personal Law Board, Dr Rasheed-Uz-Zafar, vice-chancellor at Jamia Hamdard, Maulana Zaheer Alam Badar Qasmi, general secretary of Markazi-JamiatUl-Ulama-i-Hind and Maulana Mumtaz Ahmed Qasmi, president of Tanzeem-e-Aimma (Organization of the Imams) of the Punjab Wakf Board, eminent clerics belonging to Nadwat-Ul-Ulama, Lucknow, and others. It was a good mix of religious leaders, modern scholars and journalists at the seminar.

A number of eminent Ulama who participated in the seminar dwelt at length on problems relating to the educational, health and nutritional status of children and women, all of which have a bearing on family planning. The seminar, which was presided over by Maulana Mujibullah Nadvi, member of the All India Muslim Personal Law Board, concluded that Islam specifically recognized the following rights of children, and specified award and punishment to enforce them:

- Babies' right to mother's milk.
- Right to be cared for by parents.
- Right to proper education and training.
- Right to enjoyment of the highest attainable standard of health and nutrition.
- Complete equality of opportunities to both boys and girls.

The seminar unanimously asserted that 'denying these rights to children was against the spirit of Islam' (*Wakf News*, February, 1994, Ambala).

The participants also welcomed the new trend of rising enrolments of Muslim children in primary schools in various states, particularly in the south. They agreed it was the prime responsibility of parents to send their children to school, which was a sure way of removing social and economic backwardness among Muslims. They also emphasized that the family, as the basic social unit, should provide a natural environment for the growth and well-being of its members, particularly children.

Maulana Mujibullah Nadvi cited numerous directions of Prophet Muhammad (PBUH), to the effect that an obligation was cast on parents to provide good education to their children, male and female alike, and that it was 'much better to provide education to children than to give kilos of food grains in alms'. He also clarified that in Islam there was no conflict in acquiring knowledge of religion and education in modern subjects like science and mathematics. Also, Muslims were under a mandate that they should in no way treat the girl child as inferior to the boy child. The religion also recognized certain basic rights of the child.

Maulana Nadvi felt there was a double responsibility cast on Muslims – to enable their children to become good Muslims, a model for others, and to become good citizens, to become the pride of the nation. That would be the most valuable accomplishment for parents in the upbringing of their children. Another eminent scholar and seminar participant, Maulana Zaheer Alam Badr Qasmi, stressed that for Muslims, education does not mean only acquisition of knowledge of the Quran and Hadith; Islam attached equal importance to modern subjects like science and mathematics to enable a Muslim to equip himself to meet the challenges of contemporary life in society.

It is significant that family planning was not the subject of the seminar, for fear of arousing suspicion of the participating Imams, if not hostility. However, several participants themselves highlighted the importance of small families, particularly in the context of the right of children to good health and decent upbringing, and out of concern for women's health. Against the backdrop of a few unpleasant incidents, like the sacking of an Imam in Rajasthan for speaking in favour of family planning, and a public furore in Punjab against an Imam whose wife had undergone tubectomy, these positive views presented a pleasant contrast. It proved that if the ulama are properly approached and problems are presented in proper perspective without offending the sensitivities of the orthodox, the importance of family planning can be impressed upon the people in general, and Muslims in particular.

The seminar unanimously made the following recommendations:

1. Islam prescribes a wide range of rights for children.
2. No discrimination is allowed between girls and boys.
3. Education, health, and proper upbringing are the most important rights of children.

4. There is a need to analyse the reasons why Muslim lagged in education, when Islam has categorically given them the right to education.

5. The ulama and the Imams have a great responsibility in this context. The seminar urged the Imams of the Punjab Wakf Board to analyse why Muslim children are not getting what is due to them in matters of education and health.

6. Arabic madrasas should include in their curricula modern secular education, including vocational training, besides religious education.

7. Information on women and child health should be disseminated widely.

8. *The Quranic injunction of breast feeding for at least two years must be propagated; and the meaning and implication of Quranic verse (2:233) should be suitably explained through posters displayed prominently in mosques, madaaris and other places.*

9. Abortion of female foetus after amniocentesis tests should be condemned. The seminar noted with satisfaction that this practice among Muslims is non-existent.

10. These messages should be displayed on posters in every mosque and madrasa in Punjab, Himachal Pradesh, Haryana and Chandigarh.

11. Booklets on the subject should be published and widely distributed.

12. Seminars and conferences should be organized at the district and even village level on this subject.

13. The Punjab Wakf Board and its Tanzim-e-Aimma (Organization of Imams) will observe 1994 as the Year of Rights of the Children.

The Pulse Polio campaign led by them in Gurgaon district, which topped the country, was the crowning glory of this effort .

74

THE HINDUSTAN TIMES, NEW DELHI, SATURDAY DECEMBER 9 1995 CITY

Imams launch polio drive in Mewat

HT Correspondent

GURGAON, Dec. 8
Breaking all barriers of fanaticism, the Imams and Ulemas of Haryana and Himachal Pradesh have joined hands to go to masses to alleviate their lives by educating them about the importance of pulse polio. Apart from exercising spiritual guidance, they have launched door-to-door contact programme along with the officials of Wakf Board, to make people of Mewat aware of the importance of child health, immunisation and cleanliness.

The pulse polio drive being motivated by the Punjab Wakf Board was launched in Nuh, 45 km from here, yesterday, and they have pledged to work for 100 per cent immunisation. Pamphlets, posters, leaflets etc designed in Urdu and Hindi which also show the importance of health and sanitation in Islam were being freely distributed. The campaign in Haryana has been prepared in collaboration with district administration, especially the Mewar Development Agency, Gurgaon.

The campaign is in pursuance of the historic decision taken by the Tanzeem-e-Aimma of Punjab Wakf Board (an organisation of Imams) to participate in fully immunisation and school enrolment drive at a regional seminar of Imams organised by the Board in Faridabad recently.

Dr S. Y. Quraishi, joint secretary, Government of India, Department of Youth Affairs and Sports and Administrator, Punjab Wakf Board told this correspondent that around 300 teams of Imams of Ulemas will coordinate with the district health officials in the social mobilisation. Dr Quraishi said that "Khutba" of Friday prayers prepared by religious scholars of Darul Uloom (Deoband), will be focussed on the problems of children and need for immunisation.

To monitor the whole campaign, a 12-member committee of religious scholars has also been constituted. Noted among them are Mufti Rasheed Ahmed, Mufti-e-Mewat Maulana Mumtaz Ahmed Quasmi, Maulana Bashir Ahmed, president, Tanzeem-e-Aimma PWB, Rashidul Amini of Delhi, Maulana Abdus Subhan and Maulana Siddique of Mewat. These Ulemas have, in a joint statement, appealed to the community to go for Pulse Polio on large scale.

SATURDAY DECEMBER 9 1995

Imams to preach literacy, immunisation on Fridays

EXPRESS NEWS SERVICE

NEW DELHI, Dec 8: In a historic move, Imams and Muslim religious leaders in Punjab, Haryana and Himachal Pradesh will for the first time, discuss the need of immunisation against polio in their sermon before the Friday prayers. They will also discuss the importance of education.

And they will not stop at this alone. They will propagate family planning. They believe that the Imams can not only impart religious education but also help people find solutions to their social and economic problems

For this the Imams will campaign door-to-door and visit primary schools. Special pamphlets, leaflets and posters have been printed in Hindi and Urdu showing the importance of health and sanitation in Islam, for the campaign.

The Fatehpuri Imam, Mufti Mukarram however noted that there was no similar campaign on the anvil in Delhi. Appreciating the effort made by the religious leaders for educating the masses, he said that anything which was done for public welfare was good. But the religious leaders had no right to preach family planning as it was against the teachings of the Holy Quran.

Nearly 300 Imams and Ulemas will coordinate with district health officials in Haryana, Punjab and Himachal Pradesh, to create mass awareness among the people.

Considering that there are over half a million Imams in the country, in direct and close contact with millions of Muslims, they are extremely influential within the community, particularly among the poorest and the most illiterate. It was decided that the findings and resolutions from the seminar would be disseminated to them, spelling out the clear and specific role of Imams in enforcement of the rights of children and women, as granted by Islam, especially for their education and health. The seminar has far-reaching significance, since there is a Wakf board (Muslim Endowment Trust) in every state which is entrusted with the responsibilities of looking after the mosques, madrasas, schools, orphanages and several other welfare activities of the community. These boards could be involved in promotion of education, health and family welfare programmes among Muslims in the country. They could be an effective instrument for implementation of the resolutions of the seminar of Imams of the Punjab Wakf Board.

Conclusion

Given these explicit views on the subject from the religious authorities, jurists and scholars, it would be a truism to say that Islam is, in fact, the forerunner of the concept of family planning. It is important to note that 1,400 years ago, when Islam appeared on the scene, there was no population problem anywhere on the globe. Even so, Islam, directly or indirectly, encouraged family planning.

Prof. Abdel Rahim Omran (1992)[49] of the most respected Islamic University, Al Azhar, observes, 'It is a wonder to the thinkers of today that Islam should give so much (importance) to child spacing and family planning so early in human history, and in the absence of compelling population pressures.' He explains that the term 'family planning' as used in his text refers to the use of contraceptive methods by husband and wife with mutual agreement, to regulate their fertility with a view to warding off ill-health and social and economic hardships, and to enable them to shoulder their responsibilities towards their children and society. Such a choice should be voluntary, with no coercion or law fixing the number of children a couple should beget.

The above analysis should cause a rethink among those who tirelessly condemn the entire Muslim community for producing large families with political motives in mind. No such motive is in evidence. Muslims are indeed the most backward in family planning practices, but the reason for this lies in their socioeconomic backwardness. Literacy, income and better delivery of health services hold the key to reverse this situation among them.

Those Muslims who think that Islam is opposed to family planning should, on their part, understand that Islam, on the contrary, is indeed the originator of the concept.

---

49 Omran, *Family Planning in the Legacy of Islam.*

6

Population Policies in Islamic Nations

THOSE who hold the common belief that Islam is against family planning might also presume that Muslim countries would not officially encourage family planning. To determine whether this perception is indeed correct, let us look at some of the countries where Islam is the official religion and Muslims constitute the majority of the population. I have chosen ten countries, in descending order of their total fertility rates (TFR, World Bank, 2020): Nigeria, Afghanistan, Pakistan, Egypt, Saudi Arabia, Indonesia, Bangladesh, Turkey, Malaysia and Iran.

Table 6.1: TFR, CPR and unmet need in Muslim countries

Country	Total Fertility Rate (World Bank, 2020)	Contraception prevalence rate, women currently married or in union, aged 15–49, any method, 2019 (UNFPA 2019)	Unmet need for family planning, women currently married or in union, aged 15–49, 2019 (UNFPA 2019)
Nigeria	5.281	19%	23%
Afghanistan	4.412	27%	24%
Pakistan	3.377	42%	19%
Egypt	3.155	61%	12%
Saudi Arabia	2.481	31%	26%
Indonesia	2.32	61%	13%
Bangladesh	2.067	64%	11%
Turkey	2.024	75%	6%
Malaysia	2.01	53%	17%
Iran	1.621	78%	5%

NIGERIA

Nigeria is one of the most densely populated countries of Africa, with approximately 200 million people in an area of 9 lakh sq. kms. It is also the country with the largest population in Africa,[1] and the

---

1   The World Factbook—Central Intelligence Agency, www.cia.gov, accessed on 10 April 2018.

seventh largest globally.[2] It is estimated that about 53.5 per cent of the population of Nigeria is Muslim, Roman Catholics are 10.6 per cent, other Christians are 35.3 per cent, and others constitute 0.6 per cent.[3]

The number of children a Nigerian woman gives birth to in her lifetime averages 5.3. Although the government has had numerous population policies since the 1960s and had also run education and communication campaigns on reproductive health, family planning was not given priority, and 'little to nothing was spent on contraception procurement'.[4] However, in the beginning of 2010, the government undertook several initiatives to improve the status of family planning, the efforts being largely credited to President Goodluck Jonathan.[5] Nigeria allocated $3 million for family planning for the fiscal year 2011 and also for the following year. It also announced a 'Primary Health Care Free Maternal Health Package', which included family planning services and devices; and the national health Insurance scheme extended coverage to contraception.[6] Talking about the country's family planning policy in 2012, President Jonathan acknowledged upfront that family planning was a sensitive topic:

'We are extremely religious people . . . It is a very sensitive thing. Both Christians and Muslims, and even traditionalist and all the other religions, believe that children are God's gift to man. So, it

---

2   Nigeria: People, *CIA World Factbook*, 2018.

3   See https://www.cia.gov/library/publications/the-world-factbook/fields/401.html#NI

4   Nigeria Country Page, Advance Family Planning: Baltimore, MD, http://advancefamilyplanning.org/nigeria.

5   'Nigeria: FG Commits US $3 Million for Procurement of Contraceptives', All Africa, 13 December 2011, https://www.vanguardngr.com/2011/12/fg-commits-3m-for-procurement-of-contraceptives, accessed on 16 October 2020.

6   Nigeria Country Page, Advance Family Planning: Baltimore, MD.

is difficult for you to tell any Nigerian to number their children because ... it is not expected to reject God's gifts.'[7]

Empirical studies conducted in Nigeria reveal that even though the predominant determinants of women's contraceptive behaviour continue to be concerns about personal health, the side effects of contraception and their husbands' approval of contraception, religion still persists as a determining factor.[8] Many religious leaders in Nigeria have not been very receptive to family planning initiatives.[9] The role of the faith leaders, therefore, has been immensely crucial in Nigeria's family planning initiatives. The 2012 National Family Planning Conference addressed the role of religion in influencing family planning behaviour, and in January 2013 a Nigerian faith-based non-profit organization, the Christian Rural and Urban Development Association of Nigeria (CRUDAN) in the south-west zone, issued a position paper to urge the government to formulate and enact laws to support family planning and childbirth-spacing policies, along with creation of budget lines and funding provisions for it.[10] The Nigerian Urban Reproductive Health Initiative is a project funded by the Bill and Melinda Gates Foundation and is a partner in the government's family planning and maternal and child health programmes. It has established inter-faith forums where

---

7   'Nigerian President Goodluck Jonathan Urges Birth Control', BBC News, 27 June 2012, http://www.bbc.co.uk/news/ world-africa-18610751, accessed 2 October 2020.

8   O.A. Moronkola, M.M, Ojediran and A. Amosu, 'Reproductive Health Knowledge, Beliefs and Determinants of Contraceptives Use Among Women Attending Family Planning Clinics in Ibadan, Nigeria', *African Health Science* 6, no. 3 (2006): 155–59, doi: 10.5555/afhs.2006.6.3.155.

9   'Success Story: Unreceptive Muslim Religious Leaders Promote and Practice Family Planning in Nasarawa State' (Washington, DC. USAID, 2008).

10 Abimbola Akosile, 'Nigeria: Formulate Family Planning, Childbirth Spacing Policy, FG Urged', *All Africa*, 10 January 2013, http://allafrica. com/stories/201301110307.html, accessed on 6 October 2020.

groups of religious leaders meet each year to discuss family planning; they are also trained in the positive aspects of family planning.[11]

In 2004, Nigeria's Supreme Council for Islamic Affairs conducted an exhaustive research on Islamic source material to figure out how Nigerian Muslims can be encouraged to improve their reproductive health while adhering to religious doctrine at the same time. Initiatives by Pathfinder International and the Policy Project, and funding from USAID and Packard Foundation helped the council to explore a broad array of issues ranging from HIV/AIDS and STIs to harmful health practices and family planning, and concluded that despite popular opinion, most forms of contraception are allowed in Islam. While they determined that explicit 'population control' was not acceptable, allowing spacing of births was an important practice for the well-being of the family. For instance, the Quran states that mothers should breastfeed their child for two years, which is indicative of the fact that a mother should wait at least two years before having another child.[12]

AFGHANISTAN

Afghanistan has a current population of 38 million, which is expected to increase to 64 million by 2050.[13] The majority of the population is Muslim. Afghanistan has a total fertility rate of 4.41. According to a UNFPA study, in 2013 only a tenth of Afghans used modern

---

11 'Engaging Religious Leaders', Nigerian Urban Reproductive Health Initiative, http://nurhitoolkit.org/program-areas/advocacy/religious-leaders#.X3cHA2gzbIU, accessed on 2 October 2020.

12 'Reproductive Health Issues in Nigeria: The Islamic Perspectives', Supreme Council for Islamic Affairs, Abuja, Nigeria, 2004, http://pdf.usaid.gov/pdf_docs/PNADR681. pdf.

13 Afghanistan Population Live, https://www.worldometers.info/world-population/afghanistan-population/, accessed on 10 October 2020.

methods of family planning. In a little over a decade, this usage doubled, as a consequence of a decline in child mortality rates.[14]

Three decades of an internecine war damaged the infrastructure, economy and social services in that country to such a great extent that women's access to health also suffered as a consequence.[15] Continued high levels of fertility, along with a decline in child and maternal mortality, has resulted in population growth, which is even more challenging than for many other countries because of the sociopolitical interference and death threats from the Taliban. Groups like the Taliban prohibit women from pursuing education.[16] Therefore, in Afghanistan, the high fertility rate is not a consequence of religious opposition to family planning as such but of lack of education of girls which they oppose vehemently.

The Taliban's hindering of education for women leaves them with limited family planning choices. This has also resulted in 50 per cent of Afghan girls being married before they turn eighteen, and 33 per cent of these girls having their first child before they turn eighteen.[17]

Another consequence of early marriage is that 50 per cent of Afghanistan's population is under the age of fifteen, which has

---

14 UNFPA, 'Family Planning, Afghanistan', https://afghanistan.unfpa. org/en/node/15224, accessed on 19 October 2020.

15 Mohammad H. Rasooly, Mohamed M. Ali, Nick J.W. Brown and Bashir Noormal, 'Uptake and Predictors of Contraceptive Use in Afghan Women', *BMC Womens Health* 15, no. 9 (2015), doi: 10.1186/ s12905-015-0173-6 PMCID: PMC4336684.

16 Said Ahmad Maisam Najafizada, Ivy Lynn Bourgealt and Ronald Labonte, 'Social Determinants of Maternal Health in Afghanistan: A Review', *Central Asian Journal of Global Health* 6, no. 1 (2017): 240, http://www.ncbi.nlm.nih.gov/pmc/articles/PMC5675389/, doi: 10.5195/cajgh.2017.240.

17 Douglas Huber, Nika Saeedi and Abdul Khalil Samadi, 'Achieving Success with Family Planning in Rural Afghanistan', *Bulletin of the World Health Organization* 88 (2010): 227–31, http://www.who.int/ bulletin/volumes/88/3/08-059410/en/, accessed on 10 October 2020.

resulted in lack of employment opportunities for youth and resource shortages. This has also retarded the country's development and security. Realizing these dangers, the government has been trying to make available family planning methods and contraceptives to the masses, while at the same time generating awareness about the advantages of family planning methods, but with limited success in the rural areas.[18] The Taliban has banned family planning practices because of their ardent belief that it encourages young women to commit adultery,[19] and healthcare workers who continued to advocate family planning and use of contraceptives have been murdered in the past. Another issue that stems from prohibiting education for women is the scarcity of female medical practitioners. This discourages women from consulting or being treated for their reproductive health. The preference for a male child also is a reason for multiple pregnancies and the increased birth rate.[20]

The Afghan government, however, with assistance from various national and international organizations, has strived to improve acceptance and practice of family planning and contraception to limit the number of children per woman, and many religious leaders have also joined the struggle to contribute to the process of family planning. Some of the measures taken by them are:

---

18 UN Assistance Mission in Afghanistan, 'Family Planning a Basic Human Right', Relief Web, UNFPA, 19 November 2012, http://reliefweb.int/report/afghanistan/family-planning-basic-human-right-unfpa, accessed on 2 October 2020.

19 Tom Blackwell, 'Death for Birth Control: Taliban Targets Kandahar Health-care workers', *National Post*, 3 November 2008, http://www.nationalpost.com/news/world/afghanistan/story.html?id=929966, accessed on 2 October 2020.

20 Miho Sato, 'Challenges and Successes in Family Planning in Afghanistan', Management Sciences for Health, Occasional Papers, Number 6, 2007, http://www.msh.org/documents/occasionalpapers/upload/challenges-and-successes-in-family-planning-in-afghanistan.pdf.

- Distribution of condoms after the night prayer as medical stores shut after 4 p.m.
- Speaking to the masses about family planning to encourage acceptance of it; reading out quotations from the Quran that recognize and support the importance of family planning and birth spacing.
- Dispelling the common notion that contraceptives cause infertility and physiological weakness as side effects.[21]

Religious leaders are a key to spreading awareness and acceptance of family planning, especially in countries like Afghanistan. The UNFPA has organized various religious conferences, publications and direct advocacy programmes. These have been attended by influential religious leaders and community gate-keepers to build on their statements in favour of family planning. Realizing the importance of the media and the role of women in civil society, the UNFPA has engaged 120 female civil society leaders and twenty journalists for its family planning and birth-spacing activities.[22]

Afghanistan, despite the challenges, has made strides since making its first FP2020 commitment in 2016 by increasing the number of public health facilities[23] that offer family planning and offering wider contraceptive choice to the people. It is continuing to work towards promoting public and private partnerships and engagement with religious leaders, the youth and civil societies. To attain their modern contraceptive prevalence rate goal of 30 per cent and reduction in unmet need by 10 per cent by 2020, Afghanistan has focused on

---

21 Margie Mason, 'Mullahs Help Promote Birth Control in Afghanistan', *The Guardian*, 2 March 2010, http://www.guardian.co.uk/world/feedarticle/8970751.

22 UNFPA, 'Family Planning, Afghanistan'.

23 Family Planning 2020, 'Afghanistan: Commitment Maker since 2016', https://www.familyplanning2020.org/afghanistan, accessed on 2 October 2020.

strengthening the supply chain management, addressing cultural and religious barriers to family planning, and engaging inter-sectoral coordination. The country has multiple family planning committees for contraceptive security, and for coordination of reproductive, maternal, newborn and child health, which demonstrates its strong political will and leadership in the family planning sphere.[24]

PAKISTAN

The right to decide the number, spacing, and time of childbirths has a crucial impact on the life of a woman. But one in five married women in Pakistan are unable to access effective methods of avoiding pregnancy.[25] According to the World Bank, the total fertility rate in Pakistan in 2020 is 3.3, and the population of the country is 219 million. Pakistan has been rather controversial in its approach to family planning, primarily because many religious leaders have been quite vocal about their stance against it.

One such Islamic scholar, Maulana Syed Abul A'la Maudoudi, who moved to Pakistan after Partition, wrote a book *Islam aur Zabt-e-Wiladat* (Islam and Birth Control) in 1943, in which he rejected family planning and birth control saying they were ideas opposed to Islam.[26] Interestingly, his opinions were based on the idea that family planning would result in sexual promiscuity and spread of sexually transmitted diseases along with the breakdown of the family, as women would feel free to join the workforce and abandon their traditional roles. On the other hand, he endorsed the permissibility

---

24 Ibid.

25 Ibid.

26 Nasiruddin Haider Khan, 'Challenging Myths and Misconceptions: Communicating Women's Rights in Islam', (Reproductive Health and Islam), *Islam and Muslim Societies: A Social Science Journal* 5, no. 2 (2012): 60–118.

of al-azl (coitus interruptus) but restricted it to individuals with medical necessity.

The history of Pakistan's family planning strategies dates back to as early as the 1950s, when the government included family planning in their first Five-Year Development Plan (1955–1960). However, this inclusion was met with much hostility, as the common perception of family planning being against Islam prevailed. Despite the opposition, the Family Planning Association of Pakistan (FPAP), started by Begum Saeeda Waheed, continued with its efforts, with governmental support.

The primary focus of the FPAP lay in improving female health and empowering women. This was also the time when the government realized that the high rate of fertility and population growth in the country were detrimental to the economy as well as to development. Following the coup of 1958, Field Marshall Ayub Khan became the leader of Pakistan, and he was very much inclined towards family planning. However, the exclusion of the ulama from the family planning initiatives resulted in their failure.

However, General Yahya Khan, who took over in 1969, sought to raise society's familiarity with contraceptive methods, but the operational model was changed. It was now hinged on motivation, whereas the previous model had emphasized supply. Under the leadership of Zulfikar Ali Bhutto, the policies and importance of family planning seemingly underwent a change, as family planning was formally accorded lower priority to placate the religious leaders. In reality, though, family planning was given high importance. However, constant opposition ensured that Bhutto's efforts remained unsuccessful.

Shops refused to stock contraceptives, and distribution was a problem in the rural areas. The conservative culture that prevailed meant that only a few women workers could be employed. When Zia ul-Haq took over control from Bhutto in 1977, he remained outwardly aligned with the religious leaders, but in fact allowed various programmes to bring about a decline in the fertility and the population growth rates. These programmes too, however, received their share of opposition, especially from the religious groups that followed the interpretation that the Prophet was against family planning, and that contraceptives and other methods of family planning were against Islam.

Recognizing the importance of inclusion of the religious leaders if any scheme was to work, there was an increase in efforts to include and involve the ulama in the family planning programmes since 2002.[27] Iran was used as an example of an orthodox Muslim country committed to family planning and strategies to reduce fertility and population growth rate. According to Pakistan Demographic and Health Survey (PDHS) 2012–13, 56 per cent of married women of reproductive age intended to use family planning services but only 35 per cent of them were actually using these services. Thus the prevalence of overall unmet need for family planning was 21 per cent in the country.[28]

It is interesting to note that in Pakistan, family planning gains in rural areas have outpaced gains in the urban areas. The urban contraception rate doubled, whereas rural rates rose almost six times and usage of traditional methods about ten times. One explanation for this increase could be the large unmet need for contraception in the rural areas.

Since making a commitment to FP 2020 in 2012, Pakistan has shown on-going efforts in promoting strategies for family planning. Currently, all four provinces of Pakistan have drafted the 'Costed Implementation Plan' (CIP) for family planning, and have developed

---

27 Katrina Riddel, *Islam and the Securitisation of Population Policies: Muslim States and Sustainability* (England: Ashgate Publishing Limited, 2009), 153–211.

28 M.F. Asif and Z. Pervaiz, 'Socio-demographic Determinants of Unmet Need for Family Planning Among Married Women in Pakistan', *BMC Public Health* 19, no. 1 (2019): 1–8.

task forces comprising both private and public stakeholders. A CIP is a multi-year roadmap designed to help national and subnational governments achieve their family planning goals, thereby saving lives and improving the health and well-being of women, families, and communities.[29] Each province is focused on utilizing domestic resources for procurement of contraceptives. The government is also committed to ensuring a wide range of available contraceptive methods and has trained mid-level service providers to provide IUDs and implants. The plan also provides for substantial collaboration with men and religious leaders as part of its social mobilization efforts. Pakistan was working to strengthen such collaborations in order to increase the contraceptive prevalence rate (CPR) to 50 per cent by 2020.[30]

EGYPT

Egypt is a dominant player in Arab dynamics and is the seat of Al-Azhar University, Islam's most prestigious university. The country has a spiralling population of 101 million, which is the highest in the region, and a high fertility rate of 3.1 (World Bank, 2020). Large families are perceived to generate more income, and birth control is regarded as anti-Islamic in rural Egypt. However, the 1937 fatwa of Al-Azhar University had questioned this belief by approving family-spacing methods.

Family planning in Egypt was first envisioned in the 1960s and was given a formal structure in 1977. It was introduced through the Framework for Population, Human Resource Development and

---

29 Plan Implementation Unit, Costed Implementation Plan, Population Welfare Department, Government of Sindh, 'A Summary of the Costed Implementation Plan (CIP) on Family Planning for Sindh', June 2017, http://www.healthpolicyplus.com/ns/pubs/2127-3226_PakistanCIPBriefJune.pdf, accessed on 19 October 2020.

30 See http://www.familyplanning2020.org/pakistan.

Family Planning Program in 1980. Key developments were witnessed in 1986 in the form of formulation of the third National Population Plan, and in 1996 when the plan extended family planning services to low-income and rural populations, re-emphasizing the relationship between population and development.

Historically, the first efforts towards family planning policies were met by religious extremism. That resulted in the perception of the government's efforts as controversial and provocative. Complicating this was a skeptical leadership that diluted the family planning efforts as it saw birth control as western idea; also, a populous Egypt was perceived as crucial for influencing regional dynamics.

Family planning initiatives did not receive much success until Dr Maher Mahran, with President Mubarak's outspoken support, achieved a milestone in the Egyptian family planning programme, in the sense that contraceptive prevalence rose and fertility fell between 1985 and 1988, continuing well into the 2000s and beyond.[31] To overcome the absence of specificity concerning contraceptive methods and its nuances,[32] the government launched a campaign employing posters, leaflets and active outreach by field workers. Simultaneously, electronic mass media, especially television, was put to use, as the second demographic and health survey in 1992 showed that more than 90 per cent of urban households and 70 per cent of rural households owned televisions. The mass medium would now be used to encourage change in behaviour instead of just providing information.[33]

---

31 Hesham H. Makhlouf (ed.), *Population of Egypt in the Twentieth Century*, (Cairo, Cairo Demographic Center, 2003).

32 Donald J. Bogue, 'How to Evaluate a Communications Campaign for Family Planning: A Demonstration Based on Data from the SIS Program in Egypt, 1980–82', Research Report 6, Carolina Population Center (Chapel Hill, NC, University of North Carolina Press, 1983).

33 Warren C. Robinson and Gary Lewis, 'Cost-Effectiveness Analysis of Behaviour Change Interventions: A Proposed New Approach and

The single most popular method of contraception was the IUD, but the problem lay in its availability. Until the mid-1980s, the Egyptian Medical Association ruled that only fully trained obstetricians and gynaecologists working in hospitals or large clinics could implant IUDs, thereby excluding the majority of the physicians from this work. Changing this rule and making IUDs generally available required pressure from the government, along with considerable staff retraining. In 1987, USAID funded the Clinical Services Improvement Project, which involved upgradation of a group of Egyptian Family Planning Association clinics, setting up new ones and expanding in-service training for service providers.[34]

Demographic research and surveys have demonstrably linked level of education, autonomy of women and consensual marriage to higher acceptance of contraception. However, some people consider it state intervention in the intimate family sphere. 'The state, under the guise of the family planning programme, seeks to enter the domestic space of the Egyptian household as an authoritative voice on fertility decisions.'[35]

To counter the Islamic political groups who had been a critical voice against the state's fertility control policies, the state and the donor agencies have turned to state-sponsored religious leaders like the sheikhs of Al-Azhar University to interpret Islam's teachings in

an Application to Egypt', *Journal of Biosocial Science* 35, no. 4 (2003): 499–512.

34 Maher Mahran, 'The National Population Council's Huge Achievement for the Last Ten Years' (in Arabic), *Al Wafd*, 23 January 1995; Maher Mahran, Fatma H. El-Zanaty and Ann Way (eds), *Perspectives on Fertility and Family Planning in Egypt* (Calverton, MD, and Cairo: National Population Council and Macro International, 1995); Warren C. Robinson and Fatma H. El-Zanaty, *The Demographic Revolution in Modern Egypt* (Lanham, MD: Lexington Books, 2006).

35 K. Ali, 'The Politics of Family Planning in Egypt', *Anthropology Today* 12, no. 5 (1996): 14–19, doi:10.2307/2783544.

favour of family planning. Basing its proposition on the Islamic idea that harm should be eliminated at all costs, the state argues that although procreation is important, a large population dominated by ill health and weakness is useless.

The size of Egypt's population was regarded as such a crisis by the government that President Abdel-Fatah al-Sisi declared at a conference in 2017 that the two real challenges the country faced were terrorism and overpopulation. In Egypt, a baby is born every fifteen seconds, and Egypt is already in the thirteenth spot globally in terms of population size. This has put a strain on the already scarce resources of the country and amplified the existing problems for families that are already struggling to put food on the table following the 2016 financial crisis. The crisis had resulted in inflation and devaluation of the country's currency.

The heart of the problem in Egypt lies in the mentality of the citizens and their lack of motivation to have smaller families. In the rural areas, a child is considered as an extra source of income; the idea that a child is a gift from God is quite popular among people. Simply explaining to them that one more child would mean another mouth to feed and a greater strain on the country's depleting water resources is not enough. Family planning and sex education need to be perceived as a multi-disciplinary programme. Sex education needs to begin in school, where young kids must be taught about contraception, the hazards of marrying early, and about population explosion. It should then focus on people who are about to get married, and next on married people. If there is a legislation in place that punishes couples for having a third child, then there should also be provision for exit routes for them, like permitting medical termination of pregnancy and allowing even abortion clinics.[36]

---

36 Ruth Michaelson, 'Experts Urge Egypt to Rethink Two-child Population Strategy', *The Guardian*, 3 January 2019, https://www.theguardian.com/global-development/2019/jan/03/experts-urge-

A study conducted in the Al-Qassim region of Saudi Arabia of married women at the government primary health centres in the age group 18–49 with at least one child[44] found that the average number of children per woman was five, and while half of the respondents knew about contraceptives, most of them wanted to have between five and ten children. As many as 62 per cent of these women wanted about two to three years of birth spacing; 12 per cent preferred spacing of less than two years, and only 26 per cent preferred spacing of more than three years. The three main reasons for their not using contraceptives were:

1. 69 per cent thought that children are considered a blessing from God.
2. 20 per cent thought contraceptives had harmful effects.
3. 11 per cent thought contraceptives would have a bad effect on their marital relationship.

Saudi Arabia's population has increased almost 86 per cent in the last twenty years. The population was 22 million in 2000, and has increased to 34 million as of March 2020. It is expected to reach about 59.8 million by 2050. This increase in population has put a strain on the country's limited water resources. Even though Saudi Arabia is a developed country, limited resources and an increasing population can pose serious threats to its continued growth. The country's total fertility rate is 2.4, according to 2020 World Bank data. However, family planning still remains a controversial issue in Saudi Arabia, as many perceive it as a threat to survival of the society, while others view it as a social necessity.

---

44 Mounira Al Sheeha, 'Awareness and Use of Contraceptives Among Saudi Women Attending Primary Care Centers in Al-Qassim, Saudi Arabia', *International Journal of Health Sciences* 4, no. 1 (January 2010): 11–21.

INDONESIA

As of March 2020, the population of Indonesia was 272 million, making it the fourth most populated country in the world. Indonesia is rich in diversity and has a mix of ethnicities and religions. However, Muslims constitute the majority (87 per cent) of the population, while the rest consist of Christians (Protestant and Catholic), Hindus and those with indigenous beliefs. In the 1960s, Indonesia had one of the fastest growing populations, with the average number of children per woman being 6, of which at least 2 died before they reached school-going age.

In 1967, President Suharto started a government-funded family programme, Perkumpulan Keluarga Berencana Indonesia, or the Indonesian Family Planning Association (PKBI), which aimed to reduce the fertility rate and achieve universal education in the country. Initially, the main focus of its activities were advocacy and increasing awareness about family planning by providing birth-spacing information as well as marital and infertility counselling. The programme was quite successful; there was almost universal counselling, and the results showed a lowered fertility rate. The PKBI was directly under the president's control and the programme thus fetched a lot of political leverage. The slogan 'Two children is enough, whether boy or girl' spread awareness about the importance of small families across the nation.[45]

The primary reason for the success of the programme was that it involved the religious leaders from recognized religions like Islam, Christianity and Hinduism to spread the message. Leaders from

---

45 Taara Chandani, Barbara O'Hanlon and Sara Zellner, 'Unraveling the Factors Behind the Growth of the Indonesian Family Planning Private Sector', PSP-One Technical Report Series prepared for USAID (Bethesda, MD: Private Sector Partnerships-One project, Abt Associates Inc., April 2006), 3–7, https://www.shopsplusproject. org/sites/default/files/resources/3050_file_Technical_Report_004.pdf, accessed on 10 October 2020.

these three religions were included in a panel discussion for the design of a pamphlet that would explain their religion's acceptance of family planning. This pamphlet was then distributed across the nation, helping the community at large to accept the importance of family planning and contraception. Muslim leaders also issued a fatwa that declared all forms of contraceptives – except for permanent methods or sterilization – as permissible under Islam.

Apart from involving the religious leaders in the exercise, field workers at the grassroots level were employed by the government. They would, going door to door, brief married couples about the benefits of smaller families. In order to make the idea of contraception even more attractive to women in the villages, financial benefits were also provided as a part of the programme, through provision of micro-credit and low-interest loans if the women practised family planning for a certain period. There was also an increase in the age of marriage, from 18.6 years in 1997 to 19.2 years in 2002.[46] The success of these programme has also led to a decline in the annual population growth rate, from 2.34 per cent in 1970–1980 to 1.49 per cent in 2000,[47] and to 1.1 per cent in 2018.[48] Indonesia's total fertility rate in 2020, according to World Bank, is 2.32.

---

46 Eleanor Randall, 'Family Planning Programmes Review', Population Matters, January 2012, 16; 13–17, https://www.slideshare.net/HarveyDiaz/multicountry-study-on-family-planning, accessed on 10 October 2020.

47 Fachruddin Majeri Mangunjaya and Jatna Supriatna, 'Indonesian Moslem Responding to the Environmental Crises: Notes to Nature Conservation', paper presented in Research Seminar 'Religion and Ecology' held by Center for Religious & Cross-cultural Studies (CRCS), Graduate Program, Gajah Mada University, Yogyakarta, 9–13 August 2005, http://www.academia.edu/2629837/Indonesian_Muslim_in_Response_to_the_Environmental_Crises, accessed on 3 October 2020.

48 See 'Population growth (annual %) - Indonesia, World', https://data.worldbank.org/indicator/SP.POP.GROW?locations=ID-1W, accessed 3 October 2020.

Following the success of the family planning in the country in the 1980s, the programme was privatized. The core idea was to keep unplanned pregnancies to a minimum and ensure continued practice of contraception and family planning. In accordance with these goals, the slogan of 'A small family is a prosperous family' was launched. The programme wanted to ensure:

- Families practised contraception.
- Delayed age of marriage.
- Families did not have their first child immediately after marriage.
- Children were breastfed.
- Families practised birth spacing.

The people of the country took ownership of these goals, and this programme was more appropriately referred to as a movement rather than a policy or programme, given the level of change it inspired among the people. Indonesians were encouraged to become self-reliant when it came to contraception and contribute financially to the country's family planning expenses.[49]

Indonesia's non-governmental agencies have realized the importance of involving men too in family planning decisions. This was necessary if the country was to continue on its successful path. In 2007, the proportion of condom usage was 1.2 per cent and male sterilization 0.2 per cent. These ratios fell to 1.1 per cent and 0.1 per cent, respectively, in 2010. While family planning has been successful in the country, Indonesian men have limited or no knowledge of family planning and contraceptive methods. The family planning programmes have been designed to target only women, as from a social and cultural perspective this is considered a woman's domain.

---

49 Chandani, O'Hanlon and Zellner, 'Unraveling the Factors Behind the Growth of the Indonesian Family Planning Private Sector', 9–17.

In order to improve acceptance of family planning methods among Indonesian men, new strategies have been adopted. They will include programmes specific to men in every area of family planning. Male family planning groups have been envisaged as a forum where doubts can be cleared and where men who are convinced about the programme can motivate others in their community to join.[50]

BANGLADESH

Since its independence from Pakistan in 1971, Bangladesh encouraged family planning and tried to improve the position of women in the society. The country adopted a population policy as early as in 1973, and this was followed by the government for twenty-five years, leading to a dramatic increase in the use of contraception, from 7 per cent in 1975 to 49 per cent in 1997. However, the country still had a high rate of maternal mortality and a fairly high fertility rate of 6.82 in 1975, which fell to 3.48 in 1997. During the International Conference on Population and Development (ICDP) held in Cairo in 1994, Bangladesh decided to adopt the ICDP definition of reproductive health, and the country's policymakers agreed to start an integrated service delivery structure.

As a part of this programme, stakeholders committed to improve the policies for family planning and deliver better healthcare services.[51] The earlier structure had been a vertical one, in the sense

---

50 Hon. Dr Nova Riyanti Yusuf, 'Family Planning and The Importance of Co-Opting Men (Case Study Indonesia)', Asean Inter-Parliamentary Assembly, Seminar on 'Accelerating the Achievement of MDGs-5 through the Role of Women Parliamentarians', Phnom Penh, Cambodia, 9–12 March 2011.

51 Karen Hardee, Kokila Agarwal, Nancy Luke, Ellen Wilson, Margaret Pendzich, Marguerite Farrell and Harry Cross, 'Reproductive Health Policies and Programs in Eight Countries: Progress Since Cairo', *International* Family Planning Perspectives 25, no. 9999 (January

that married women were trained and employed as 'family welfare assistants' to deliver family planning services and counselling to the rural population of Bangladesh. While the government promoted sterilization as a method of family planning, these family welfare assistants offered information and access to many other contraceptive methods, like the pill, to women in the rural areas. About 85 per cent of all contraceptive pills used in rural Bangladesh between 1978 and 1997 were provided by these family welfare assistants. However, the drawback remained that these women were not trained to provide healthcare services and were unable to deal with the side effects of the pill. It was also found that they visited women who were more educated, rather than uneducated women who would have actually benefited more from the pills. In a patriarchal society like Bangladesh where the status of women is low, this programme, which was designed only for women, had a very limited range of services as men were not included in the programme.[52]

In 1997, Bangladesh formed a Health and Population Sector Strategy that included the ICDP mandates. The salient features of this strategy included:

- Combining family planning with other reproductive healthcare services.
- Shifting to a client-centered approach rather than the demographic focus approach.
- Better quality of care.

1999): S2–S9, https://www.guttmacher.org/sites/default/files/pdfs/pubs/journals/25s0299.pdf, accessed on 10 October 2020.

52 James F. Phillips and Mian Bazle Hossain, 'The Impact of Household Delivery of Family Planning Services on Women's Status in Bangladesh', *International Perspectives on Sexual and Reproductive Health* 29, no. 3 (2003): 128–45, https://www.guttmacher.org/journals/ipsrh/2003/09/impact-household-delivery-family-planning-services-womens-status-bangladesh.

- Continuous involvement of stakeholders in the design and monitoring of the programme.

With these goals in mind, the family welfare associates were based in health facilities that were now placed where the communities lived, and their upkeep was undertaken by the communities themselves. These facilities delivered essential and other services, but delivery of services has not been very substantial. The focus was on families that had difficulty in accessing these facilities. That was why the earlier door-to-door system was modified to that of a village depot, which would to provide the families living in the vicinity the necessary contraceptives.[53]

Despite these changes, a USAID study found that 17 per cent of Bangladeshi women did not have access to modern methods of family planning even though 99 per cent of them were aware of at least seven different methods of family planning. The study also found that 63 per cent of women in urban areas and 62 per cent in rural areas did not wish to have more children. Despite these numbers, only 6 per cent (from rural and urban areas combined) opted for the permanent method of sterilization, while 52 per cent used oral contraceptives.[54] One of the reasons behind this could also be the perception that Islam prohibits permanent methods of sterilization.

A UNFPA study in 2003 found that 54 per cent of couples in the country practised contraception and out of these only 4 per cent used

---

53 Lisa M. Bates, Md. Khairul Islam, Ahmed Al-Kabir and Sidney Ruth Schuler, 'From Home to Clinic and Family Planning to Family Health: Client and Community Responses to Health Sector Reforms in Bangladesh', International Perspectives on Sexual and Reproductive Health 29, no. 2 (2003): 88–94.

54 SHOPS Project, Bangladesh Family Planning: Private Health Sector Assessment, Brief (Bethesda, MD: SHOPS Project, Abt Associates, 2013).

condoms. Bangladesh is a patriarchal country, yet, paradoxically, its family planning programmes tend to exclude men, while women are not allowed to take decisions for their families. This study also found that women who had male child/children had smaller families.[55]

While the population of Bangladesh is predominantly Muslim, it is a secular country and the government has supported family planning measures since the country's independence and has also tried to get clerics involved in the programmes. It is interesting to note that although the clerics in Bangladesh are not entirely opposed to the practice of family planning, they are against women becoming more independent and more than just wives and mothers.[56] Concerted efforts of Pathfinder and USAID in training Imams to collaborate with them in order to increase awareness and acceptance of family planning methods among the citizens has resulted in the Imams allowing announcements about the importance of family planning and availability of resources to be made on the loudspeaker at the mosques. They were also roped in to promote special days like National Immunization Day, World Breastfeeding Day and the like. This proved very beneficial in promoting family planning practices in Bangladesh, as people are more likely to be open to accepting information from a mosque or an Imam.[57] Bangladesh's TFR as of

---

55 Unnati Rani Saha and Radheshyam Bairagi, 'Inconsistencies in the Relationship Between Contraceptive Use and Fertility in Bangladesh', *International Perspectives on Sexual and Reproductive Health* 33, no. 1 (2007): 31–37.

56 Heather D. Boonstra, 'Islam, Women and Family Planning: A Primer', *The Guttmacher Policy Review* 4, no. 6 (December 2001), https://www.guttmacher.org/gpr/2001/12/islam-women-and-family-planning-primer, accessed on 19 October 2020.

57 Mary K. Burket, 'Advancing Reproductive Health and Family Planning through Religious Leaders and Faith-Based Organizations', *Pathfinder International*, August 2006, http://www2.pathfinder.org/site/DocServer/FBO_final_reference.pdf?docID=6901, accessed on 3 October 2020.

2020 is 2.067, which indicates that its efforts towards implementation of family planning strategies have been phenomenally fruitful.

TURKEY

Turkey is a Middle Eastern country covering an area of approximately 770,000 sq.km, with a current population of 84 million, of which 98.6 per cent is Muslim. The population growth was rapid between 1927 and 2000, although the growth rate varied from 1.06 per cent per year in 1940–45 to the highest of 2.85 per cent per year in 1955–60. Turkey is the seventeenth most populated country in the world, with the present population growth rate at 1.09 per cent and the total fertility rate at 2.02. Clearly, there has been a profound demographic shift in Turkey in recent years.

As of the early 1920s, the population was only 13 million and heavy casualties during the wars of 1911–1920 resulted in the country adopting a pro-natalist population policy. Import of contraceptives was prohibited, and the state provided financial incentives to larger families.[58] Kemal Ataturk's (dictatorial president of Turkey [1923–1938]) desire to increase the population led to adoption of a state policy along the same lines. Consequently, the minimum age of marriage was reduced to seventeen for men and fifteen for women in 1938. The Law on General Hygiene was an explicit pro-natalist law that obliged the ministry of health to encourage larger families through grants and monetary awards to women with six or more children and prohibited the import and sale of contraceptives.[59] The

---

58 T. Tokgöz and Ays¸e Akın, 'Türkiye'de Aile Planlaması Çalıs¸malar'ı', in *Hekimler ·İçin Aile Planlaması El Kitabı içinde*, ed. A. Akın (Ankara: Tanıt Matbaası, 1983), 22–29.

59 Esen Altıok, 'The Development of a Population Policy and Its Implementation', in *Population Policy Formation and Implementation in Turkey*, ed. Ned Levine and Sunday Üner (Ankara: Hacettepe University Publications, 1978), 53–74; Nusret H. Fis¸ek, 'Türkiye'de

1926 Turkish Penal Code, which declared induced abortion a crime, was not effective in its implementation. Several studies showed that abortion continued to be widespread.[60] In 1958, obstetricians and gynecologists such as Dr Ziya Durmuş, Dr Necdet Erenus, Professor Naşit Erez, and Dr Zekai Tahir Burak launched an initiative to change the population policy and legalize methods of contraception. Burak was a prominent specialist and head of a large maternity hospital in Ankara, and he had noticed that many women were admitted in a serious condition because of self-induced abortions and that most of them died. He documented these hospital cases to demonstrate the extent to which women were suffering from the adverse effects of unwanted pregnancies and unsafe abortions. He then sent a letter to the Ministry of Health stating that maternal mortality had increased

---

Nüfus Planlaması Çalış maları,' reprinted in 1998 in *Kitaplaş mamış, Yazıları-II içinde-Ana Çocuk Sa'glı'gı, Nüfus Sorunları ve Aile Planlaması,* ed. R. Derleyen Dirican (Ankara: Türk Tabipleri Birli'gi Publications, 1963), 171–72; Nusret H. Fis ek, 'Türkiye'de Nüfus Sorunlarının Ele Alını s Tarzı ve Planlar',' reprinted in 1998 in *Kitaplaş mamış, Yazıları-II içinde- Ana Çocuk Sa'glı'gı, Nüfus Sorunları ve Aile Planlaması,* ed. R. Derleyen Dirican (Ankara: Türk Tabipleri Birli'gi Publications, 1964), 161–70; Nusret H. Fis ek and Frederic C. Shorter,, 'Fertility Control in Turkey', *Demography* 5, no.2 (1968): 578–89.

60 Nusret H. Fis ek, 'Çocuk Dü sürmenin Sosyal Yönü', reprinted in 1998 in *Kitaplaş mamış, Yazıları-II içinde- Ana Çocuk Sa'glı'gı, Nüfus Sorunları ve Aile Planlaması,* ed. R. Derleyen Dirican (Ankara: Türk Tabipleri Birli'gi Publications, 1967), 151–60; 'Türkiye'de Do'gurganlık, Çocuk Düs ürme ve Gebeli'gi Önleyici Yöntem Kullanma Arasındaki Ilis kiler', reprinted in 1998 in *Kitaplaş mamış, Yazıları-II içindeAna Çocuk Sa'glı'gı, Nüfus Sorunları ve Aile Planlaması,* ed. R. Derleyen Dirican (Ankara: Türk Tabipleri Birli'gi Publications, 1972), 195–203; H. Kis,nis,çi and A. Akın, 'Türkiye'de Düs üklerle ilgili Epidemiyolojik Bir Aras,tırma', in *Türkiye'de Nüfusun Yapısı ve Nüfus Sorunları—1973 Aras,tırması* (Ankara: Hacettepe University Publications, 1978), 113–32.

because of unsafe abortions, that measures should therefore be taken to prevent such deaths, and that contraception should be legalized.[61] Consequently, a series of events resulted in the ministry acknowledging the need for safe abortions under certain medical conditions. Even though it did not result in a change in the policy, this acknowledgement formed the basis of legalization of family planning in Turkey for the first time.[62] The military revolution of 1960 resulted in a number of legislative and regulatory reforms that focused on the objective of population planning.[63] Discussions between the ministry of health and the State Planning Organization resulted in a unanimous conclusion that a change in the traditional policy was necessary.

The first Five-Year Development Plan, therefore, focused on the problems of high population growth and advocated repeal of the

---

61 Ayse Akin, 'Emergence of Family Planning Program in Turkey', in *The Global Family Planning Revolution, Three Decades of Population Policies and Programs*, ed. J. Robinson and J. A. Ross (Washington DC: The World Bank, 2007), 85-102.

62 Esen Altıok, 'The Development of a Population Policy and its Implementation', in *Population Policy Formation and Implementation in Turkey*, ed. Ned Levine and Sunday Üner (Ankara: Hacettepe University Publications, 1978), 53–74; Fis,ek, 'Türkiye'de Nüfus Planlaması Çalıs,maları', 171–72; Fis,ek, 'Türkiye'de Nüfus Sorunlarının Ele Alını,s Tarzı ve Planlar', 161–70; Nusret H. Fis,ek, 'Çocuk Dü,sürmenin Sosyal Yönü', 151–60; W. Holzhausen, 'The Population Problem in Turkey (as Seen from the Perspective of a Foreign Donor)', *Nüfusbilim Dergisi* (Turkish Journal of Population Studies) 9 (1987): 63–73; State Planning Organization, *Turkey: National Report to the 1994 International Conference on Population and Development* (Ankara: State Planning Organization, 1993); R. Üner and Nusret H. Fis,ek, *Türkiye'de Doğum Kontrolünün Uygulanması Üzerinde İncelemeler* (Ankara: Ministry of Health and Social Affairs, 1961).

63 Lewis S. Anderson, Turkey, Country Profiles Series (New York: Population Council, 1970), https://files.eric.ed.gov/fulltext/ED088656.pdf, accessed on 10 October 2020.

anti-contraception laws, replacing them with family planning laws. Family planning education would be provided to the masses. This change in policy was primarily due to the large number of abortions that was happening annually. Additionally, the mechanization of agriculture and rapid urbanization were posing a challenge for Turkey's cities, with their limited space and resources. The Population Planning Law (1983), therefore, sought to provide the legal framework for funding and implementation of a nation-wide family planning programme.

Opposition, however, came from educated but ill-informed groups, who held the view that a bigger population would mean a bigger market, and that if Turkey had a bigger population it would mean a bigger army and a more powerful voice in international affairs. In addition, many gynaecologists were opposed to the family planning programme because they were concerned that it would affect their practice. Therefore, from time to time, adverse propaganda that was medical in nature suggested that contraceptives were harmful. In general, no opposition that was of a religious nature emerged.

As of 2019, the president of Turkey had denounced birth control because of the perception that birth control and family planning had resulted in a decline in the country's population. He has also criticized the media for the perceived role it played in eroding the family as an institution.[64] A current look at the Turkish demographics shows that the population is fairly young, with 67 per cent in the age group of

---

64 'Turkey's Erdoğan denounces birth control, family planning', Ahval, 2 May 2019,https://ahvalnews.com/family/turkeys-erdogan-denounces-birth-control-family-planning, accessed 3 October 2020.

15–64. But the population has a slow growth rate of 1.09 per cent,[65] with the total fertility rate at 2.046 births per woman.[66]

MALAYSIA

For the major part of the twentieth century, the population of peninsular Malaysia increased at more than 2.4 per cent per year, rising from about 3.8 million in 1931 to 18.5 million in 2001 and to 32 million in 2020 (increasing 1.30 per cent from the previous year). The official religion of the Malays is Islam, but Malaysia boasts of a diverse range of ethnicities, comprising Indians and Chinese. Before World War II, the main reason for the growth in population was the large-scale immigration of the Chinese, who were attracted by employment opportunities in the tin mines and in commerce, and of Indians, who were recruited to work in the rapidly growing rubber industry. However, with the cessation of immigration, the population began to grow naturally, and from the late 1950s Malaysia started showing rapid population growth as a result of high fertility. A large number of post-war baby boomers began to marry and have children. Currently, the total fertility rate of Malaysia is 2.01.

It is interesting to note, however, that until the early 1960s, family planning had no place in the development plans of the country, and Malaysia was perceived to be relatively underpopulated. Therefore the government did not consider population growth as an obstacle to development. However, economic problems and growing awareness of the socioeconomic and health implications of a high population growth rate in the long run resulted in a change of stance. Income disparities, surveys on employment, unemployment and under-

---

65 See https://worldpopulationreview.com/countries/turkey-population/, accessed 3 October 2020.

66 Turkey Fertility Rate 1950–2000, https://www.macrotrends.net/countries/TUR/turkey/fertility-rate, accessed 3 October 2020.

employment, as well as increasing strain on the limited resources of the country, resulted in an urgency for adoption of family planning policies. These policies would also address the adverse effects of frequent births on maternal and child health. M. Khir Johari, minister for agriculture and cooperatives from 1962 to 1965, and later minister for education, was one of the first leaders in the country to express concern about the population and suggested that the government took positive efforts to incorporate the National Family Planning Programme (NFPP) in the national development plan (1966). Consequently, the government advocated family planning as a way of life and a necessary measure to improve maternal and child health, as well as for the general welfare of the family.

Contrary to the popular fear of possible widespread religious opposition to family planning, it was surprisingly minimal in Malaysia. In addition, the medical profession had assured the government that it would provide active support to and participation in the national programme. This resulted in the availability of good medical and health facilities and good family planning services across the country.[67] The main concern about family planning was in regard to whether it was against the teachings of Islam, which Khir Johari addressed using the examples of other Islamic countries that had taken up family planning. He assured the people that the government had no intention of compelling anyone, Muslim or non-Muslim, to accept the government's family planning initiatives.[68]

The Population Project (1973–78) initiated a multi-disciplinary approach towards the population problem, enlarging the scope

---

67 M. Khir Johari, 'Malaysia: A Bold Attack', in *Population: Challenging World Crisis*, ed. Bernard Berelson, Voice of America Forum Lectures (Washington, DC: Government Printing Office, 1969).

68 Eddy Lee, Michael Ong and T. E. Smith, 'Family Planning in West Malaysia: The Triumph of Economics and Health over Politics', in *The Politics of Family Planning in the Third World*, ed. T. E. Smith (London, George Allen & Unwin, 1973), 256–90.

of family planning from simple fertility reduction to overall improvement in family welfare. The project was designed to strengthen and intensify family planning initiatives, along with provision of maternal and child health services and incorporation of population education in the education system. It provided infrastructure for specialized family planning services, which included marriage and genetic counselling, treatment of infertility, cancer screening and a follow-up system that promoted biomedical research. The multi-disciplinary approach of the NFPP supported related social programmes and activities that focused on improving the quality of life and status of women.[69]

In the late 1970s and early 1980s, several developments led to a reversal of the anti-natalist policy to a pro-natalist one. These developments included a revival of Islamic fundamentalism, labour shortages due to industrialization and Dr Mahathir Mohamad's becoming the fourth prime minister of Malaysia. The resurgence of Islamic fundamentalism had a role to play in the change as Islamic teachings were interpreted to be pro-natalist. Consequently, there was a de-emphasis on family planning, and focus shifted to family development and reproductive health. However, forces of social change, including delayed marriage, resulted in a rapid decline in the fertility rate, and the effects of the new pro-natalist population policy lasted only a few years.

IRAN

Iran remains one of the best examples of the effectiveness of family planning programmes. It has managed to drastically reduce the birth rate in the country without enforcing it and without abortions. The

69 A. Noor Laily, B.A. Tan, O. Ramli and L.C. Kuan, *Facts and Figures: Malaysia National Population and Family Development Programme* (Kuala Lumpur: National Family Planning Board, 1982).

country's achievement is comparable with that of many developed countries. Iran was one of the first nations to include a family planning programme in its development plans. Its family planning programmes have been recognized as models by the World Health Organisation (WHO). From a birth rate of 5.6 per woman in 1985 to a birth rate of 1.6 in 2020, there has been a phenomenal decline on this score in the urban as well as rural areas of the country. Adoption of family planning methods, which rose from 34 per cent in 1976 to 74 per cent in 2000, and increase in the average female age of marriage, from 19.7 in 1976 to 22.4 in 2000, were seen as the major reasons for the decline in population.[70]

The decision to control and decrease the birth rate was taken in the 1960s, and a birth control programme and population policy were adopted in 1967. There was some improvement in adoption of family planning methods under Mohammad Reza Shah (the last Shah of Iran), but the change was not substantial, mainly because of the exclusion of the ulama in the execution of the policies. The western ideals of the Shah led him to think that the ulama would hinder the progress of policies aimed at reducing the population growth rate, even though most of the clerics believed that family planning was beneficial and permissible in Islam. This exclusion resulted in confusion among the more religious Iranians, especially in the rural areas, where they were largely illiterate and depended on the clerics for guidance. Many of the religious Iranians, in both cities and villages, who were against the Shah would have still practised family planning had they been encouraged by the clerics' acceptance of family planning methods. The programme could have been more successful if Shah's government had sought religious support and introduced pro-family planning fatwas.

---

70 Farzaneh Roudi-Fahimi, 'Iran's Family Planning Programme: Responding to a Nation's Needs', Population Reference Bureau, Middle East and North Africa, MENA Policy Brief, 2002.

Despite the country's adoption of family planning policies, the political unrest (1977–1979), and eventually the revolution of 1979, meant that these measures were not given much importance by the government. While contraceptives and other family planning methods were provided by the ministry of health and medical education, these programmes remained short-staffed and did not cover all the rural areas. Amidst the country's war with Iraq (1980–1988), the problem of population growth was overlooked, and Iran witnessed a population growth rate of 3.4 per cent between 1976 and 1986.

In fact, there was actually a shift in policy, from pro-family planning to anti-family planning, as clerics asked women to have more children as part of the war efforts. It was only after the end of the war that the government had to deal with the repercussions of an increasing population in the form of increased demand for food and healthcare. The clerics also realized that a large population would go against the principle of a happy Islamic nation. The main concern of the government was as to how the public would respond to its new policies as they were a reversal of the previous policies that had been propagated by religious leaders.

Once Ayatollah Khomeini, supreme leader of Iran, supported the change in policies, it was easier for the government and the clerics to advocate for the changes. Fatwas by Ayatollah Khomeini saying that the health of parents and the children they already had were of utmost importance, and his permitting family planning within Islam, helped the masses to accept these new policies. In one such fatwa, Ayatollah Khomeini tells a woman that due to her ill-health and the associated risks of another childbirth, sterilization, which is generally not permitted in Islam, would be an acceptable decision. The media campaign predominantly focused on Imam Ali's (son-in-law of the Prophet and an important figure in Shia Islam) views that smaller families were happy families, as well as on the verses from the Quran and the Hadith that promote family planning.[71]

---

71 Riddel, Islam and the Securitisation of Population Policies, 97–152.

The main reason behind the success of these programmes was the government's assurance to the people, with examples from the religious texts, that family planning is a part of Islamic beliefs. This message was spread throughout the country, especially in the rural areas through educative and awareness campaigns. This awareness is integral to the adoption of family planning in countries that have a Muslim population. Many people have denounced family planning as anti-Islamic in the past, and that has had its impact on a large number of Muslims around the world. Assurance from religious leaders of the permissibility of contraceptive methods, therefore, makes a substantial difference when it comes to adoption of family planning measures by the community, especially in the rural areas of developing countries.[72]

Following the success of the country's family planning methods, Ayatollah Ali Khamenei has now asked women to have more children as the average age of the country's population has increased. An intense change in the total fertility rate has resulted in changes in the population's age structure, and the UN has projected that by 2100 as much as 30.9 per cent of Iran's population is likely to be aged sixty-five and older.[73] The government introduced a baby bonus scheme in order to encourage larger families, under which for every child born to them the parents would receive $950 into their account and $95 every year until the child turned eighteen. Upon attaining twenty years of age, the child can withdraw this amount, to use for education, housing or marriage. However, the growing rate of inflation and the rising costs of living deter most families from having more children. With improvement in their quality of life as

72 Amir Erfani, 'The Impact of Family Planning on Women's Educational Advancement in Tehran, Iran', International Center for Research on Women Fertility and Empowerment Working Paper Series 008-2012-ICRW-FE (December 2012): 1–27.

73 Safoora Javadi, 'Essays in Women's Fertility and Public Policies', Diss., University of Wisconsin-Milwaukee, 2019.

a result of fewer children, it is doubtful whether Iranian women will want to have more children.[74]

CONCLUSION

In nearly all the examples of the countries discussed above, it is evident that birth control or the population control programmes have been challenging. There is an essence of voluntarism associated with acceptance of family planning by the community, which is influenced by their religious and sociocultural beliefs. In the context of family planning, the belief is that the teachings of Islam are against the idea. The family planning policies adopted by various countries whose official religion is Islam and majority of their population Muslim, show a pattern that illustrates one thing – that the perception of Islam being against family planning is rather misplaced.

All the examples clearly demonstrate that increase in the literacy rate, especially among women, and participation of women in the labour force result in a decrease in the total fertility rate, as women become aware of modern methods of contraception, their associated side effects and how to address them. In many instances, women, especially from rural areas, shy away from family planning initiatives because they prefer to consult female medical practitioners. A shortage of women in the workforce and in the medical discipline often results in the failure of family planning schemes. The socioeconomic status and the state of the healthcare delivery system of a country also determine contraception usage in that country.

The other factor that is highlighted from these examples pertains to participation of men in the family planning process. The idea that family planning is a woman's business is not entirely correct and should involve men too for its successful implementation.

---

74 Farzaneh Roudi-Fahimi, Iran is Reversing its Population Policy (Woodrow Wilson International Center for Scholars, 2012).

However, what emerged most clearly is that theological perspectives can often hinder family planning projects. Success stories of family planning in orthodox Muslim countries like Iran and Bangladesh are the result of the involvement of the religious leaders and their inferences from religious texts to support the exercise. Their involvement has always led to success, as people, especially in the rural areas in developing nations, mostly look up to their religious leaders for guidance and advice. Wherever theological resistance was successfully addressed and the clerics converted from adversaries to allies, success has followed.

7

Attitude towards Family Planning among the Major Religions

MANKIND has always believed in some immortal power or force. In the very beginning, human beings worshipped the forces of nature. With the improvement of human society from its rude beginnings to a more refined existence, polytheism or idolatry was, and necessarily must have been, the first and most ancient religion of mankind. The definition of religion is a rather controversial and complicated matter in religious studies, as scholars fail to agree on any. The Oxford dictionary defines religion as 'the belief in and worship of a superhuman controlling power, especially a personal God or Gods'.

As a religion grows, different sects emerge as a result of disagreement among human beings over various aspects of their religion. Something uttered by, say, a realized soul, and is passed on by oral tradition from first-hand accounts of his or her contemporaries, is distorted in every successive narration, and may eventually convey only a small part of the original saying. The frail memories of men, their love for exaggeration, and human carelessness, often result in dilution of the truth.[1]

According to three major monotheistic religions of the world, God has spoken to only a chosen few directly.

Therefore mankind must now rely on these human leaders who are perceived to be more aware of God's will than others to guide and lead the people live better lives.

The most prominent among the religions of the world is Christianity, with the largest following in the world, the second being Islam, and the third Hinduism. There is now a growing trend towards atheism, which has had a profound effect on how people perceive death, what they teach their children, and even how they vote.

Another growing trend is that of alternative religions, which people from the major religions around the world have begun to follow. Jediism[2] is the second most popular new faith, a study in 2017 said. Although it is more of a philosophy than a religion in the true sense, it highlights the fact that as the needs of people change, there is a growing need for changes in religion too.

Though many theologians may disagree that there have been changes within religious beliefs and teachings, in fact there have been several changes with the passage of time. The most obvious of these are perhaps the changes in the status of women in society and in religious perceptions about and attitudes towards family

---

1   David Hume, *Natural History of Religion* (London: Aegitas, 2017).

2   Jediism is a philosophy primarily inspired by certain elements of Star Wars, namely the fictional religion of Jedi. It attracted public attention in 2001 when a number of people recorded their religion as 'Jedi' on national censuses.

planning. This, in turn, increases the burden on religions to guide their followers to better lives.

To understand the impact of religions on birth rate and fertility, this chapter will take a look at the main religions around the world and in India, and their attitudes towards family planning, historically as well as in the present. This chapter excludes Islam, which has already been elaborated upon in Chapter 5.

The three main sub-groups of Christianity – Catholicism, Protestantism and the Orthodox Church – have differing views on family planning, so these three are studied separately. The other religions discussed are Buddhism, Judaism, Confucianism, Taoism, and the like. Even though Hinduism is the third largest religion in the world, it is practised primarily in the Indian subcontinent, so it will be covered in the section on Indian religions, which would also include Sikhism, Jainism and a variety of others that make for a small percentage of the Indian population.

CHRISTIANITY

As of 2010, there were 2.2 billion Christians in the world, accounting for 31 per cent of the world's population.[3] Catholics constitute the largest group among them, accounting for more than 50 per cent of the Christian population, followed by Protestants, at 37 per cent, and the Orthodox Christians, at 12 per cent. Other groups, like Jehovah's Witnesses and Mormons, account for 1 per cent of the Christian population. While Christianity is not growing in the

---

3   'The Future of World Religions: Population Growth Projections, 2010–2050', Pew Research Center: Religion and Public Life, 2 April 2015, https://www.pewforum.org/2015/04/02/main-factors-driving-population-growth/, accessed on 19 October 2020.

western countries as it had been during the last few centuries, it is expanding in African and Asian countries.[4]

The ideas about contraception in Christianity mainly come from church teachings rather than the scriptures, as the Bible has very little to say on the subject. As a result, Christian teachings on birth control are often based on different Christian interpretations of the meaning of marriage, sex and family. Christian acceptance of contraception is relatively new as all churches disapproved of artificial contraception until the beginning of the twentieth century. Different churches hold different views. Liberal Protestant churches often teach that it is acceptable to use birth control as long as it does not allow promiscuity. More conservative churches only approve of contraception between married couples as they perceive sex outside marriage as morally wrong. According to them, contraception should be limited to married couples only, to regulate the size and spacing of their family.

Catholicism

Roman Catholicism remains the most influential religion in the world. The Vatican, whose population is composed entirely of Catholics, has a seat in the United Nations. The global Catholic population is around 1.28 billion, with Brazil at the top of the list of Catholic nations, with a population 112 million, followed by Mexico, with 98 million. The Philippines comes third, with a population of 85 million Catholics.[5] The Catholic Church is the

---

4   The Pew Forum, 'Global Christianity: A Report on the Size and Distribution of the World's Christian Population', 19 December 2011, http://www.pewforum.org/Christian/Global-Christianity-exec.aspx, accessed on 6 October 2020.

5   'Highest Catholic Population 2020', https://worldpopulationreview. com/countries/highest-catholic-population/, accessed on 12 April 2020.

oldest of all Christian institutions, and for a long time remained the sole church for all Christians. Although there are now several branches of Christianity, yet in places where Catholics are present they continue to be the majority group.

Many scholars are of the opinion that knowledge of contraception preceded Christianity in the ancient world.[6] Various contraceptive methods, like coitus interruptus, potions and condoms, were widely used by the Egyptians, Jews, Greeks and Romans. Abortion was also perceived to be a universal practice. However, as most abortions were self-induced or administered by mid-wives, there is no recorded history of 'cases', in medical terms. 'Abortion was perceived to be similar to mental illness and homosexuality.'[7] However, neither contraception nor abortion was the primary method of limiting fertility; it was infanticide.[8] Infanticide was often disguised as accident or stillbirth, but the numbers were so high that they could not be passed off as the latter without suspicion. The other perceivably more civilized substitute for infanticide as a fertility control measure was abandonment.

In the Middle Ages, families with too many children gave away some of them as 'human gifts' to the church, and these children would not only be raised by the religious orders but were raised to join them.[9] This served to lower the general fertility, because these

---

6   John T. Noonan, *Contraception: A History of Its Treatment by Catholic Theologians and Canonists* (Cambridge, Mass.: Harvard University Press, 1965), 1–29; Rosalind P. Petchesky, *Abortion and Women's Choice: State, Sexuality, and Reproductive Freedom*, rev. ed. (Boston: Northeastern University Press, 1990), 25–35; Linda Gordon, *Woman's Body, Woman's Right: Birth Control in America*, rev. ed. (New York: Penguin, 1990), 35–46.

7   Petchesky, *Abortion and Women's Choice*, 30.

8   Gordon, *Woman's Body, Woman's Right*, 32–35.

9   The medieval theologian Thomas Aquinas, for example, was a younger son in a large family who was sent as an oblate to Monte Cassino in

children would grow up to live a life of celibacy.[10] Abandonment was a more convenient option as parents felt less guilty about it, in the sense that it did not require killing. By the beginning of the modern period (circa 1500 AD), abandonment numbers had reached epidemic proportions as a result of the influence of the Roman Empire and the church that advocated abandonment instead of infanticide.[11]

The Church consistently frowned upon contraception and abortion, and they were generally forbidden. The only allowed methods of limiting fertility were sexual abstinence and breastfeeding. Direct methods of abortion after the period of time when it was believed ensoulment of the foetus took place, was forbidden, although there remained room for indirect abortions if the life of the mother depended on it. This negative perspective of Catholic teachings with regard to contraception was based on the idea that the primary blessing of marriage is children, and only those who desired children should marry. Therefore, fertility control was perceived to be a characteristic of promiscuity. Fertility control methods were considered illegal and condemned by the Church.

The Church's attitudes towards family planning can also be looked at in terms of the attitude towards women obtaining in those times.

1230 at age five. See Elizabeth Clark and Herbert Richardson, eds., *Women and Religion: A Feminist Sourcebook of Christian Thought* (New York: Harper, 1977), 79.

10 In the late medieval and early modern period, a remarkably high percentage, between 10 and 15, of the European population was celibate. S. Ryan Johansson, 'The Moral Imperatives of Christian Marriage: Their Biological, Economic, and Demographic Implications in Changing Historical Contexts', in *One Hundred Years of Catholic Social Thought: Celebration and Challenge*, ed. John A. Coleman, (Maryknoll: Orbis Books, 1991), 136.

11 John Boswell, *The Kindness of Strangers: The Abandonment of Children in Western Europe from Late Antiquity to the Renaissance* (New York: Pantheon Books, 1988), 209–10.

The belief that women were created by God with the intention of being subjugated by men is still prevalent today in some pockets. As early as in the twentieth century these beliefs were present even at the formal level. In 1930, Pope Pius XI condemned women's rights movements for going against the divine role of the woman as being solely an obedient wife and mother.[12]

In 1968, Pope Paul VI issued an encyclical that shook the Catholic Church to its core. It declared that every use of artificial contraceptives is immoral. The document, *Humanae Vitae* ('Of Human Life'), was a shocker, because many Catholics had hoped the pope, with the widening availability of the pill after its appearance in 1960, would open the way for Catholics to practise birth control. The encyclical continues to be controversial, with the hierarchy, including Pope Francis, the current head of the Catholic Church, supporting it while most Catholics ignore it.[13]

The long-standing arguments on why contraception is wrong have gradually changed and have eventually been dropped by the hierarchy in the church, in the sense that even though a ban on contraceptives is still in place, it is only a restriction of unnatural means of contraception.[14] There is, however, dispute concerning classification of the banned methods, as to which of them can be used to prevent implantation of the fertilized ovum. The only method

12 Rosemary Radford Ruether, 'Women, Reproductive Rights and the Catholic Church', Catholics for Choice, May 2006, http://www.catholicsforchoice.org/topics/reform/documents/2006womenreproductiverightsandthecatholicchurch.asp, accessed 3 October 2020.

13 Thomas Reese, 'Humanae Vitae: Sex and Authority in the Catholic Church', *National Catholic Reporter*, 20 July 2018,https://www.ncronline.org/news/opinion/signs-times/humanae-vitae-sex-and-authority-catholic-church, accessed on 3 October 2020.

14 Reese, 'Humanae Vitae'; see also 'Catechism of the Catholic Church, 1652–1654', http://www.vatican.va/archive/ccc_css/archive/catechism/p2s2c3a7.htm, accessed on 19 October 2020.

that is deemed natural is abstinence during fertility, because of the understanding that the purpose of union between a man and woman is solely procreation. One of the ideas that led to contraception being considered unnatural was its perception as a misuse of women, as women were presumed to be solely created for the purpose of reproduction.

Africa has the fastest growing population of Catholics, and there use of condoms has been deemed immoral. The biggest problem now is that sub-Saharan Africa has the largest number of people living with HIV/AIDS. With condoms banned, there appears to be no decline in the spread of the disease.[15] However, many NGOs and some liberal Catholic priests in Africa agree that while monogamy is a basic tenet for Catholics, condoms should be used when a man has more than one sexual partner.

Protestantism

Nearly 40 per cent of the Christian population of the world (900 million) are Protestant.[16] Protestantism is a form of Christianity that does not recognize the authority of the Roman Catholic Church and is not loyal to Eastern Orthodox Christianity either. For about three centuries, from AD 1500 to AD 1750, political, economic and cultural turmoil in Europe resulted in war and religious persecution. Protestants of various denominations crossed borders in search of safety and a place where they could practise their religion. They

---

15 Rod McCullom, 'An African Pope Won't Change the Vatican's Views on Condoms and AIDS', *The Atlantic*, 26 February 2013, http://www.theatlantic.com/sexes/archive/2013/02/an-african-pope-wont-change-the-vaticans-views-on-condoms-and-aids/273535/, accessed on 3 October 2020.

16 See Victor Kiprop, 'Countries With The Most Protestant Christians', 21 June 2017, https://www.worldatlas.com/articles/countries-with-the-most-protestant-christians.html, accessed on 19 October 2020.

perceived themselves to the authentic followers of the Christian faith and their practice has having remained undistorted for centuries. The desire to return to the very roots of Christianity, and revolutionary inventions like the printing press, resulted in the Bible becoming the centre of all Protestant deliberations.

Protestant fundamentalism, however, speaks a patriarchal language, and this is the very aspect that has shaped the debates on contraception and abortion in the world of Protestants. It has shown resistance to full and equal status for women in public and private places, as well as in the church. Generally, views on contraception and abortion among a community are rooted in their cultural understanding of human sexuality, especially women's sexuality. Salvation of the non-material soul is perceived to be the goal of religion. The female body that provides material pleasure is believed to imprison the soul, and that is why desire for the female body is feared.[17] Among Protestants, marriage committed to sexual abstinence was presumed to be holier than even marriage in which spouses had intercourse only for procreation. Thus, sex outside marriage, use of contraception and non-procreative sex were denounced as murderous.[18] A foetus was assumed to be a God-given product of sexual activity, and thus sexual activity was to be limited to creation of this product alone. In fact, abortion was perceived as something that hid the results of illicit or non-procreative sex. Contraception and abortion were, therefore, considered to be impediments to the real purpose of sexuality. The Protestants actually had a more conservative stance on abortion than their Roman Catholic counterparts.

Women have experienced both the blessings and curse of fertility from ancient times and have practised a number of methods to

---

17 Joan Timmerman, *The Mardi Gras Syndrome: Rethinking Christian Sexuality* (New York: Crossroad, 1984), 35–38.

18 James B. Nelson, *Embodiment: An Approach to Sexuality and Christian Theology* (Minneapolis: Augsburg Publishing House, 1978), 52–53.

control their procreative capacities through the use of contraceptives and early abortion.[19] The sixteenth and seventeenth centuries were also the period when witchcraft was presumed prevalent, and mid-wives, with their knowledge of birth-control, both contraceptive and abortive, were the usual targets accused of this practice.[20]

Sex between engaged couples was tolerated since marriage would follow, but women who gave birth outside marriage were severely punished. After marriage, high infant and child mortality rates resulted in frequent pregnancies. This trend, however, underwent a change in the nineteenth century as a consequence of industrial capitalism and urbanization, and there was a reconfiguration of the family unit and gender roles. Holland, in 1882, became the first country to have a birth control clinic. It was run by Holland's first female physician, Aletta Jacobs.[21] The growing power of women to wield some influence in the governance of the household was also an added factor.

The willingness among the people to practise contraception and abortion significantly rose in the nineteenth century. Yet, by the end of the nineteenth century, the U.S. Congress had banned abortion and made contraception illegal. This was primarily because of the evolution of a new gender identity for women. Women, therefore, began to organize themselves into groups to demand political equality, especially suffrage, to reform the evils in society. The second half of the nineteenth century saw Protestant women develop expanded roles at home even while missionary societies were socially

---

19 John M. Riddle, J. Worth Estes and Josiah C. Russell, 'Ever Since Eve: Birth Control in the Ancient World', *Archaeology*, March/April 1994: 29–35.

20 Anne Llewellyn Barstow, *Witchcraze: A New History of the European Witch Hunts* (San Francisco: Pandora, 1994), 129–135.

21 See https://www.encyclopedia.com/women/encyclopedias-almanacs-transcripts-and-maps/jacobs-aletta-1854-1929

active, bringing the gospel to poor and immigrant women.[22] These Protestant women advocated for 'voluntary motherhood', which meant that wives could choose to submit to marital intercourse only when they themselves wanted to bear the burden of motherhood.

The other reason for the ban on contraception by the US government was, in part, due to the fear that white birth rates were dipping in comparison to the much higher birth rates among the foreign immigrants as well among the local population of people of colour.[23]

This U-turn in the Protestant perception was, however, short-lived. In the early twentieth century, Protestant ministers joined the campaign to reverse the laws against contraception. Support for legalization of abortion came slowly. Most western European countries, as well as Canada and the United States, began to legalize abortion only after 1950. Even though the major Protestant denominations would not endorse abortion, they did acknowledge the need for women to be free to take their own decisions on unwanted pregnancies. In the recent decades, most Protestant denominations have supported the idea that it is a woman's choice to terminate her pregnancy and that it is a moral decision on her part. She should be the one to take the final decision in the matter. Protestants have supported public policies legalizing medical abortion services and making them accessible to all women in order to safeguard this freedom of choice.[24]

---

22 Rosemary Radford Ruether and Rosemary Skinner Keller, eds., *Women and Religion in America*, Vol. I, *The Nineteenth Century, A Documentary History* (San Francisco, Harper and Row, 1983), 242–53.

23 Gordon, *Woman's Body, Woman's Right*, Chapter 7.

24 Gloria H. Albrecht, 'Contraception and Abortion Within Protestant Christianity', in *Sacred Rights: The Case for Contraception and Abortion in World Religions*, ed. Daniel C. Maguire (New York: Oxford University Press, 2003), 79–99, doi:10.1093/acprof:oso/9780195160017.003.0004.

Orthodox Christianity

Orthodox Christianity, or Eastern Orthodox Christianity, is one of the three major sects of Christianity that originated and grew in the Eastern Roman Empire. It was often influenced by the people and politics of Byzantium, its capital city.

Over the last century, the Orthodox Christian population around the world has more than doubled and now stands at nearly 260 million, with the population surpassing 100 million in Russia alone, a sharp resurgence after the fall of the Soviet Union. Even so, currently 12 per cent of Christians around the world belong to the Orthodox sect and only 4 per cent of the total global population is Orthodox, compared with an estimated 7 per cent in 1910. The ecumenical Patriarch, who is the Archbishop of the Orthodox Church, resides in Turkey, though Turkey does not have a very high population of Orthodox Christians.

According to estimates, in 2017, as much as 77 per cent of Orthodox Christians lived in Europe, whereas only 24 per cent of Catholics and 12 per cent of Protestants in the world lived there.[25]

The Orthodox Church is often divided in its views on contraception, yet the majority here shares the same views as the Catholic Church on contraception and family planning. Intercourse after marriage is permitted, as it is for the purpose of procreation, which is given primary importance. Union of husband and wife in sexual intercourse within marriage is perceived to be a harmonious act, yet the Orthodox Church encourages its disciples to restrict their appetites, not only for sex but also for food. Sexual relations before or outside marriage are considered sinful and against the will of God.

---

25 The Pew Forum, 'Orthodox Christianity in the 21st Century', 8 November 2018, https://www.pewforum.org/2017/11/08/orthodox-christianity-in-the-21st-century/, accessed on 19 October 2020.

The church preaches that if a couple decide to wed but do not plan to have children immediately or at all, they are probably not ready to be married. The Church regards such a marriage as a means of 'legal fornication', which is against its teachings. For the same reason, sterilization is not accepted. The Church does not recognize divorce or remarriage, but in case of infertility of either spouse, divorce followed by remarriage for the purpose of procreation is considered acceptable.

Even though the population crisis is a source of debate and constant concern worldwide, the Church still believes that if a couple is blessed with a child, God will provide for it. The Orthodox Church believes that life begins at conception, and therefore practise of contraception, which harms the foetus, is against the teachings of the Church. Abortion is also prohibited for the same reasons. Other artificial means of birth control, like use of condoms, are also against the Church but the institution allows couples to use these methods in some circumstances as long as they confer with their priest. This is because the Orthodox Church considers creation of children the primary reason for a couple's union but also acknowledges the wish of the people to want to limit the size of their families. So, a few methods such as abstinence and natural family planning have been allowed by the Church.

In Russia, where the majority of Orthodox Christians live today, many theologians and bishops agree that practice of birth control is a personal choice. Father Alexander Men, a Russian theologian, has said that if couples have more children than they can support there is little to separate them from animals. Many Russian theologians believe that all forms of contraception are acceptable, apart from abortion and those methods that are abortifacient.[26]

---

26 Taras Baytsar, 'Eastern Orthodoxy and Contraception: Contemporary Vs. Traditional Views: Teaching on Contraception among Orthodox Churches', Orthodox Christianity, https://www.orthodox-christianity.

The Orthodox Church proclaims equality between men and women; however, it emphasizes that man and woman are meant to fulfil different roles. Women, as the Church emphasizes, are the backbone of the Church as they are the backbone of their respective parishes and homes.[27] The views among Orthodox thinkers about a woman's role in society remain conservative. Women are believed to have been essentially created for the purpose of child-bearing and cooking, and they appropriately belong to the household.[28]

As with every religion, the views of the Orthodox Christian Church have changed and evolved with the world. While initially there was a need to increase the population of the community in individual countries and for the religious order as a whole, the current status of the world's population has brought about significant changes in the views of the Church about women and their roles, both within households and in the outside world, in family planning and contraception.

BUDDHISM

Buddhism was founded by Siddhartha Gautama. There are some doubts about when exactly it was founded, but it has generally

---

com/2011/11/orthodoxy-and-contraceptiona-change/, accessed 19 October 2020.

27 Bishop Nicholas, 'The Role of Women in the Orthodox Church', Antiochian Orthodox Christian Archdiocese of North America, http://ww1.antiochian.org/role-women-orthodox-church, accessed on 3 October 2020.

28 Ariana Monique Salazar and Michael Lipika, 'On Gender Issues, Many in Orthodox Christian Countries Have Conservative Views', Pew Research Center, 16 May 2017, https://www.pewresearch.org/fact-tank/2017/05/16/on-gender-issues-many-in-orthodox-christian-countries-have-conservative-views/, accessed on 3 October 2020.

been accepted that Siddhartha Gautama lived between 563 BC and 483 BC.[29]

Buddhism spread to many parts of Asia and the rest of the world, though most of the Buddhists outside Asia are of Asian origin. There are as many as 535 million people around the world who practise Buddhism, accounting for between 8 per cent to 10 per cent of the world's population.[30]

During the time of the Buddha, women were treated poorly and regarded as the property of their husbands. The preference for a son existed even at that time in the Indian subcontinent, and the birth of a girl was not always welcome.

Despite these general attitudes, Buddha gave women equal opportunities for spiritual development and growth, and is believed to have said that some women can be better than men and have the ability to attain nirvana just as men do.

Marriage and sexuality were accepted by the Buddha for lay people who chose to live in the world. Marriage in Buddhism was not perceived as only a religious duty but as something that gratified the couple's urge for sensual pleasure.

It is clear that early Buddhism advocated that followers aim to get rid of attachment to sensual pleasure to escape the circle of rebirth. Sexuality was perceived to be an obstacle for people wishing to attain nirvana.[31] However, it was normal for men and women to have mutual passion and sexual attraction. Sexuality and reproduction were respected in Buddhism as long as sexual misconduct did not occur. People also have the right to practise

---

29 'Buddhism At a Glance', BBC Religion, 17 November 2009, http://www.bbc.co.uk/religion/religions/buddhism/ataglance/glance.shtml, accessed on 11 October 2020.

30 'Buddhist Countries 2020', https://worldpopulationreview.com/countries/buddhist -countries/.

31 R. William LaFleur, *Liquid Life: Abortion and Buddhism in Japan* (Princeton: Princeton University Press, 1992).

family planning and contraception, and no divine plans, wills and commandments are believed to be pro-natalist. According to the Tripitaka (traditional term for the Buddhist scriptures), life begins at the time of conception, when three conditions combine:

- The mother and father have sexual intercourse.
- It is the mother's fertile period.
- The 'being to be born' is present.

Any methods that prevent the process of this conception are welcome as long as no life is destroyed under any circumstances. Buddhism says that both husband and wife have a right to family planning and contraception. Ideally, it is a duty that is shared between a couple. Buddhism stresses on the ethics of reciprocity and interdependence, based on responsibility.[32] Therefore, it is possible to say that women have the right to practise family planning and safe methods of contraception to contain the size of their families.

Buddhists constitute 8 to 10 per cent of the world's population and live primarily in the Asia Pacific region where high population is a concern. Yet, as education has not yet reached all the people in the region, knowledge about religious attitudes towards contraception is not always available to many either. Most often it is women who are the users of contraceptive methods, whether natural or modern. Education is important to spread knowledge about the different available methods of contraception. Religious acceptance of contraceptive methods is important if increase in practice of family planning and birth control is to take place.

---

32 Pradmasiri De Silva, 'Human Rights in Buddhist Perspectives', in *Human Rights and Religious Values: An Uneasy Relationship*, ed. Abdullahi A. An-Na'lim et al. (Michigan: Eerdmans Publishing Co., 1995), 133–43.

JUDAISM

Jewish people originated in the Middle East, and since then they have grown to more than 14 million around the world. The enlarged Jewish population, which includes people with full or partial Jewish ancestry, tops 20 million, according to 2017 estimates.[33]

While Jews can be found in every country in the world, some nations have significant Jewish populations. In 2020, 74.8 per cent of the global Jewish population lived in Israel, followed by the United States (1.75 per cent), and Canada (1.06 per cent).[34]

Historically, Jews have been open to the idea of family planning. A couple were allowed to have two children, one son and one daughter, or two sons, and then they could drink the 'sterilization potion' to prevent further births if they wished to. The religious leaders encouraged women to use contraceptives even before they had two children in three situations:

• The wife was a minor (under twelve years of age).
• The wife was pregnant (in order to avoid superfetation).
• The wife was breastfeeding (to avoid early weaning).

Followers of Judaism understand that women are not responsible for propagation of the religion by producing more children. Jewish men are charged with this responsibility, and they are allowed to divorce a woman if, even after ten years she is unable to have children. In case a man dies before he is able to impregnate his wife, she can marry his brother, and the children born would be considered the children of her dead husband and eligible to his inheritance.

---

33 'Jewish Population by Country 2020', https://worldpopulationreview.com/country-rankings/jewish-population-by-country.

34 Ibid.

Paradoxically, however, the use of condoms is not allowed. The religion considers it a 'wastage of seed'. As the responsibility rests with the man to procreate, methods of contraceptives that stop sperm from entering the womb are not allowed.

There are three schools of Judaism: the Orthodox, the Liberal and the Reform. Among these, the Orthodox is restrictive when it comes to certain types of birth control devices for women, like diaphragms, while the other two allow them.[35]

Judaism believes that a man and woman should only have sexual intercourse after they have been married. Unlike the Catholic and Orthodox Church, sex is not seen as a sinful act but rather as a union, with procreation as one of the main goals, along with companionship, love and intimacy. Some Jewish groups have accepted sex before marriage, as long as it is within a committed relationship, as many people cohabit before they get married. Judaism believes that life starts when the head comes out of the womb, but abortion is allowed only in special circumstances, such as risk to the mother's life.[36]

Since the Holocaust, there have, however, been differing views about the practice of contraception and family planning. Six million Jews died in the Holocaust, and their numbers have been dwindling ever since. The global population of Jews is now 0.2 per cent, which has raised concerns about the continuation of Judaism.[37] Some religious leaders have said that couples should have more children who will be raised in the Jewish faith. Those concerned about the global population crisis have raised objections to such views. Others

35 'Judaism and Contraception', BBC Religion, 21 July 2009, http://www.bbc.co.uk/religion/religions/judaism/jewishethics/contraception.shtml, accessed on 19 October 2020.

36 'Family Planning in the Jewish Religion', Epigee, http://www.epigee.org/guide/judaism.html, accessed on 3 October 2020.

37 'Jews', in 'The Future of World Religions: Population Growth Projections, 2010-2050', Pew Research Center, 2 April 2015, https://www.pewforum.org/2015/04/02/jews/.

have suggested that in the Jewish tradition, taking on a student is perceived the same as having a child, so Jewish couples should be encouraged to adopt and raise children to pursue the Jewish faith.[38]

Having experienced the horror of the Holocaust, it is understandable that the Jews would want to ensure the survival of their faith, even if it meant overlooking the threat of limited resources. An event of the magnitude of the Holocaust is bound to shift a community's beliefs and priorities. After all, in many societies it took some time before families started having fewer children when infant and child mortality rates dropped. There are also views among the community that the Jewish people have experienced several horrors in the past but their survival had more to do with ensuring that their faith was learned by a few than by increasing their numbers.

Confucianism and Taoism

The chief Chinese religious traditions are the major indigenous religions of Confucianism and Taoism. Both traditions are similar in their representation of peace and harmony as the ultimate state of the whole universe and, in fact, the ultimate goal of human life.

Family has always occupied a central position among the highest values in the 'human world', according to the Chinese. The most important responsibility of a traditional Chinese family is to reproduce, and the biggest tragedy for them is perceived to be absence of descendants. It is important to understand here that the Chinese do not merely want to have children, but want to have good and healthy children. Hence, the Chinese people have been very conscious about 'planning' to have quality children, especially sons.[39]

---

38 Laurie Zoloth, 'Each One an Entire World: A Jewish Perspective on Family Planning', in *Sacred Rights*, ed. Daniel C. Maguire, 21–53.

39 Geling Shang, 'Excess, Lack and Harmony. Some Confucian and Taoist Approaches to Family Planning and Population Management-Tradition and the Modern Challenge', in *Sacred Rights*, 223.

Sexuality is not an unknown or avoided topic among the Chinese, but has been one of the main themes that early Chinese thinkers explored in order to understand the universe in its entirety. It is interesting to note here that the early Chinese did not perceive sexuality as something obscene, but affirmed it to be a positive force responsible for the origin, growth and flourishing of both the natural as well as the human worlds. The Chinese had successfully made a distinction between the functions of sexuality and reproduction, and believed that human sexuality is not just for the purpose of reproduction but also for health, pleasure, and even cultivation of the self. Coitus reservatus, or the idea of controlling unwanted pregnancies, has long been understood and practised in the Chinese traditions. This is perhaps one of the reasons why contraception as a concept does not receive any opposition among the Chinese.

There is no evidence that indicates exactly when the Chinese began to practise abortion, but one thing remains certain – the Chinese have practised abortion for various purposes since ancient times. Even though abortion was not endorsed, there was no explicit code that prohibited it either. However, many frowned upon abortion because of the stigma associated with it. Abortions, therefore were carried out in secret by mid-wives rather than doctors. There was no ban on abortion, and Chinese attitudes towards and perceptions about abortion were rather tolerant and compassionate; they believed that a necessary abortion was a matter of the parents' choice. These ideas were strongly rooted in the Chinese traditions, and therefore very little resistance occurred when the communist government propagated a coercive family planning campaign and use of abortion as a way of birth control in 1979. The main issue about this policy related to the number and gender of children a couple wanted for themselves. There has been criticism about the poor medical conditions under which abortions took place in China and the country's aggressiveness in enforcing the policy.

Infanticide – rather, female infanticide – used to be a common practice in China, and the primary reason why people resorted to it was economic – as a result of their struggles of poverty and starvation. However, this indicates that the concept of family planning had developed among the lower classes too and was not exclusive to the political or social elite.

Despite the acceptance and permissibility of all forms of contraception methods in the Chinese faiths, there still remain certain barriers to effective and proper usage of contraception among the Chinese.

Indian religious traditions

India is a traditional society where religion plays a huge role in defining identities and determining one's belief system and conduct. Therefore, from the Indian perspective, the concept of family planning is rather challenging, as religion and society in India are perceived to be inclined towards big families and sons.

HINDUISM

The ancient religion of India, Hinduism, otherwise known as *sanatan dharma* or the eternal tradition, is rather a confederation of religions and not a dogmatically unified system, holding its faith in multiple deities.

During the Vedic times the family constituted the basic unit of the Aryan society. The Rig Veda viewed marriage as sacred rather than just a contract. Marriage was perceived to be a harmonious union of the biological and spiritual elements. However, the main purpose of marriage was to beget children, especially sons, so that the lineage could be carried forward in a strictly patriarchal society. This did not devalue female children, and there was considerable emphasis on intellectual achievement for both male and female children. Women during the Vedic period (circa 1500–500 BC) had a say in the selection of their husbands, which translates to their being married at a mature age. They had strong marital rights and social rights that allowed them to move freely in society and participate in public life and even debate in assemblies.

This, however, does not last in the era that follows because of the perception that only a male child can enable the dead to survive in the heavens by making regular offerings to them. This led to a ritualistic preference for sons over daughters and eroded the role of the woman as a partner and an equal in marriage.[40] There was a rise in the status of women during the period of the *Upanishads* (circa 700–500 BC), and women were given the right to study the Vedas, a privilege denied to them later. It must be pointed out that even though the status of women varied through the ages, the basic purpose of marriage remained to be continuance of family.

From the beginning there was awareness about abortion, which was widely condemned by the traditions. However, it is unclear if this aversion to abortion among religious leaders encompasses the modern-day idea of rational limitation of family size. This apparent aversion is rooted in the Hindu theory of conception, that is perceived to be a consequence of a divine act and is therefore holy and worthy of reverence. Irrespective of the widespread disapproval of abortion through the ages, there are numerous Ayurvedic texts that address methods of avoiding pregnancy (contraception) and terminating unwanted pregnancies (abortion). They attest to the fact that human beings have always felt the need to control the consequences of sexual activity. The principal concern of the medical scientists remained that of healthy conception, but there is no doubt that abortion was practised in times of need. Due to the formal disapproval of the

---

40 Sandhya Jain, 'The Right to Family Planning, Contraception and Abortion: The Hindu View', in *Sacred Rights*, 134–35.

religious teachers, this knowledge was preserved in texts, allowing only a section of the medical hierarchy to provide these services to women in distress.

In the twentieth century, advancements in medical science have negated the necessity to reproduce more, as one could drastically reduce infant and maternal mortality and increase life span. In order to stabilize the social order, adoption of the small-family norm becomes necessary. As *dharma* includes the idea of public duty and public responsibility, it necessitates the small-family norm, which is achievable through contraception and family planning methods. Therefore, family planning is entirely consistent with and nowhere opposed to the Hindu concept of dharma, and is backed by social consensus. The forms of social resistance to the idea of family planning among the lower classes or insistence on the part of some families on begetting a male child even after the birth of three or four daughters does not stem from religious pressure on them, but in fact is an instance of society lagging behind the spirit of faith.

The scenario is that young women and men often have no education regarding sexual intercourse, contraception or sexually transmitted infections, nor any understanding of ovulation and timing of and between pregnancies. Women are usually not aware about contraceptives until after the birth of their first child, which is basically an assurance for the families involved that the marriage was a good match. Thus, birth control might be forbidden among some couples until the first child is born. Studies demonstrate that Indian men do not desire fertility regulations, and attempts made by women to influence this decision might result in their physical abuse, allegations of infidelity against them or even threat of divorce.

Despite the permissibility of contraception, it is unfortunate that not all Hindu women utilize contraceptive methods. The lack of success of family planning initiatives among the community can be attributed to cultural resistance, the prevalent desire for a male child and lack of female empowerment, especially in the rural areas. Low

levels of education and decreased accessibility to services are related
to low rates of contraceptive prevalence among Hindu women.[41]

SIKHISM

Sikhism originated in the Punjab area of south Asia, a territory that
in the present day spans India and Pakistan. The main religions at
that time were Hinduism and Islam. The Sikh faith began around
AD 1500 with the teachings of Guru Nanak. It was a faith that was
quite distinct from both Hinduism and Islam.

Sikhism took a radical departure from Hinduism by destroying
the barriers that existed in the Hindu society between man and man,
and also between man and woman. The foundation of Sikhism lay
in a healthy, egalitarian and progressive social order that advocated
the principles of universal equality and brotherhood as the only true
basis of social relations. Sikhism's concept of equality transcended
the boundaries of caste, creed, sex and colour. Women were treated
as equal to men in every field of life. Sikhism does not debar a
woman from reading the scriptures and attaining salvation, and she
can attain the highest religious goal without having to take birth as
a man to attain mukti.

The transformation brought about by the Sikh gurus in the
status of women was truly revolutionary, in the sense that not only
did it give women an identity of their own but also freed her from
the shackles to which she was bound in traditional Hindu society.
Guru Nanak, the founder of the Sikh faith, advocated for justice for
women and provided the scriptural basis for equality, which is not
found in other religious scriptures of India. As the Sikh faith grew,
it eventually demolished the traditional biases against women one
by one. Women were no longer perceived to be an evil that led men

---

41 Jain, 'The Right to Family Planning, Contraception and Abortion',
    139–41.

astray, nor were they regarded as an obstacle in the realization of a man's spiritual ideals.

Sikhism is perceived to be a householder's religion for both men and women, and the Sikh gurus honoured the institution of marriage and denounced asceticism. They perceived sexuality as nothing abnormal and as a temperate gratification of bodily desires. The religion approves the institution of marriage as the practical and natural outlet for taming and controlling the human biological instincts and does not perceive sexual abstinence and vowed celibacy as virtues. It is perceived that a Sikh, by leading a householder's life, shares the riches of life but also does not lose sight of the ultimate reality. Men and women are equal companions in life and their roles are complementary and not competitive. A married woman performs a very useful role in society as she maintains sexual discipline for herself and establishes a morally healthy society. She is an embodiment of virtues and fortitude, and she must be respected because man and all of his social life would be incomplete without her.

In Sikhism, marriage is considered essential. Marriage is also not regarded as a contract that can be dissolved at will. It is an unbreakable spiritual union whose basis lies in everlasting true love. It aims to fuse two souls into one and is a means by which two souls attain spiritual growth. Married life is perceived to enable a person to fulfil his obligations to the society effectively, as production gets augmented if there is trusting companionship, shared work and interest, tolerance and understanding, between man and woman. Sikhism ensures a regular and continuous supply of labour, which serves as both a means and an end to productive activity. However, procreative activity must not proceed in an unchecked manner. In modern parlance, it may therefore be said to mean that children should be had by choice and not by chance, thereby promoting family welfare in the community.

However, it must be noted here that there is always a gap between doctrine and reality, and this fact shows up in the operative part of the

Sikh value system. One of the important determinants of a woman's status and also that of population growth is the rate of fertility, and religion is one of the most important factors that influence the thinking, attitudes and behaviour of people in the context of fertility. Other factors include age of marriage, customs and traditions governing marital behaviour, and health and mortality conditions. Sikhism disapproves of early marriage, and to an extent approves of widow remarriage, when the widow does not have children.[42]

There are taboos against intercourse on particular days of the month and during pregnancy, as it is perceived to reduce fertility.[43] Excessive indulgence in sex is discouraged as it is perceived to be animalistic. Sikhism allows judicious organization and temperate gratification of bodily pleasures so as to improve the quality of life of the people and lays great emphasis on personal hygiene to promote physical fitness. There is no such scriptural injunction in Sikhism that goes against birth control measures and there is no evidence either indicating religious resistance to human interference in fertility. Sikhism can be perceived as encouraging its adherents to put a check on their procreative powers.

The Sikh society, however, sanctifies a patriarchal structure, in which marriage, motherhood and service to husband are perceived

---

42 Bhai Randhir Singh, ed., *Prem Sumarag Granth*, 41, 48; and *A Guide to the Sikh Way of Life* (Patiala: Academy of Sikh Religion and Culture, 1953), 13. *Prem Sumarag Granth* (the true way to love) is an anonymous work in old Punjabi evoking a model of Sikh way of life and of Sikh society. It also provides a comprehensive model of Sikh polity with details concerning civil and military administration. Although known to earlier Sikh scholars, it was published for the first time in 1953 by the Sikh History Society, Amritsar, edited with an elaborate introduction by Bhai Randhir Singh, who, in 1940, accidentally came by a partly mutilated manuscript, which he revised with the help of another manuscript preserved in the Punjab Public Library, Lahore. A second edition was brought out by New Book Company, Jalandhar, in 1965.)

43 Singh, *Prem Sumarag Granth*, 75.

to be the most valuable attributes of a woman, which in turn serves as negation of a woman's personality. Women are respected for these above-mentioned roles, but they are generally given a secondary status to men, who dominate over her in all matters of life, irrespective of her merits. Consequently, a Sikh woman does not have much of a say in decisions regarding the number of children and spacing between the children she will have. Social norms prevalent in the Sikh society are similar to those in the Hindu society, which favours high fertility rates. A sterile woman is looked down upon, and it is considered a great fortune for a family to have many sons, as sons are important for continuance of the family line, the last rites of parents, and care of the parents in their old age. All these factors stand in the way of family planning among Sikhs, which results in high fertility rates.

The value system that operates within the Sikh society is sharply at variance with the code of conduct as laid down in the scriptures. Attitudes towards family planning, fertility and women's participation in the workforce are variables that are disturbed due to this contradiction. The sex ratio in Punjab, the home state of the Sikhs, has been consistently unfavourable to women because of various sociological reasons. Therefore, there is an urgent need to dismantle the social barriers that tie down the woman so that she may be empowered to play her role as a free agent in promoting human welfare and happiness.[44]

JAINISM

Along with Hinduism and Buddhism, Jainism constitutes one of three most important Indian religions still in existence and is an integral part of south Asian belief and practice.

---

44 Upinder Jit Kaur, 'Role and Status of Women in Sikhis', All About Sikhs, https://www.allaboutsikhs.com/sikhism-articles/role-and-status-of-women-in-sikhism, accessed on 19 October 2020.

Jainism believes in the peaceful co-existence of all living beings and emphasizes reverence and respect for all life forms. It is not only a religion but also a way of life. The basic virtues of Jainism include non-violence, truthfulness, chastity and non-materialism. The fundamental belief of Jains is ahimsa or non-violence, which extends to all forms of life. It essentially translates into the belief of live and let live, and emphasizes the philosophy that animals, birds, plants and the like have souls, an idea that extends to even the elements of earth, air, fire and water, which are perceived to be made of tiny souls. Therefore, Jains do not favour contraception, and abortion is forbidden. In principle, abortion is not permitted even if it costs the mother's life. However, one may decide to practise it in certain extraneous situations, but with repentance. Jainism believes in the sanctity of life; whatever the life form. Different kinds of creatures are perceived to be embodiments of similar souls in varying and similar situations, therefore the religion's emphasis on equal regard for all forms of life.[45]

However, there remains a sense of prejudice against women, who are perceived as temptresses, symbolic of attachment, fickleness and, most importantly, treacherousness.[46] The main characteristic of a woman lies in her acts of deception, or *Maya*, and this belief is perpetuated to such an extent that it is used as a justification for sex differentiation. The main question is whether this basic inequality between man and woman can be neutralized. The theological consequence of this image of woman gives rise to debates as to whether women can gain salvation, and this debate radically separates the Digambaras and the Svetambaras on the question of nudity.

---

45 See 'Guidelines for Health Care Providers Interacting with Patients of the Jain Religion and their Families', https://www.kyha.com/assets/docs/PreparednessDocs/cg-jain.pdf, accessed 19 October 2020.

46 Manisha Sethi, 'Chastity and Desire: Representing Women in Jainism', *South Asian History and Culture* 1, no.1 (2009): 42–59, doi: 10.1080/19472490903387209.

The underlying idea is that a woman cannot go naked because of her specific physiology and innate impurity. She is perceived to be unable to reach emancipation as a woman, and therefore has to be born as a man first.[47]

INDIAN BUDDHISTS

Buddhism is an ancient Indian religion that arose in and around the ancient kingdom of Magadha, which now falls in Bihar, India. According the 2011 Census, Buddhists make up about 0.7 per cent of the Indian population. The largest concentration of Buddhism is in Maharashtra, where 77 per cent of the Buddhists in India reside.[48]

Women were perceived to be a burden on the family because, according to traditions, women are believed to be incapable of performing the last religious rites for the well-being of the departed souls of the parents. Therefore, they were considered to be of little use. This was also the reason why the birth of a female child in a family was considered a misfortune. The Buddha, however, emphasized the fruitful role of a woman as a wife and a mother in the success of family life. Husbands and wives are expected to share equal responsibilities, and must be equally dedicated to the duties of the household and family. In family affairs, women were even considered a substitute to their husbands when they were away. In fact, a wife was expected to acquaint herself with the trade, business or industry her husband is associated with so that she could manage these affairs in his absence. This is indicative of Buddhist society looking at man and woman equally. Buddhism does not restrict educational opportunities for women or religious freedom, as the Buddha accepted and preached

---

47 See https://www.encyclopedia.com/environment/encyclopedias-almanacs-transcripts-and-maps/gender-and-religion-gender-and-jainism.

48 www.census2011.co.in.

that women, too, are capable of realizing the truth, just like men. He, therefore, permitted the admission of women into the Order.[49]

The Buddha's teachings do not condemn non-reproductive sexual activity but do object to the pursuit of sensual desires, which is suggestive of the idea that Buddhists who actively seek enlightenment should refrain from practising birth control in order to pursue their sexual desires. The Buddhist attitudes towards contraception are based on the idea that it is wrong to kill for any reason. Therefore, the most common Buddhist view on birth control is that contraception is acceptable if it prevents conception, but methods that prevent development of the fertilized egg are wrong and should be avoided. The Buddhists believe that life begins when the egg is fertilized, hence birth control methods such as the IUD, which act by killing the fertilized egg and preventing its implantation, are not acceptable, as that harms the consciousness that is embodied in the fertilized egg.[50]

CONCLUSION

Most of the major religions do not condemn birth control, although they do promote fertility as they date back to eras when high fertility rates would mean the difference between survival and death for a community as a consequence of high infant and child mortality. Despite that, there is plenty of room that allows, and to some extent even promotes, family planning. The opposition to family planning methods and contraception stems from the idea that contraception

49 'Buddhism and Women: Position of Women at the Time of Buddha', Buddhist Studies: Buddha Dharma Education Association and BuddhaNet, http://www.buddhanet.net/e-learning/history/position. htm, accessed on 19 October 2020.

50 'Contraception', 23 November 2009, http://www.bbc.co.uk/religion/ religions/buddhism/buddhistethics/contraception.shtml

and birth control encourage promiscuity, especially among women.[51] However, the bigger picture that is often missed is that in the global context, family planning, meant to limit the size of the family, actually seeks to reduce the increasing strain on the planet's limited resources. Contraception brings the choice of motherhood for women and promotes their health and well-being. It is imperative to understand that a healthy mother begets healthy children. A mother's health, nutrition level, choice in the number of children she will have, and how she will space her births result in lesser chances of infant or child mortality. In the context of climate change awareness and the serious crisis of non-renewable resources, religion and faith must not come in the way of practicality, logic and the call to address the need of the hour.

---

51 Austin Cline, 'Contraception, Birth Control, and World', Learn Religions, 6 January 2019, https://www.learnreligions.com/contraception-birth-control-and-world-religions-248029, accessed on 5 October 2020.

8

The Politics of Population

THIS chapter seeks to look at the incidence of hate speech and bigotry among right-wing propagandists and their implications. It also highlights the fact that Muslims and Hindus are not really on opposite ends of the scale but at the same end of the spectrum in how they fare in various socio-economic indicators.

There has been a fundamental change in perceptions regarding the pros and cons of population growth, from population explosion to demographic dividend. But the main differences in this matter relate to the means by which population growth may be controlled. Family planning has been made a matter of heated political controversy. Right-wing Hindu religious groups have always tried to make political issue out of the higher growth rate and fertility of Muslims compared with the Hindus.[1] This is primarily because of

1   A. Dharmalingam, Kannan Navaneetham and S. Philip Morgan, 'Muslim-Hindu Fertility Differences: Evidence from National Family Health Survey-II', *Economic and Political Weekly* 40, no.5 (2005): 429–36, DOI: 10.2307/4416134.

the predominant political ideology of 'us and they' that is injected into the masses by the right wing.[2]

The BJP government's ideological agenda is dictated by the Rashtriya Swayamsevak Sangh (RSS), which had previously claimed itself to be a cultural organization and refused to acknowledge its political influence. However, currently, the RSS asserts its political influence with immense pride. 'The Bharatiya Janata Party (BJP) is today the most prominent member of the family of organizations known as the "Sangh parivar" and nurtured by the Rashtriya Swayamsevak Sangh (RSS).'[3]

The mission statement of the group says it is 'firmly rooted in genuine nationalism' and publicly denounces 'erosion of the nation's integrity in the name of secularism' and 'endless appeasement of the Muslim population'.[4]

The very basis of Hindutva politics that is practised by parties like the BJP and Shiv Sena in recent years has relied on two interlinked ideas: that Hindus are victims in secular India and that Muslims have been appeased in the name of secularism since Independence. Prime Minister, Narendra Modi, in a speech (23 September 2016) dedicated to Deen Dayal Upadhyaya, the forerunner of the Bharatiya Janata Party said: 'Fifty years ago, Pandit Upadhyaya said, do not

---

2   Kunal Purohit, 'The Islamophobic Roots of Population Control Efforts in India', Aljazeera, 9 August 2019, https://www.aljazeera.com/features/2019/08/09/the-islamophobic-roots-of-population-control-efforts-in-india/, accessed on 19 October 2020.

3   Mujibur Rehman, ed., *Rise of Saffron Power: Reflections on Indian Politics* (London: Routledge, 2018), 2.

4   Lauren Frayer and Furkan Latif Khan, 'The Powerful Group Shaping the Rise of Hindu Nationalism in India', npr, 3 May 2019, https://www.npr.org/2019/05/03/706808616/the-powerful-group-shaping-the-rise-of-hindu-nationalism-in-india, accessed on 3 October 2020; also see Rashtriya Swayamsevak Sangh, Vision and Mission, https://www.rss.org/Encyc/2012/10/22/rss-vision-and-mission.html, accessed on 15 October 2020.

reward/appease (puraskrit) Muslims, do not shun (tiraskrit) them but purify (parishkar) them. Do not treat Muslims like vote ki mandi ka maal (vote banks) or ghrina ki vastu (object of hatred). Unhe apna samjho (regard them as your own).'[5]

Modi cannot be singled out for the use of ambiguous, vague and unclear expressions in this context, as the idea of 'Muslim appeasement' has haunted Indian politics for nearly three decades but has not been countered. The phrase 'Muslim appeasement' is referred to in at least two dimensions of politics regarding Muslims: biased institutional apparatus and unfair political practices. Constitutional provisions that offer legal protection to autonomous bodies, such as Islamic endowments known as waqf, the Muslim Personal Law and educational institutions such as Aligarh Muslim University are considered to be unfair and problematic. They are perceived as being against the spirit of secularism and religious equality. The root cause of this bias lies in the Hindutva ideology and in the much-debated idea of 'Muslim appeasement'.

In a 1970s' article titled 'Minorities Problems and Its Solution', written by Balraj Madhok, one of RSS's known intellectuals, the problematic aspects of the Indian constitution are outlined. In the article, he says: 'Articles 21, 30 and 370, which are discriminatory being in favour of minorities should be abrogated from the Constitution of India. Such provisions be made in the Constitution that no discrimination between the citizens of India will be made by the Government on the basis of religions or methods of worship. ... Such Muslims and other minorities who are not prepared to abjure their separatist tendencies should be declared foreigners, and they should be divested of the right of franchise.'

'"Muslim appeasement" is also used to denote specific forms of political practices. The assurance given to Muslims by the political parties with regard to educational and/or economic empowerment,

---

5   https://www.youtube.com/watch?v=72xWEpLGlMY

distribution of tickets to Muslim candidates in elections and even declaration of holidays on Muslim religious festivals are treated as "Muslim appeasement".[6]

The publication of the Sachar Committee report in 2006 provided a new perspective to the idea of Muslim appeasement. It underlined the fact that Indian Muslims are socially, economically and educationally backward and marginalized. This report led to non-BJP parties demonstrating that 'Muslim appeasement' was in fact 'a myth created by Hindutva forces'. 'Hindutva politics also refashioned itself in the light of this response. It was argued that the Congress did not show any serious interest in the empowerment of Muslims — they were treated as a vote bank, which led to marginalisation and exclusion.[7] The idea of Muslim appeasement has been a favourite topic of politicians, while the minority itself has been pushed to the margins and is now struggling for survival, as various socioeconomic indicators show. If Muslims had really been appeased and successive governments had focused on them all these years, why would they be in such a pathetic state?

Indian Muslims are perceived as second-class citizens in their own country.[8] Table 8.1 shows the stark backwardness of Muslims in all sectors of the economy. It exposes the blatantly false charge of 'appeasement' which has been thrown against the Muslims as part of the well-orchestrated propaganda on which the hate campaign against them was originally built. The Muslim community remains

---

6   Qtd. in Hilal Ahmed, 'From Rajiv Gandhi to Modi, Nobody Defines "Muslim Appeasement" But All Use It for Votes', *The Print*, 14 November 2018, https://theprint.in/opinion/from-rajiv-gandhi-to-modi-nobody-defines-muslim-appeasement-but-all-use-it-for-votes/148566/, accessed on 14 October 2020.

7   Ibid.

8   Aijaz Zaka Syed, 'The Myth of Muslim Appeasement', Clarion, 8 October 2013, https://clarionindia.net/the-myth-of-muslim-appeasement/, accessed on 3 October 2020.

the most deprived in the Indian job market and is completely off the radar of corporate India. The affirmative action framework, which the private sector was necessitated to adopt and implement in the last decade, is more focused on Dalits, sidelining Muslims and leaving them to their own devices.[9] Muslims are also very poorly represented in defence and security-related activities, and this poses a matter of concern as it is crucially linked to their sense of well-being and security about their life and assets, as perceived by the Muslim community. The share of Muslims in the public order and safety services at the Central level is just 6 percent while that of Hindu upper-castes is 42 percent. At the state level, the share of Muslims is slightly higher at 7 per cent while only 4 per cent of Muslims are engaged in defence related activities.[10]

According to the Sachar Committee report (2005–2006),[11] the proportion of Muslim IPS officers is 4 per cent, IAS officers 3 per cent and IFS officers less than 2 per cent, indicating a history of 'systematic discrimination'. Only 4.5 per cent of employees at Indian Railways, the largest employer in India, are Muslim, of whom 98.7 per cent are placed at the lower levels, according to Sachar Committee Report.[12] The Muslim share in the police constabulary

---

9   Naren Karunakaran, 'Muslims constitute 14% of India, but just 3% of India Inc', *The Economic Times,* 7 September 2015, https://economictimes. indiatimes.com/news/politics-and-nation/muslims-constitute-14-of-india-but-just-3-of-india-inc/articleshow/48849266.cms?utm_source=contentofinterest&utm_medium=text&utm_campaign=cppst, accessed on 15 April 2020.

10 R. Robinson, 'Religion, Socio-economic Backwardness & Discrimination: The Case of Indian Muslims', *The Indian Journal of Industrial Relations* 44, no. 2 (2008): 194–200, http://www.jstor.org/stable/27768189, accessed on 22 September 2020.

11 'Government Employment and Programmes', in 'Social, Economic and Educational Status of the Muslim Community of India', Sachar Committee Report, 2005-2006, 165.

12 Ibid., 167.

is only 6 per cent, in the public health sector only 4.4 per cent, and in the public transport sector only 6.5 per cent. Their representation is also very low in the universities and banks. The average size of bank loans disbursed to Muslims is two thirds of the amount disbursed to other minorities. In some cases, it is half. The total share of Muslims in the Indian population is 14 per cent, however the total number of Muslim students in colleges is 5.23 per cent and in institutes of national importance only 2.19 per cent. Similarly, the proportion of Muslim faculty in colleges is 5.35 per cent and in institutes of national importance only 2.88 per cent.[13] Muslims, as a community, have been excluded from the formal sector. Therefore, they depend on the informal sector and self-employment as their means of livelihood. In the urban areas, the share of Muslims in self-employment is 50 per cent, against 33 per cent for Hindus, according to the NSSO (2009–2010).

Table 8.1: A list of corporations showing Muslim representation on the board of directors/governors, showing how under-represented the community is

Organization	Total membership of board of directors/ governors	Total number of Muslims
Prominent Financial Institutions of India:		
SBI	12	0
HDFC	10	0
LIC	12	0
SEBI	9	0

13 See https://twitter.com/RajatDutta13/status/1253203548076048385.

Organization	Total membership of board of directors/ governors	Total number of Muslims
RBI	14	0
NSE	9	0
BSE	8	0
PNB	9	0
ICICI	12	0
Top Ten Indian PSUs:		
ONGC	11	0
Indian Oil	17	0
NTPC	14	0
Power Grid	10	0
BPCL	8	0
Coal India	11	0
HPCL	10	1
GAIL	10	0
Power Finance	8	0
REC	4	0
Top Print Media Houses:		
Bennett Coleman (Times Group)	12	0
HT Media	6	0
Kasturi & Sons (The Hindu)	14	0
Indian Express	6	0
Dainik Jagran	18	0
Dainik Bhaskar	18	0
Manorama Malayalam	8	0

Organization	Total membership of board of directors/ governors	Total number of Muslims
Outlook	5	0
Television News:		
Aajtak (India Today)	7	0
Times Group	12	0
NDTV	5	0
ASG Media (Republic)	3	0
Zee News	5	0
ABP	7	0
India TV	5	0
Network 18 (CNBC)	8	1
Sun TV	15	0
News Broadcasting Association	10	0

Source: Twitter.com. Series of tweets by blogger Rajat Dutta (@RajatDutta13) on 23 April and 25 April 2020[14]

And, how can it be denied that the political space for India's minorities has been shrinking? In 2014, only 3.7 per cent of Members of Parliament in the lower house were Muslim, against 9 per cent in 1980, even though the share of the Muslim population rose to 14.2 per cent from 11.1 per cent during this period. The BJP in 2014 and 2019 was the only major political party with no Muslim Members of Parliament.[15]

---

14   See https://rajatdutta13.blogspot.com/2020/05/muslim-representation-in-governing-body.html.

15   Archana Chaudhary and Iain Marlow, 'Why India's Modi Has His Country's Muslims Worried', *Washington Post*, 14 December 2019,

Communal Hatred

The success of the RSS and the BJP over the past years is owed largely to their adept poisoning of public opinion. Politicians, indoctrinated media houses, the infamous IT cell of the BJP, and a huge number of social media trolls spread false information to polarize the population and demonize Muslims. [16]

And, of course, a key issue that has become religious and political is family planning, especially its lower prevalence in the Muslim community. One of the most shared WhatsApp messages of the past few years is a shrill cry about the 'shrinking' Hindu population in India. The propaganda that Muslims are about to overtake the Hindu population and capture political power is rather overwhelming. The fact is that total fertility rate of Muslims in India has seen a steep decline over the past few decades, as is evident from NFHS-4 data. The TFR of Muslims during NFHS-1 was 4.4, against the TFR of Hindus at 3.3; the gap saw a reduction during NFHS-2, when the TFR of Muslims came down to 3.6 against the TFR of 2.8 of Hindus. The TFR of Muslims further fell to 3.4, while the TFR or Hindus fell to 2.6. NFHS-4 has seen a significant reduction in the TFR of Muslims, which has come down to 2.6 while the TFR of Hindus has come down to 2.1. However, fear-mongering on the part of Hindu nationalists about Muslim population growth is a

---

https://www.washingtonpost.com/business/why-indias-modi-has-his-countrys-muslims-worried/2019/12/13/9b0e5f6a-1dbf-11ea-977a-15a6710ed6da_story.html, accessed on 6 October 2020.

16   Samanth Subramanian, 'How Hindu Supremacists Are Tearing India Apart', *The Guardian*, 20 February 2020, https://www.theguardian.com/world/2020/feb/20/hindu-supremacists-nationalism-tearing-india-apart-modi-bjp-rss-jnu-attacks, accessed on 6 October 2020. Senior journalist Swati Chaturvedi has exposed the modus operandi of this hate machine in her 2016 best-seller, *I Am A Troll - Inside the Secret World of BJP's Digital Army*.

favourite hobby. It has led to controversial hate speeches and vicious propaganda at all levels.

Narendra Modi, when chief minister of Gujarat in 2002, mockingly remarked, *'hum paanch, humare pachchees'*,[17] insinuating that every Muslim has four wives and twenty-five children. On the issue of providing relief camps for Muslims in February that year, following the carnage of the Godhra riots, he wryly said, *'What should I do? Run relief camps for them? Do we want to have baby producing centres?'* A chief minister, who had taken oath under the constitution was ridiculing an entire community that made up about 9 per cent of his state population, isolating them from the rest of Gujarat by referring to the community as 'them' and mocking them.[18]

In recent times, after the triple talaq law was passed, Modi's reference to population explosion is indicative of the strong probability that the BJP government is actively working towards fulfilling the Rashtriya Swayamsevak Sangh's long cherished dream of a uniform civil code in India.

'In our society, there is a section which is very well aware of the consequences of uncontrolled population growth. They deserve our accolades and respect,' he said. *'This (small-family policy) is an expression of their love for the nation ... a form of patriotism. We need to inspire the segment of society still not thinking on these lines. We need to worry about population explosion.'*[19] He called upon the state and the central

---

17 "'Should We Run Relief Camps? Open Child Producing Centres?'", *Outlook*, 30 September 2002, https://www.outlookindia.com/website/story/should-we-run-relief-camps-open-child-producing-centres/217398, accessed on 16 October 2020.

18 Debesh Das, 'Slanderous Campaigns against Muslims and the Facts', *Peoples Democracy* XLI, no. 25 (18 June 2017), https://peoplesdemocracy.in/2017/0618_pd/slanderous-campaigns-against-muslims-and-facts, accessed on 3 October 2020.

19 Seshadri Chari, 'Modi Govt Has Been Working for a Uniform Civil Code and We Didn't Even Notice. Until Now', *The Print*, 16 August

governments to initiate schemes in order to ensure that the country as a whole does not pass on an 'unhealthy and uneducated' society to the future generations.[20]

Many researchers have pointed out that there is a strong correlation between poverty, lack of education and family size. However, Modi drew everyone's attention to the 'irresponsible' ones, those who contribute to the already increasing population and push their children into an uncertain future.

Also, the traditional practice of polygamy among Muslim men is believed to be deeply rooted in their religious belief and is also defended by the Muslim Personal Law Board. In India, polygamy is illegal except for Muslims and tribal communities. This is where the essence of the demand for a uniform civil code lies.

In the absence of a uniform civil code, the question of the religious rights of one community in a secular society has become a rather controversial issue in India. A 'uniform population policy' (a phrase used by Mohan Bhagwat himself) for all communities, irrespective of their religious beliefs, social taboos, faith-related conduct and personal laws, has been a long-pending demand of the RSS, the ideological fountainhead of the BJP.[21] The RSS approach to the uniform civil code is rather interesting. From Golwalkar to Mohan Bhagwat, the heads of RSS, the RSS is of the opinion that community reform must happen, and the best way to achieve one law, one nation, is for the demand to come from within the community. The RSS believes that those who are against the uniform civil code misguide the community by creating an RSS-phobia, holding that the real purpose of UCC for the RSS is majoritarianism. The RSS

2019,   https://theprint.in/opinion/modi-govt-has-been-working-for-a-uniform-civil-code-and-we-didnt-even-notice-until-now/278053/, accessed on 6 October 2020.

20 Ibid.

21 Ibid.

stands for a UCC that does not address micro-issues like rituals, local and community traditions, but mainly meta issues like marriage, its dissolution, succession, and the right to property for women. The basic idea of a UCC for the country, according to the RSS, is gender equality and gender justice. On 23 August 1972, Golwalkar, sarsanghchalak (head) of the RSS (1940–1973), in an interview to K.R. Malkani, editor of the pro-RSS daily *The Motherland* (ceased after Emergency) said, '. . . *the right to marry four wives is causing a disproportionate increase in Muslim population. I am afraid this is a negative approach. If our objections to Muslim practices are on humanitarian grounds, then that becomes a valid objection. A reformist's attitude in this matter is alright. But a mechanical leveller's attitude would not be correct. Let the Muslims evolve their old laws. I would be happy if they will arrive at the conclusion that polygamy is not good for them; but I will not like to force my views on them.*'[22]

On the issue of family planning, in 2013, RSS joint secretary, Dattatraya Hosbal, said: 'According to the 2011 Census, growth rate of children in the age group of 0-6 is 15 per cent among Hindus, whereas it is 18 per cent among Muslims. Small-family norms are posing a big threat to Hindus. So, each family should have three children.' He also added that the Sangh would go all out to encourage bigger families as 'blindly following family planning norms by a community won't do any good to the country. It will trigger serious imbalance in the country'.[23] The RSS has advised Hindus to have bigger families and go for more children. The Sangh feels that big

---

22 Rakesh Sinha, 'RSS Stand on Uniform Civil Code - Don't Believe the Haters', NDTV.com, 24 August 2017, https://www.ndtv.com/opinion/rss-stand-on-uniform-civil-code-dont-believe-the-haters-1741041, accessed on 6 October 2007.

23 Ramesh Babu, 'RSS to Hindus: Shun Family Planning, Have More Kids', *Hindustan Times*, 27 October 2013, https://www.hindustantimes.com/india/rss-to-hindus-shun-family-planning-have-more-kids/story-of99bXak9KXFkvv0CtZasK.html, accessed on 6 October 2020.

Hindu families will help counter the menacing demographic changes that are taking place in many parts of the country.

To counter the perceived threat to Hindus, Rajeshwar Singh, RSS Pracharak, in December 2014, said, *'Muslims and Christians will be wiped out of India by December 31, 2021.'*

'This is a pledge taken by my colleagues,' he asserted. *'This is our pledge.'*[24]

Pravin Togadia (VHP working president) had said in this context, 'Now, we will not let population of Hindu decrease to 42 per cent from 82 per cent. Hindus need to increase their population to ensure their safety because system of the country is not able to protect Hindus.'[25]

Using instances from Hindu mythology, Indian spiritual leader, Ramanandacharya Raghavacharya said:

Lord Krishna had 16,108 wives and he had ten children from each of them. The world will be ruled by those who have maximum population. Lord Ram too had asked his brother Bharat to have more sons for protection of the religion.'[26]

An Ayodhya priest, Kanhaiyya Das, said, 'The slogan *"hum do humare do"* will not work. Each Hindu family should have at least eight children.'[27]

---

24 'Muslims and Christians Will Be Wiped Out of India by December 31, 2021: BJP Leader Rajeshwar Singh', Sabrang, 14 December 2014, https://sabrangindia.in/article/muslims-and-christians-will-be-wiped-out-india-december-31-2021-bjp-leader-rajeshwar-singh, accessed on 6 October 2020.

25 Lalmani Verma, 'Now, Saffron Leaders Ask Hindus to Have 10 Kids to Ensure Survival of Religion', *The Indian Express*, 19 January, 2015, https://indianexpress.com/article/india/india-others/now-saffron-leaders-ask-hindus-to-have-10-kids/, accessed on 6 October 2020.

26 Ibid.

27 Ibid.

Mohan Bhagwat, chief of the RSS, had made certain controversial remarks in 2016 in the context of population growth among Indian Muslims. He was asked how if, in India, where the rate of growth of Hindus was 2.1 per cent and that of Muslims 5.2 per cent, the Hindu population growth rate continued to lag behind the Muslim growth rate by two-and-half times, then would not India become an Islamic country in fifty years? Bhagwat had remarked, *'Which law says that the population of Hindus should not rise? What is stopping them when population of others is rising? The issue is not related to the system. It is because the social environment is like this.'*

The massive uproar caused by his statements pushed the RSS into 'clarifying' that he did not mean that Hindus should have more babies, but his intention was to state that there has to be a common law on population growth that is applicable to all.[28]

BJP MP Sakshi Maharaj, addressing a gathering in 2017, said: 'Those with four wives and forty children are responsible for the population increase in the country. Hindus are not responsible for the increase in population.' He was holding the Muslim community responsible for the population growth in the country.[29] He had also said that all Hindu women 'must produce four children to protect the religion'.[30]

---

28 Salman Anees Soz, 'RSS Claims About Rapid Growth of the Muslim Population are Simply False', *The Wire*, 7 September 2016, https://thewire.in/politics/rss-claims-rapid-growth-muslim-population-simply-false, accessed on 6 October 2020.

29 *The Economic Times*, 'Sakshi Maharaj Booked for "Population Control" Remarks', 7 January 2017, https://economictimes.indiatimes.com/news/politics-and-nation/sakshi-maharaj-booked-for-population-control-remarks/articleshow/56392759.cms?utm_source=contentofinterest&utm_medium=text&utm_campaign=cppst, accessed on 6 October 2020.

30 Kay Benedict, '"Hum Do Humare Do" Not For Our MPs', *The Free Press Journal*, 7 December 2019, https://www.freepressjournal.in/

In 2018, Banwari Lal Singhal, a BJP legislator from Rajasthan, said, 'Hindus giving birth to one or two children are worried about educating them. But Muslims are worried about how to take over the nation by increasing their population; education and development have no significance to them. It is my personal opinion.'[31]

In 2018, Union Minister Giriraj Singh said: 'The growing population of the country, especially Muslims, is a threat to the social fabric, social harmony, and development of the country.'[32]

BJP MP Hari Om Pandey, in 2018, said: 'The menaces such as of terrorism, rape, sexual harassment prevailing in India is (sic) only of the rising Muslim populations. If one looks closely, there is a rapid increase in the percentage of Muslim population since the time of Independence.' He asserted that a new country like Pakistan will be formed out of India if the government failed to take measures to curb the rising Muslim population.[33]

Yogi Adityanath, chief minister of Uttar Pradesh, led a campaign that blamed Muslim youths for waging a 'love jihad' by seducing

---

analysis/hum-do-humare-do-not-for-our-mps, accessed on 6 October 2020.

31 Deepika, 'Muslims Producing More Children Aiming to Corner Hindus in India: Rajasthan BJP MLA', oneindia, 1 January 2018, https://www.oneindia.com/india/muslims-producing-more-children-aiming-to-outnumber-hindus-in-india-rajasthan-bjp-mla-2612025.html, accessed on 3 October 2020.

32 Chaitanya Mallapur, 'BJP Leaders Cite Growing Muslim Population as Threat to India; Facts Don't Back their Claims', *Firstpost*, 15 January, 2018, https://www.firstpost.com/india/bjp-leaders-cite-growing-muslim-population-as-threat-to-india-facts-dont-back-their-claims-4303403.html, accessed on 6 October 2020.

33 *The Indian Express*, 'Rising Muslim Population Responsible for Increase in Rapes, Murders: BJP MP', 27 July 2018, https://indianexpress.com/article/india/bjp-mp-hari-om-pandey-rapes-murders-muslim-population-5279384/, accessed on 6 October 2020.

Hindu women to convert to Islam.[34] Sunil Bharala, labour welfare minister in Adityanath's government, said: 'Hindus should produce at least three children.' He told reporters, 'Personally, I believe that we should adopt the idea of five, there should be three children in each family…'[35]

Amit Pandey, a thirty-six-year-old pharmaceutical trader from Lucknow, has amassed over 30,000 followers in just two months on his Facebook page, Jansankhya Niyantran Kanoon (Population Control Law). He sets aside an hour a day to work on his 'cause', calling on people to write to Prime Minister Narendra Modi to legislate population control. His efforts, he claims, have seen 150,000 letters being sent to Modi on the issue. Pandey has long believed that Muslims are conspiring against the country. 'In Muslims, there is no humanity. Each of them is a jihadi in his or her own way. With a growing population, they will become huge vote banks and their votes will start mattering more than Hindu votes,' he told Al Jazeera. He also posts incessantly on his Facebook page photos, GIFs and videos that are mostly misinformation. He believes that the government data showing that Muslim population growth is slowing down is fake and manipulated. 'They don't think of themselves as Indians; they don't have the right intentions. Each Muslim thinks of how to defeat Hindus and wage a Ghazwa-e-Hind (Holy War against India),' he said.

---

34 Chaudhary and Marlow, 'Why India's Modi Has His Country's Muslims Worried'.

35 'Yogi Adityanath ke mantri boley – Hindu "Hum do-Humare Do" ko chod kar, "Hum Do, Humaare Paanch" ki Neeti Mein Par Chale' [Yogi Adityanath's minister said - Except Hindu "Hum Do-Hamare Do", follow the policy of "Hum Do, Hamare Paanch"]', NDTV India, 10 December 2019, https://khabar.ndtv.com/news/india/yogi-government-minister-says-hindus-should-follow-the-policy-of-ham-do-hamare-five-2146180, accessed on 6 October 2020.

Across northern and central India, a campaign underpinned by Islamophobia, advocating for a population control norm, is gaining momentum. The Jansankhya Samadhan Foundation (Population Resolution Foundation) is an NGO that supports a two-child norm, with punishment including jail terms for offenders. Anil Chaudhary, head of the NGO claims: '. . . *the group has held 150,000 protests and meetings across nearly half of India's 725 administrative districts, runs more than 400 WhatsApp groups, and is connected with 100,000 people.*'

He says, 'When we travel across the country, 95 per cent of the people say that Muslims are driving India's population explosion. Hindus tell me, "There is no point in telling us to control the population, you should tell the Muslims." The thing is, this is the fact.'Chaudhary insists that his organization is non-political. He says, 'Initially, we tried to advocate this with the (Muslim) community. But we were reportedly told by them that for religious reasons, the community will never accept such a law.'[36]

In July 2019, BJP Member of Parliament Rakesh Sinha proposed a private member's bill – Population Regulation Bill, 2019 – in the Indian parliament. The bill suggests that people with more than two living children should be 'disqualified' from running for the post of MP, MLA, or for membership of any body of local self-government. It also suggests that government employees must give an undertaking that they will not have more than two children. Those employees who have more than two children on or before the commencement of the act should be exempted. Other penalties include reduction in subsidies on loans and interest rates on savings instruments, reduction in benefits under the public distribution system, and higher-than-normal interest rates on loans taken from banks and other financial institutions. According to Sinha, India's growing population has made the country agitated. He talked about

---

36 Purohit, 'The Islamophobic Roots of Population Control Efforts in India'.

a 'religious imbalance' as a consequence of the growing population.[37] It will be interesting to see the debate on the bill and its outcome.

Earlier in November 2019, Ajay Bhatt (BJP), Member of Parliament, introduced a Private Member's Bill for 'Population control by adoption of small family norms', clearly defining small family as two living children.

The worthy MPs need to be reminded that coercive measures have never succeeded in the past. In fact, these have faced tremendous backlash. What comes to mind is the popular backlash for a similar policy of Congress leader Sanjay Gandhi during the emergency (1975–77) which gave a setback to a programme from which the country is yet to recover.

There is no evidence on the effectiveness of a two-child policy. Similar policies in few states (such as Bihar) have failed to bring down the fertility rates to the desired level. A five-state study (comprising Madhya Pradesh, Andhra Pradesh, Haryana, Odisha and Rajasthan) by Nirmala Buch found that there was a rise in sex-selective and unsafe abortions; men divorced their wives to run for local body elections, and families gave up children for adoption to avoid disqualification.

The overall size of population will continue to increase for some more time as two thirds of India's population is under 35 years.[38] Even if this cohort of young population produces only one or two children per couple, it will still result in a quantum increase in population size before stabilizing, which as per current projections will happen around 2050.

---

37 *The Indian Express*, 'Private Member's Bill Calls for Two-child Norm', 13 July 2019, https://indianexpress.com/article/india/private-members-bill-two-child-norm-population-regulation-rakesh-sinha-5827145/, accessed on 6 October 2020.

38 Census 2011, https://censusindia.gov.in/2011census/population_enumeration.html, accessed on 19 October 2020. The above link can be used for all Census data.

That is why the Mission Parivar Vikas program of the Government of India in 146 high fertility districts in the country to provide the intensive and improved family planning services is an important and much needed initiative.

In 2019, BJP MLA Surendra Singh from Ballia, said, 'If population control law is not made in India then in next fifty years, Hindutva will not be safe even in India. You can see that in Jammu and Kashmir, security has to be deployed. Workers of Bharatiya Janata Party (BJP) and Rashtriya Swayamsevak Sangh (RSS) are being killed in West Bengal and no one is taking action. Wherever BJP is not in ruling, you must have experienced Islamist terrorism and Islamic extremism.'[39] His next communal onslaught was: 'Those who desisted from saying "Bharat mata ki Jai" are Pakistanis!'[40]

In 2017, Ananth Kumar Hegde, incumbent Member of Parliament from Uttar Kannada constituency, made a provocative statement 'Till Islam is in the world there can be no end to terrorism!' He faced no consequences for saying that.[41] While demonizing the Muslims for the country's population growth, Hindu ideologues, paradoxically, have projected birth control as an 'anti-Hindu' measure while at the same time complaining that the Muslims refuse to practise it. However, writing in the RSS-affiliated magazine, *Organiser*, many decades ago (21 August 1971), Kaka Bhusandi had

---

39 *The New Indian Express*, '"Hindutva" Won't be Safe if Population Control Law is Not Made: BJP MLA Surendra Singh', 28 October 2019,   https://www.newindianexpress.com/nation/2019/oct/28/ hindutva-wont-be-safe-if-population-control-law-is-not-made-bjp-mla-surendra-singh-2053729.html, accessed on 19 October 2020.

40 Humra Quraishi, 'List of Hate Mongering Leaders of BJP Is Long, But No Action Against Them', *National Herald*, 6 February 2020, https:// www.nationalheraldindia.com/opinion/list-of-hate-mongering-leaders-of-bjp-is-long-but-no-action-against-them, accessed on 19 October 2020.

41 Ibid.

said, in a piece titled 'Birth Control Has Ruined Many Countries': 'The thesis that birth control is necessary to ensure sufficient food for the existing population in our country is questionable.'[42]

Organiser, in its edition of 4 May 1974, had reported that the Hindu sammelan organized by the Hindu Raksha Dal had passed a resolution advising Hindus to not fall prey to the family planning propaganda of the government. M.W. Onkar, writing in the magazine (in its issue of 18 November 1990) claimed, *'The government machinery compels the Hindu population to resort to family planning devices and undergo vasectomy and tubectomy operations.'*

Another hardcore Hindu propagandist, Bishen Swaroop Goyal, in a booklet explicitly titled *Family Planning is a Conspiracy Against Hindu Society*,[43] claimed that only the well off among the Hindus practised family planning, because of which "Muslims, Christians, Sikhs and Parsis think that the Hindus are fools'.[44] He believed that the poor and the backward social groups were not inclined towards population control, so he declared: 'What is most painfully worrying is that because the nationalist intellectual classes (a euphemism for educated and better off, and presumably 'upper-' caste Hindus) are adopting family planning, they shall turn very soon into an even smaller minority.'[45] As every issue for which the Hindutva brigade mobilizes support is by giving it a communal colour that is strongly anti-Muslim, family planning too has been projected as something pro-Muslim and anti-Hindu. Goyal wrote: 'The family planning programme has been introduced with the sole purpose of reducing

---

42 Yoginder Sikand, 'Hindutva Hypocrisy on Family Planning', Sabrang, 1 March 2005, https://sabrangindia.in/ann/hindutva-hypocrisy-family-planning, accessed on 19 October 2020.

43 Bishen Swaroop Goyal, *Parivar Niyojan Hindu Samaj Ke Virudh Shadyantra* (New Delhi: Vikalp Prakashan, n.d.).

44 Ibid., 1.

45 Ibid., 2.

Hindus into a minority. The world knows that wherever in India the Hindus became a minority, those areas were separated from the country. So, is it that family planning is being propagated solely to break up India and thereby revive Muslim rule?'[46]

An appeal to Hindus to rapidly multiply while simultaneously condemning the Muslims for allegedly refusing to limit their families appeared some years ago in a writ petition filed by a group of 'upper'-caste Hindus from Gorakhpur in the Supreme Court (No. 15, 1993)[47] against the Union of India, asking for a ban on the Quran. They declared in their petition: 'It may be noted that Hinduism has not restricted Hindus to have one wife only. It is the sectarian Indian Parliament which has restricted the population growth of Hindus to meet her (sic.) nefarious designs, viz. appease Mohamdens (sic.) to grab Muslims' vote-banks and rob and slay Hindus ...' They went on to declare that 'The one and only reason of [sic.] the Hindus' survival is their population strength. The Indian Government and Constitution are colluding with Muslims to finish this barrier.'[48]

The list of hate speeches against the Muslim community runs long, especially from the current dominant sections who appear to be hell-bent on threatening the very existence and survival of Indian Muslims in the country. The most disturbing dimension to the hate speeches is that an entire generation of Muslim haters is being trained, nurtured and tutored to come out and chant *'Desh ke gaddaron ko, goli maaron saalon ko'* [49] (shoot the traitors of the

---

46 Ibid.

47 Writ petition No. 15 of 1993-A.P. Tripathi, R.C. Agarwal, R.P. Gupta and I.L. Shrivastava versus Union of India, http://www.islaminterfaith. org/.

48 Ibid.

49 Quraishi, 'List of Hate Mongering Leaders of BJP is Long, But No Action Against Them'.

nation), spewing hatred towards the Muslim community and calling them traitors. Anti-Muslim slogans create a sense of divide in young minds. The RSS's educational and political agenda include both use of violence against the minorities and the absorption of subaltern groups into the Hindu fold and involving them in this mission.

The degree of militarization that follows this training extends to both men and women. However, the confidence pumped up in both the boys and the girls can quickly turn into aggression and a chauvinistic attitude towards non-Hindu 'others'.[50]

In the book *Religious Demography of India*, written by A.P. Joshi, M.D. Srinivas and J.K. Bajaj, the authors have said there is much that Indian Religionists need to fear (the term Indian Religionists here is a euphemism for Hindus, Buddhists, Sikhs and Jains). 'The proportion of Indian Religionists in the population of India has declined by 11 percentage points during the period of 110 years . . . Indian religionists formed 79.32% of the population in 1881 and 68.03% in 1991 . . . If the trend . . . continues, then the proportion of Indian Religionists in India is likely to fall below 50% in the latter half of the 21st century.'[51]

However, it becomes important to note that India here means undivided India, the author having considered the combined population of India, Pakistan and Bangladesh. For the present Indian Union, the decline is more nominal, from 86.64 per cent in 1901 to 85.09 per cent in 1991. But, according to the book, a 'pocket of high Muslim influence seems to be now developing in the northern

---

50 Nandini   Sundar,   'Teaching   to   Hate: RSS'   Pedagogical Programme', *Economic and Political Weekly* 39, no. 16 (2004): 1605–1612, www.jstor.org/stable/4414900.

51 Qtd in Swapan Dasgupta, Book Review of *Religious Demography of India* by A.P. Joshi, M.D. Srinivas and J.K. Bajaj (Chennai, India: Centre for Policy Studies, 2003), India Today, 19 May 2003, https://www.indiatoday.in/magazine/society-the-arts/books/story/20030512-book-review-of-religious-demography-of-india-793763-2003-05-19.

border belt covering Uttar Pradesh, Bihar, West Bengal and Assam. And a border pocket of even more intense Christian influence has developed in the north-eastern states.' The data presented in this book is startling and can be misinterpreted to the extent that the book can be used as a ready reckoner for a Hindu backlash against secularism.[52]

From 1 April 2020 onwards, amidst the global COVID-19 pandemic, there was a call for the socioeconomic boycott of Muslims and the coining of a deeply communal term, 'Corona Jihad'.[53] In a blatant example of hate speech, especially designed to incite an economic boycott of Muslims, Uttar Pradesh BJP MLA Suresh Tiwari asked the people of Deoria district to not purchase vegetables from Muslim vendors, *Indian Express* reported. The legislator from the district's Barhaj constituency said in a viral video, 'Keep one thing in mind, I am telling everyone openly, no one should purchase vegetables from Muslims.' He later tried to explain it away, saying, 'After hearing complaints that people of a community were selling vegetables after contaminating them with saliva in an attempt to spread coronavirus disease, I advised them not to purchase vegetables from them . . . After the situation gets normal, then decide what they want.'[54]

The Aurangabad bench of the Bombay High Court ruled on 21 August 2020 that the foreign nationals who had attended the Tablighi Jamaat event earlier in March 2020 were simply made the 'scapegoat'

---

52 Qtd in Ibid.

53 'Continued and Systematic Vilification of Minorities During Lockdown: Report', Sabrang, 30 May 2020, https://sabrangindia. in/article/continued-and-systematic-vilification-minorities-during-lockdown-report, accessed on 19 October 2020.

54 Sabrang, 'UP BJP MLA Asks People Not to Buy Vegetables from Muslim Vendors', 28 April 2020, https://sabrangindia.in/article/bjp-mla-asks-people-not-buy-vegetables-muslim-vendors, accessed on 5 October 2020.

and allegations were made that they were responsible for the spread of COVID-19 in the country. The bench of Justices T.V. Nalawade and M.G. Sewliker noted that it was a huge propaganda against the foreigners who had come to the Markaz in Delhi and quashed the FIRs against these foreign nationals. 'A political government tries to find the scapegoat when there is pandemic or calamity and the circumstances show that there is probability that these foreigners were chosen to make them a scapegoat,' the court said in its order. 'The propaganda against the so-called religious activity (Tablighi Jamaat) was unwarranted. The activity was going on for more than 50 years and it is there throughout the year,' it added.[55]

Unfortunately, this hate campaign is here to stay, as it has proved to be a tool for polarization and consolidation of the Hindu vote bank, a tested strategy for winning elections. And since, despite abundance of law, all these utterances go unpunished and have the tacit or blatant support of the ruling dispensation, there is no deterrence in sight.[56]

The laws of the land are strictly against hate and divisive speech.

Sections 153A and 153B of the Indian Penal Code 1860 make any act that incites or promotes disharmony or feelings of enmity

---

55 *The Economic Times*, 'Foreign Attendees of Tablighi Jamaat Event Made Scapegoat, says Bombay High Court', 22 August 2020, https://economictimes.indiatimes.com/news/politics-and-nation/foreign-attendees-of-tablighi-jamaat-event-made-scapegoat-says-bombay-high-court/articleshow/77691420.cms?utm_source=contentofinterest&utm_medium=text&utm_campaign=cppst, accessed on 5 October 2020.

56 In order to prevent this narrative from becoming partial and one-dimensional, the author had investigated similar hate speech and propaganda from Muslims regarding Hindus, specific to the context of family planning.

or hatred between different religious, racial, linguistic or regional groups, castes or communities a punishable criminal offence. Section 295A of Indian Penal Code 1860 provides punishment for any act done by anyone with deliberate or malicious intention to outrage the religious feelings of any class of the citizens, or insults or attempts to insult the religion or religious beliefs of that class of citizens. Under Section 298, punishment is prescribed for any act committed with the deliberate and malicious intention of hurting the religious feelings of any person. Sections 505(1) and 505(2) make the making, publishing or circulating of any statement or rumour an offence, if the statement or rumour is likely to incite any class or group of persons to commit any offence against another class or group of persons, or promotes or is likely to promote feelings of enmity, hatred or ill-will between different religious, racial, linguistic or regional groups, castes or communities.

Section 8 of the Representation of People's Act 1951 bars from contesting elections a person who has been convicted of illegitimate use of freedom of speech and expression. Sections 123(3A) and 125 prohibit promotion of animosity on the grounds of religion, race, caste community or language in reference to elections, terming such acts as corrupt electoral practices. Despite the existence of such provisions, hate speech is surprisingly common and prevalent in the political dynamics of the country, and it leads to communalism and bigotry. The fundamental reality of hate speech in India is not abuse of the law, but the persistent refusal by the authorities to enforcing the laws. If hate speech is protected in the name of freedom of speech and expression, then the consequences would primarily consist of violation of the principles on which the foundation of democracy stands.[57]

---

57 Diya Vaishnav and Nihal Deo, 'The Peril of Hate Speech in India', The Criminal Law Blog, 3 February 2020, https://criminallawstudiesnluj. wordpress.com/2020/02/03/the-peril-of-hate-speech-in-india/, accessed on 19 October 2020.

Fertility Behaviour of Communities – a comparison

The fertility behaviour of different communities is interesting to study in detail and this book has attempted it. It is noteworthy that the fertility gap between Hindus and Muslims in India has narrowed considerably over the years, and the greatest birth-rate disparities now remain between states and not among religions. It is interesting also to note that Hindu women in the state of Bihar have two children more each compared with Muslim women in the more developed state of Andhra Pradesh.

The perception that Muslims produce more children because of their religion is stronger and much common in regions where Muslims are culturally distinct minorities in sizeable numbers. Islam, in fact, is not particularly a pro-natalist religion. Eight of the nine classic schools of Islamic law permit contraception, and many Muslim states like Iran have supported family planning, as explained in detail in Chapters 5 and 6. However, all of this is conveniently disregarded by divisive groups.[58]

On one hand, the debate is all about how Muslims are the reason behind the population growth in India, but on the other hand, little to nothing is done to alleviate their deplorable conditions which are responsible for their higher fertility rate as explained in detail in Chapter 4. On top of all this, attempts are made to boycott them and deny them the very source of their livelihood. Also, solving the problem of Muslim overpopulation by encouraging Hindus to have more children does not in any way solve the problem of population explosion that India faces as a country. Neither do the hate speeches

---

58 Krithika Varagur, 'The Muslim Overpopulation Myth That Just Won't Die', *The Atlantic*, 14 November 2017, https://www.theatlantic. com/international/archive/2017/11/muslim-overpopulation-myth/545318/, accessed on 6 October 2020.

and mudslinging help the cause. It is highly unlikely that any facts about Muslim demographics will change minds anywhere, especially if misleading information is given to the masses by religious and political leaders.

In this context, there are two possibilities. One, that these hate-mongers are ignorant; two, that their sole intention is to create mischief, by deliberately distorting facts to create a wedge of hate between the two major communities in India. Considering that the right-wing propagandists are well educated and well informed, do deep study and thorough research, we can rule out the first possibility. That leaves us with the second. The propagandists have a mischievous intent – to create hatred for Muslims and bring about social polarization. How effective it is proving in electoral politics is for everyone to see. It has proved to be a foolproof strategy for the BJP to win elections.

Interestingly, the population problem by itself is not a Hindu-versus-Muslim issue, as commonly projected, and as the analysis below demonstrates. It will be noticed that Hindus and Muslims are in fact at same end of the spectrum. If the fertility rate of the Muslims is the highest, at 2.61, the Hindus have second highest rate, at 2.13, and for the same reasons of socioeconomic backwardness, as we will see below.

Literature suggests that the Muslim-Hindu differences in the context of fertility may not be 'real'.[59] Muslim-Hindu fertility differentials will disappear once differences in socioeconomic factors

---

59	S. Philip Morgan, S. Stash, H.L. Smith and K.O. Mason, 'Muslim and non-Muslim Differences in Female Autonomy and Fertility: Evidence from Four Asian Countries', *Population and Development Review* 28 (2002): 515–38, https://doi.org/10.1111/j.1728-4457.2002.00515.x; and A. Dharmalingam and S. Philip Morgan, 'Pervasive Muslim-Hindu Fertility Differences in India', *Demography* 41, no. 3 (2004): 529–45.

are taken into account.[60] In the context of these factors, Hindus and Muslims are almost at the same end of the spectrum.

LITERACY AND FERTILITY

While the ratio of literacy among Muslim men is the lowest in India, at 80.3 per cent, Hindus follow right after, at 86.4 per cent; the rate is 89.4 per cent among Christians, 88.3 per cent among Sikhs, 94.2 per cent among Buddhists/Neo-Buddhists, and 97.1 per cent among Jains. Muslims and Hindus, therefore, fare almost the same when it comes to literacy.

The literacy ratios are not very different when it comes to women either. While the literacy percentage for Muslim women is 64.2, Hindu women fall right behind, with a literacy percentage of 68.3. Both Hindus and Muslims are right at the bottom when it comes to education of women.

If we take a look at the net attendance ratio (NAR) by religion for middle, secondary and higher secondary schooling, we find it is the lowest for Muslims, at 56.2, and next lowest for Hindus, at 69.8 (refer to Chapter 4).

POVERTY

We have seen earlier that level of poverty is a determining factor in family planning. Once again, the Muslim community has the highest incidence of poverty, but Hindus are not far behind, coming second in rural poverty, and third in urban poverty (refer to Chapter 4).

---

60 Dharmalingam, Navaneetham and Morgan, 'Muslim-Hindu Fertility Differences'.

AVAILABILITY OF INFRASTRUCTURE AND SERVICES:

Access to healthcare providers is critical for the practice of family planning. We see that the percentage of women in the age group of 15–49 who have had a live birth (preceding the NFHS survey in 2015–16) and have received antenatal care (ANC) from a skilled provider is lowest among Muslims, at 77 per cent, and next lowest among Hindus, 79.3 per cent. Comparing the status of these two communities with other religious communities like the Christians, Sikhs, Buddhists/Neo-Buddhists and Jains, it is clear that Hindu and Muslim women both fare poorly in this respect.

The percentage of child deliveries in a healthcare facility is lowest among Muslim women, at 69.2 per cent, followed by Christian women, at 78.5 per cent, then Hindu women, at 80.8 per cent.

The percentage of women in the age group of 15–49 who have received family planning advice is lowest among Muslims, at 65.2 per cent, and next among Hindus, at 69.7 per cent. Both communities are at the bottom in this respect, in comparison to other religious communities, like the Christians, Sikhs, Buddhists/Neo-Buddhists and Jains (refer to Chapter 4).

AGE AT MARRIAGE

Early marriage means early pregnancy. If we take a look at women aged 15–19 who are pregnant with their first child, we can see that Muslims have the highest percentage, at 3.1, followed by Hindus, at 2.7. The percentage ratios for other communities are significantly lower. Similarly, the percentage of women aged 15–19 who have already begun childbearing is highest for Muslims, at 9, and second highest for Hindus, at 7.8. Here too, both communities have a higher percentage of women in this category and in this age group than other communities do. (Refer to Chapter 4.)

EXPOSURE TO MASS MEDIA

The practice of family planning depends a lot on awareness about it among the community. Here, the mass media are a crucial factor. Here too, analysis of the date shows that Hindus and Muslims are not very different. The percentage of women who have heard or seen a family planning message on radio, television, in a newspaper or magazine, or on a wall painting or hoarding in the past few months varies across religious communities, but Muslims and Hindus stand shoulder to shoulder. While exposure to family planning messages via radio is lowest among Sikhs, at 5.5 per cent, which is possibly because they have high television exposure, among Muslims and Hindus the exposure is 15.9 per cent and 18.5 per cent, respectively.

Muslim women have the lowest exposure among all communities to family planning messages via television, at 50.8 per cent, followed by Christian women (58.1 per cent) and Hindu women (at 59.5 per cent). Exposure to family planning messages through newspapers/ magazines and wall paintings/hoardings is lowest for Muslim women, at 30.5 per cent and 46.9 per cent, respectively. Hindu women have the second lowest exposure to family planning messages via newspapers/magazines and wall paintings/hoardings, at 37.1 per cent and 54 per cent, respectively. No exposure to family planning messages via any of the above-mentioned media is highest among Muslim women, at 34.4 per cent, and then among Hindu women, at 27.7 per cent.

The pattern is not very different among men. The percentage of men in the age group of 15–49 who have heard or seen a family planning message via radio among Muslims and Hindus is 20.4 and 22.5, respectively. Exposure to family planning messages via television is lowest among Muslim men, at 53.7 per cent, and Hindu men, at 62 per cent, with Christians in between, at 57.2 per cent. This trend is similar in other categories of mass media too. In exposure to family planning messages via television, newspapers/magazines, wall-paintings/hoardings, Muslim men are at the bottom, followed by Christian men and then Hindu men. No exposure to mass media messages on family planning is highest among Muslim men, at 28.5 per cent, followed by Christian men, at 26.7 per cent, and then by Hindu men, at 23 per cent (refer to Chapter 4).

Unmet need for limiting child births as well as in total (including spacing), is highest among Muslims, at 7.1, followed by Christians, at 6.9, and Hindus, at 5.4. In the need for limiting the number of children, the two communities stand close, with Muslims at 9.4 and Hindus coming right next, at 7 (refer to Chapter 4).

Political Participation in Family Planning

Growth in population has an undeniable impact on health, food security, education, labour force and employment, and the economy. Poor family planning can lead to hunger, illiteracy, and living conditions that are far from optimal. Failing to recognize this link will result in India missing out the opportunity of reaping the demographic dividend.

The political class, however, has shown very little interest in the population and development issue, particularly after the backlash of forced family planning during the emergency (1975–77). There is hardly any debate or questions asked about this issue in the legislatures. It is time to shed our indifference and reticence and make it an important development agenda.

Political Distancing from Family Planning

The political discourse on population vis-à-vis development and reproductive rights has gone down abysmally. A committee called the Technical Committee on Population and Development of National Institute of Health and Family Welfare chaired by the author (2014) studied this issue in detail and developed a Resource Book for

Elected Representatives in India to facilitate their understanding of the importance of the subject and its linkages with other everyday concerns of development, like poverty, literacy, employment etc.[61]

An analysis of the questions raised in four Lok Sabha terms (LS 13–16) showed that of all the questions raised, those on health and family welfare were about 5 per cent, of which questions on population and family planning constituted only 3 per cent – amounting to just 0.15 per cent of all Parliament questions. The situation in state Vidhan Sabhas is least likely to be any different.

While a number of questions highlighted the issue of increasing population growth and its impact on limited natural resources, there seemed to be little awareness of its association with sociocultural factors such as literacy, early age of marriage, availability of information on family planning methods, infant mortality, etc.

The legislators need to realize that investing in family planning will help improve health and development in not only the constituency, but also the state and even the country as a whole. It is critical to work towards ensuring that there is a school at an accessible distance, for everyone, that girls complete their schooling, attain higher education, and undertake income generation activities. Such factors should, in turn, enable them to delay marriage and first birth, and empower them to make smart reproductive choices, take control of their fertility, bear healthy children and stay healthy

---

61 *Family Planning: An Investment in Health and Development; A Resource Booklet for Elected Representatives of India* was developed by the Technical Committee for Population and Development, constituted by the National Institute of Health and Family Welfare, under the chairmanship of Dr S.Y. Quraishi, former Election Commissioner of India, facilitated by the Policy Unit and the Citizens' Alliance for Reproductive Health and Rights, in partnership with the United States Agency for International Development supported Health Policy Project, 2013–14, in New Delhi, India, and implemented by Futures Group.

themselves. Smaller and economically empowered families do help control national population growth and accelerate economic growth.

Elected representatives can contribute in myriad ways as members of Parliament or Vidhan Sabha or Panchayat at the constituency level, in the media, and on other public platforms. A few suggestions on these lines are to be found in Chapter 9.

CONCLUSION

From the above analysis it is clear that family planning is not a Hindu-versus-Muslim issue as the two communities have similar statistics. In socioeconomic indicators which influence family planning behaviour, they stand shoulder to shoulder. It will not be incorrect to say that they are on the same end of the spectrum and not at opposite ends, as the widespread narrative goes. Their socioeconomic conditions are almost similar and region specific, and that is what determines their fertility behaviours.

Prejudice against other communities, which arises out of false notions based on myths and misconceptions, leads to stereotyping of whole groups. It leads to strong contempt and hatred, and a wish to oust the 'other'.[62] As we have seen, Hindu-Muslim polarization originally started with the concocted narrative that Muslims are deliberately producing more children to capture political power. Since this right-wing fixation has gone practically unchallenged for decades, it has penetrated deep into the psyche of the Hindu masses, old and young. Their minds have to be cleansed of these false notions without further delay, to create better understanding and goodwill between the two communities.

It is worth understanding that the gap between Hindus and Muslims has actually increased manifold in favour of the Hindus.

---

62 Vaishnav and Deo, 'The Peril of Hate Speech in India'

While there were 30 crore more Hindus than Muslims in 1951 the gap had increased to over 80 crores by 2011.

Understanding the need for overall development of the country for the well-being of its citizens, irrespective of their religion, is of utmost importance. And it is the responsibility of the government to protect the rights and respect the religious freedom of every individual, as each of them belongs to India. *Sab ka saath, sab ka vikas* is a beautiful concept, if followed sincerely. Equal socioeconomic development of all classes is the key to transforming India economically and build a secular country, which is the basic tenet of India's sovereignty and integrity as the world's biggest democracy.

9
The Way Ahead

POPULATION explosion has been a matter of concern for India ever since the country became independent. As early as in 1952, India launched a national family planning programme, the first country in the world to do so. Throughout the subsequent seven decades, family planning continued to be a subject of great importance in the five-year plans, though it ceased to be projected as a national disaster as had been in the beginning.

Initial fears that the food shortages of the 1950s – when the total population of India was well under 400 million – would aggravate so much that the country would face starvation deaths, becoming increasingly dependent on American charity, also proved wrong. Food deficits turned into food surpluses, despite the population increasing nearly four times.

Moreover, somewhere along the way, instead of 'population explosion', 'demographic dividend' became the popular narrative. Demographic dividend comes from increase in the working population's productivity, which boosts per-capita income. Soon enough, the burgeoning population increasingly got to be viewed as 'human resource'.

The more the human resources were trained and galvanized, more of them found demand for their skills abroad. Indians who went abroad to work transformed the country's economy enormously with their remittances in foreign exchange. Those who went abroad and stayed back contributed to the development of their host countries and became India's soft power.

Our population has now become our soft power, although the proportion of formally skilled workers in India itself is extremely low, at 4.69 per cent of total workforce, compared with 24 per cent in China, 52 per cent in the US, 68 per cent in the UK, 75 per cent in Germany, 80 per cent in Japan and 96 per cent in South Korea. Imagine, if with just 5 per cent of skilled workforce we transformed so dramatically, what would be our strength if we could improve the quality and skills of the remaining 95 per cent of the youth force, or even a fraction of it! We can also learn a lesson from China which, by transforming its teeming millions of youth into a productive force, has captured the global economy.

Changing wrong narratives

One more narrative that deserves to be changed in the country is that Muslims are responsible for the population explosion in India, but this narrative still persists. Right-wing Hindu propaganda has continued to feed this myth, creating alarm among the Hindus that they will soon be outnumbered by the Muslims, who will capture political power (see Chapter 8).

This book is about understanding this misinformation propagated and deliberately perpetuated to create a rift between Hindus and Muslims and polarize them for political gains.

Upon the author's request, a Mathematical Model was prepared by two distinguished mathematicians, Professor Dinesh Singh, former vice chancellor, Delhi University, and Professor Ajay Kumar, of K.R. Mangalam University. This model conclusively proves that the Muslim population will never exceed the Hindu population. The population difference is never going to be zero no matter how much time we take into account. In fact, this difference is on a constant rise (Figure 9.1; also see Appendix 1 for details).

Figure 9.1: Population growth comparison: Polynomial growth model

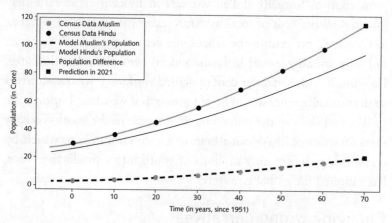

This book leads us to the following conclusions:

- The assertion that the all-India birth rate among Muslims has been the highest among all communities in the country is correct.
- It is also true that the demographic ratio has been affected. Muslims have gone up from 9.8 per cent of the population in 1951 to 14.2 per cent in 2011, in sixty years. Hindus, on the other hand, have come down from 84 per cent of the population to 79.8 per cent. However, the situation is far from the exaggerated and provocative narrative that Muslims will overtake Hindus very soon and capture political power in India. If it took sixty years

for the Muslims to increase their percentage in the population by 4 percentage points, it should logically take 600 years to increase it by 40 percentage points! That, too, provided the growth rate remains what it has been all these years. The mathematical model (Appendix 1) has amply demonstrated that, forget any time soon, the Muslims can *never* overtake the Hindus in India.

- An established fact is that Muslims in India have been adopting family planning, and pretty fast. For several decades, their rate of adoption of modern family planning methods has been faster than that of Hindus. The National Family Health Surveys have shown that over the past twenty-four years, new-generation Muslim families have done a better job at family planning than their Hindu counterparts, though their statistical figures still trail that of Hindu families.[1] It is important to note, however, that Muslim fertility is falling in line with Hindu fertility, and the difference is narrowing. According to NFHS-1, the TFR of Muslims was 4.4, which reduced to 3.6 in NFHS-2, and further to 3.4 in NFHS-3. NFHS-4 data show a significant reduction in the fertility differentials between Hindus and Muslims, with the TFR of Muslims at 2.61 and that of Hindus at 2.13. The TFR gap came down from 1.1 points to 0.8 points, remained at 0.8 points in the next survey and again declined to the present 0.5 points over the course of four surveys.

- Although the unanimous opinion is that Islam is against permanent methods of birth control, namely sterilization, whether of males or females, a large proportion (20.8 per cent)

1 Nikhil Rampal, 'New-gen Muslim Women are Better at Family Planning', *India Today*, 23 August 2019, https://www.indiatoday.in/diu/story/muslim-women-family-planning-india-1590955-2019-08-23, accessed on 6 October 2020.

of Muslims[2] has undergone sterilization, which shows their eagerness to adopt family planning.

- No organized attempt, much less a political conspiracy, has been noticed among Muslims to produce more children to overtake the Hindus.

- On the contrary, the right-wing organizations have been trying to feed the Hindus the fear that Muslims will overtake them in numbers and capture political power in India within years. They have been trying to provoke them to produce more children by starting a procreation war. There is no prima facie evidence, however, that the right wing has succeeded in this mission. There seems to have been no study of the impact of this appeal on birth rates among the Hindus, though its impact on hate and polarization in the society is writ large everywhere. This has a marked influence on electoral results, presumably the real objective of the propaganda.

- *We also find that Hindus are a close second to Muslims in almost all indicators of family planning, and that the two communities are on the same end of the spectrum, not opposite. So, making population growth in India a Hindu-versus-Muslim issue is uncalled for.*

- We have also seen in great detail that Islam is not against family planning at all. On the contrary, it is the pioneer of the concept, a fact that has got blurred over the years because of lack of awareness about it and skewed interpretations of the Quran and Hadith.

- It is not surprising that most of the Muslim countries in the world have adopted family planning as a state policy and have achieved commendable results, mostly with the support of religious leaders.

---

2   National Family Health Survey-4, 2015–16, India; Mumbai, IIPS.

Factors affecting Family Planning among Muslims

Socioeconomic backwardness:

The real factors holding Indian Muslims back from family planning are their socioeconomic backwardness and failure of the administration to address their issues.

As seen in Chapter 4, the Muslims are lagging behind other communities in education, income and access to health services. Their socioeconomic backwardness is the main reason for the higher birth rate among them. However, there is hardly any evidence of attempts to address these problems on the part of the authorities. It would be interesting if the right-wing leaders who have been provoking a procreation war would do something about the educational backwardness and acute poverty of the Muslims. Instead, what we have heard about increasingly in the recent years is their repeated efforts to weaken the Muslims economically by advocating their social and economic boycott. Despite this being a criminal offence under the laws of the land, hate groups on social media have gone berserk posting such messages, unhindered. And the government's apathy – if not tacit or explicit support to these offenders – is helping them in their vitriolic campaign.

There has been some improvement in the socioeconomic situation of Indian Muslims. However, according to Sachar Committee Report (2005–2006), this change is marginal, and much lower than the improvements in the socioeconomic situation of the scheduled caste/scheduled tribe (SC/ST) communities. Only a few development indicators for Muslims have shown some nominal growth. The report shows that more Muslims than SC/STs are poor in the urban areas and more Muslims than OBCs are poor in the rural areas. Also, Muslims find it difficult to live away from their homes if they want to pursue their education away from their home city, town or village.[3] The rate of decrease in poverty among Muslims vis-a-vis the other minority/backward communities clearly highlights the fact that poverty alleviation programmes and developmental efforts have either failed to reach Muslims or have conveniently sidelined them from social and welfare schemes.

According to a study on family planning practices in rural India, many men in rural India, irrespective of their religion, do not have adequate information about the different methods of family planning and are also, in many cases, unaware of its benefits. Without proper guidance, the men, as heads and sole decision makers of the family, generally opt for female sterilization, as this is thought to be the only available option.[4]

Education

Many religious leaders, especially the local Imams, whom most common Muslims look up to, believe that family planning is against the religion of Islam. However, as discussed in the chapters before, this is based on ignorance. Their influence on the Muslim community's willingness to adopt contraception is, however, limited, but can be easily addressed by taking the route that emphasizes the rights of women and children in Islam. This has been elaborated in the communication strategy later in this chapter.

Education or *ilm* is considered the foremost Islamic duty for both men and women. It is especially important for girls to be educated,

3   Prime Minister's High Level Committee Chairperson Rajindar Sachar, 'Social, Economic and Educational Status of the Muslim Community of India', Chapter 8, 'Poverty, Consumption and Standards of Living', p. 157. November 2006.

4   Arundhati Char, Minna Saavala and Teija Kulmala, 'Male Perceptions on Female Sterilization: A Community-Based Study in Rural Central India', *International Perspectives on Sexual and Reproductive Health* 35, no. 3 (September 2009): 131–38.

as studies have shown that empowering women decisively changes attitudes towards family planning. As women become literate and educated, larger numbers will find work, not only delaying their marriage but also shortening their fertile years.

Access to family planning services

There is enough evidence showing that access and availability of health services in a sustained way at the community level results in greater acceptance of any welfare programme. Considering that child survival and infant mortality rates have a direct bearing on acceptance of family planning, it should be ensured that immunization and other child survival programmes must be scaled up in a big way in areas where there is a large concentration of Muslims. These schemes will find easy acceptance. It has also been reported that wherever mother and child health delivery has been efficient, acceptance of family planning is higher. This is because the doctor-patient relationship is one of trust and confidence, and the motivational role of doctors and paramedics among the people is much greater than anybody else's.

It is common knowledge that doctors, unfortunately, are reluctant to be posted in the villages and in the backward areas of cities and towns. Since areas of high Muslim concentration are generally backward, it has been found that a large number of posts at primary health centres and health sub-centres have been vacant for years.

Quite a bit of the poor performance of family planning programmes may be attributable to the lack of staff at these centres rather than the reluctance of the community to adopt the programmes. The fact that the unmet need of the Muslim community for family planning services is the highest (16.5 per cent)[5] proves the point conclusively.

---

5   Total unmet need for family planning is highest among Muslims at 16.5 per cent. (Refer to Chapter 4.)

It is sheer common sense that without adequate staff in position, no public welfare programme, much less family planning, can succeed.

Undoubtedly, training of the field outreach staff is crucial. It is quite evident that the staff, inadequate as they may be, have not been trained and oriented to deal with communities reluctant to take on family planning. Unless they are trained to identify the peculiar problem of Muslim reluctance in this matter, the reasons thereof, and the possible strategies that will convert their resistance into acceptance, they cannot deal with the problem effectively. Suitable training and publication of literature explaining the true Islamic position on family planning need to be provided to the community so that they are able to effectively overcome their resistance to it.

Recommendations

1. Muslims must adopt family planning proactively:

Since it has been established beyond doubt that a small family is a happy family and that Islam expects young people to marry only when they have the wherewithal to look after a family and provide for their health, educational needs and financial comfort (see Chapter 5), Muslims must adopt family planning practices proactively. They should not pay heed to the right-wing call to produce a large number of children and start a procreation war between the two communities. They should wholeheartedly focus on educating their boys and girls, nurture their skills, and marry them off only when they are physically mature and financially capable of raising a family. They must remember that primacy of quality over numbers is a good Islamic principle.

2. For effectively tackling the high birth rate among Muslims, the foremost need is to understand the problem in its entirety and in depth. For that we require to do a needs assessment, as very little effort has been made in that direction. Research should be conducted

to analyse the reasons for the slack in development among Muslims, including their fears and apprehensions, real or unfounded. It is important to identify the sources of information and the opinion leaders that influence the Muslim mind and attitude. (Appendix 2 lists some of the research issues identified by the author for pursuit by interested scholars.)

3. Create Legislators' Interest in Family Planning

As seen in Chapter 8, legislators' interest in the subject needs to be cultivated. They must keep abreast with the status of family planning in the constituency, state, and the country. They need to take the following steps:

- Seek updated information about new family planning methods and products from non-government and civil society organizations.
- Advocate for the gravity of family planning in Parliament, state assemblies, raise relevant queries surrounding the same and also make it an important part of the party manifesto.
- Ask relevant questions in Parliament and Vidhan Sabhas.
- Speak about the benefits of a small family in public fora.
- Highlight the links between family planning and development concerns like education, poverty, employment, access to health services, etc.
- Ensure proper utilization of family planning funds, at least through the District Vigilance, Grievances and Monitoring Committee - or any other relevant committee.
- Prepare panchayats to become community monitors so as to ensure the availability of family planning products and support couples to delay first child, space and limit family size.

4. An analysis of the communication efforts made so far towards behavioural change among the community must be undertaken.

Family planning is one programme of its kind, and it can only succeed with the support of large-scale communication. Our performance on that score has been less than desirable.

As we have repeatedly seen, it is a widespread myth, both among the Muslims and the Hindus, that Islam prohibits contraception. But hardly any effort seems to have been made so far to counter this myth. It would be worthwhile to study the efforts that may have been made in this direction by the government, the NGOs, the scholars and others, and the outcomes of these efforts. Based on the outcomes of the previous efforts, a carefully planned strategy has to be evolved to dispel the misconceptions effectively.

It would be necessary to review the communication material that has been produced specifically for the Muslim target audience and subject it to critical analysis for its adequacy, dissemination pattern and effectiveness. Regrettably, not much information is available on this aspect of communication exercises. It seems that the efforts so far have been limited to a few short feature films set in Muslim locales and scenarios, and a few posters and advertisements in Urdu.

In a communication sent by the author to the Ministry of Health and Family Welfare asking what special efforts have been made to dispel misinformation among the Muslims on the subject of family planning, the ministry said the following: 'Regarding special efforts made to communicate to the Muslim population, it is stated that this Department generally brings out material for the information of common people and not specifically aimed at a particular target group.'[6] This response is prima facie secular and 'politically correct', but this omnibus approach is unscientific as it runs contrary to the importance of segmentation of the target audience – as anybody familiar with the science of social marketing would know – and

---

6   Ministry of Health and Family Welfare, 1995 (correspondence between the author and the Ministry).

contrary to the need of specifically designing communication strategies for each segment to achieve the desired behaviour change.[7]

If the Muslims have fears about their identity and survival – a recent phenomenon – they have to be allayed. Similarly, we have to remove the apprehension among those Hindus who actively oppose family planning on account of their fear that Muslims will soon outnumber them. They need to be assured that there is no organized resistance on the part of the Muslim community to family planning.

5. Desirable Communication Strategy

The subject of persuading Muslims to adopt family planning being undoubtedly sensitive, the communication strategy has to be creatively devised and disseminated. Instead of directly preaching birth control, it is advisable to build the campaign around concepts that Islam fully supports, such as the importance of child spacing, breastfeeding, the need for proper upbringing of children, their health and educational needs, concerns for health of the mothers, etc., It will be advisable to create the campaign around these aspects rather than push the terminal methods which, by all accounts, Islamic jurists reject. In any case, such an approach would also be totally in line with the current family planning policy of the country, which too lays greater emphasis on temporary, spacing methods rather than sterilization.

It would be a good strategy to appeal to Muslim pride in Islam's eternal and universal nature, its pioneering role in laying down the multiple rights of women and children, and its quintessential modernism, which creates scope for reforms as per the needs of the time. If we take this position – and there is full evidence that Islam was actually a pioneer of the family planning concept even when there was no population pressure – this may work well with

---

7   Richard K. Manoff, *Social Marketing – New Imperative for Public Health* (New York: Praeger, 1985).

the Muslim audience, giving them the feeling of 'ownership' of the programme.

An integrated communication strategy addressing the rights of women, the rights of children, literacy, education, income generation and the importance of delayed marriage, etc., is imperative. The disparity between Islam's concern for the health and well-being of women and children and the actual conditions, as reflected in the high infant mortality rate, maternal mortality rate, morbidity and stillbirths, needs to be brought out.

Since this is a highly sensitive subject, the communication strategy has to be evolved with extreme care and caution. The approach has to be rational rather than emotional, informative rather than didactic, and, most importantly, persuasive rather than antagonistic. This is necessary to prevent the possibility of a backlash of the clergy.

Operational Possibilities

The following actions are suggested for reaching out to the Muslims to dispel their misconceptions about family planning:

1. Since most Muslims know Urdu better than any other language, it is necessary to communicate with them in the language they understand. Therefore, information on the subject should be regularly communicated to them in the Urdu newspapers, magazines and journals. Credible writers need to be commissioned for this. The writers themselves need to be sensitized, which could be done by providing them with authentic literature, and by holding seminars and workshops for them.

2. Meetings with Muslim community representatives, particularly opinion leaders, need to be organized at various levels, with the help of field staff specially trained for the purpose.

3. There are quite a few liberal ulama (religious scholars) who understand the true Islamic position on family planning and are open to public discourse on it. These ulama should be identified to actively communicate to the people the real Islamic position favouring family planning.

4. Given the current widespread belief that Islam is against family planning, free discussion/debate on the subject should be encouraged. This conversion of a universal *belief* into a *debate* would be a step forward in helping people to know the true Islamic position regarding education, health and family planning.

5. To generate such a debate, a series of seminars at national, regional and local levels may be organized, where scholarly papers would be presented citing the verses from the Quran and the Hadith showing that Islam is supportive of family planning. The ripple effect of these seminars is bound to prove useful. The first Fiqhi Seminar organized in Patna in 1989, oft cited in Chapter 5, is a great model.

6. There has been a number of success stories where Muslim NGOs and others have done commendable work in family planning. Success stories from Kerala, Tamil Nadu and Maharashtra and others should be identified and publicized. Some of these success stories could be documented for use in training programmes, at seminars and workshops, and also communicated through print and electronic media.

7. A proper orientation of health workers posted in the Muslim areas needs to be conducted and effective techniques of communication imparted to them.

8. Since Muslim health workers may have better rapport with the community, they should be identified, trained and deployed in such

areas. If necessary, for some specific pockets, a special recruitment drive to hire motivated Muslim workers may be considered.

9. Muslim opinion leaders like the ulama, journalists and scholars need to be exposed to the successful family planning efforts in major Muslim countries like Indonesia, Egypt, Iran and Bangladesh to dispel the notion among Indian Muslims that Islam is opposed to family planning. It is expected that this kind of exposure to writings and discourses would convert a large number of opinion leaders to the realistic and right Islamic position on family planning.

10. It is also advisable to invite the ulama and senior journalists and scholars from Muslim countries to India for international conferences or individual lecture tours. This would enable cross-border learnings and help Indian Muslims understand better that if the Muslims in Indonesia, Iran and Egypt, etc., could enthusiastically adopt family planning within the Islamic parameters, then why not Indian Muslims.

11. Wakf boards can play a nodal role in this effort. The Punjab Wakf Board had indeed played a pioneering role by organizing the National Seminar on the Rights of Women and Children in Islam in 1994, where the Islamic approach to family planning was examined. The positive response from almost all of the participants, most of whom were Imams from the states of Punjab and Haryana, was heartwarming. Encouraged by this, the author, as the administrator of the Punjab Wakf Board at the time, requested them to adopt the Pulse Polio campaign in Gurgaon district. They willingly obliged, enthusiastically mobilizing nearly 1,000 Imams and organizing them into 300 teams. Their effort was such a thundering success that the district topped the country in the Pulse Polio campaign and earned them laurels, winning praise in a widely read editorial in the *Indian Express*.

12.   It would be a good idea to rope the Muslim youth into these efforts by involving them in the design of posters, creation of slogans, songs, jingles, etc. Essay and debate competitions in Urdu and various regional languages could be held. This will create a chain of peer educators who can take the messages to a wider group in their community.

13. Since authentic information is generally not available and, in its absence, negative propaganda flourishes, it is necessary to develop for the Muslim audience at least one good resource book explaining the Islamic tenets, as explained in Chapter 5. This could be translated into regional languages and supplemented with fact sheets based on local needs.

A SWOT analysis (Appendix 3) shows that if serious and sincere efforts are made, it will be possible to devise and implement a feasible communication and administrative strategy capable of producing positive results in family planning among Muslims within a reasonable period of time.

Family planning in India is actually a success story that cannot be lightly dismissed. Except for two years of forced sterilizations during the dark period of the Emergency in 1975–77, it has been a voluntary programme bolstered by small incentives. As a backlash to the Emergency, the programme had completely gone off the political radar, and political leaders treated the subject as taboo. There have hardly been any questions asked in parliament or the state legislative assemblies on this subject. The ministry of health and family welfare has, however, gone about its business in a low-key manner without arousing any hostility. The strategy has paid off, and we are not very far from reaching the replacement rate. As many as twenty-four states in India have already reached replacement levels of TFR. Some states have, in fact, gone below the line.

Population stabilization is now well within sight. If our collective march towards the cherished goal continues uninterrupted, the country can hope to reap the benefits of demographic dividend and replace China as the global economic super power very soon.

Appendix 1[1]

Will Muslim Population Overtake Hindus?

A Mathematical Model

The census data, from 1951 to 2011, of the Hindu and Muslim communities in India is given in the following table.

Population (in crores)	1951	1961	1971	1981	1991	2001	2011
Muslim	3.5856	4.6941	6.1418	8.0286	10.6715	13.8188	17.2245
Hindu	30.3675	36.6528	45.3292	56.2389	69.006	82.7579	98.0378

There are two mathematical models – the polynomial growth model and exponential growth model – that are fitted into the population data.

---

1 Mathematical Model courtesy Professor Dinesh Singh, former Vice Chancellor, Delhi University and Professor Ajay Kumar, KR Mangalam University, Gurugram.

We first fit a second-degree polynomial in this data. The polynomial function that describes the growth of the Muslim population is

$$f(x)=0.002559x^2+0.07394x+3.621,$$

Population Growth Comparison: Polynomial Growth Model

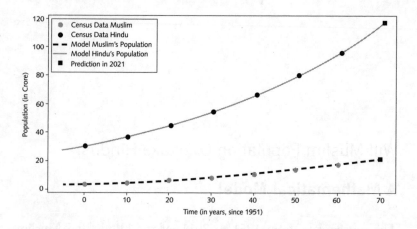

where x denotes the time in years and $f(x)$ denotes the population in crores.
Similarly, the function

$$g(x)=0.008817x^2+0.6099x+30.01,$$

represents the Hindu population. In Figure 1, $f(x)$ and $g(x)$ are plotted in solid line and dotted line curves respectively.
According to this model,

Muslims in 2021 = 21.3367crore

and

| Population in Crores | | | | | | |
Year	Muslim	Absolute Increase in Muslims	% increase in Muslims	Hindu	Absolute Increase in Hindus	% increase in Hindus	Difference in increase (in %)
1951	3.5856			30.3675			
1961	4.6941	1.1085	30.91	36.6528	6.2853	20.69	10.22
1971	6.1418	1.4477	30.84	45.3292	8.6764	23.67	7.17
1981	8.0286	1.8868	30.72	56.2389	10.9097	24.06	6.66
1991	10.6715	2.6429	32.91	69.006	12.7671	22.7	10.21
2001	13.8188	3.1473	29.49	82.7579	13.7519	19.92	9.57
2011	17.2245	3.4057	24.64	98.0378	15.2799	18.46	6.18
2021	21.3367	4.1122	23.87	115.9076	17.8698	18.22	5.65

Hindus in 2021 = 115.9076 crore. The per cent increase in Muslims is 23.87 per cent and in Hindus is 18.22 per cent, so the difference is 5.65 per cent.

Now the question is when will the population of Muslims be higher than the population of Hindus? Mathematically we can say that for what value of x,

$$f(x) \geq g(x),$$

or in terms of graphs, when will the dotted curve cross the orange one?

Let us elaborate it a little more. The variable x denotes the time in years and $f(x)$ and $g(x)$ represents the population of Muslims and Hindus respectively. We are curious to know whether Muslims and Hindus will be equal or surpass Hindus after a certain number of years, that is, for what value of time x population of Muslims $f(x)$ will be greater than or equal to the population of Hindus $g(x)$.

The time when the number of Muslims will be equal to that of Hindus, the two curves will intersect each other, that is,

$$f(x) = g(x)$$

or

$$f(x) - g(x) = 0$$

There is no such real x which satisfies the above equation. *In fact, the dotted line curve will never cross the solid line one. This means, the Muslim population will never exceed the Hindu population.*

Let us try to understand this in another way. Consider $h(x) = f(x) - g(x)$. Then the function $h(x)$ represents the population difference. The purple curve represents the function $h(x)$. As we see from the graph in Figure 1, the purple curve will never touch the X-axis, that the population difference is never going to be zero no matter how much time we take into account. In fact, this difference is rising constantly.

Another model we fit into the population is the exponential growth model. The function that describes the growth of Muslim population is

$$f(x) = 3.71931389e^{0.02580116x},$$

Figure 2, Exponential Growth Model

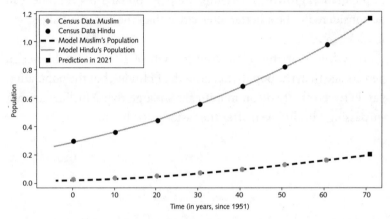

where x denotes the time in years and $f(x)$ denotes the population in crores. Similarly, the function

$$g(x) = 31.0405068e^{0.0193993028x},$$

represents the Hindu population. In Figure 2, $f(x)$ and $g(x)$ are plotted in dotted (Muslim) and solid (Hindu) curves.

The same mathematical logic is also valid in this situation too, and hence we make the same inference from this model as well.

According to this model,

Muslims in 2021 = 22.6377 crore

and

Hindus in 2021 = 120.6922 crore.

The percentage increase in Muslims is 31.43 and 23.11, and the difference is 8.32.

The percentage increase seems to be much larger in both populations as per the exponential model than in the polynomial growth model. Such an increase in population does not seem possible because the family planning program has caused a decline in population growth. Therefore, the polynomial growth model can be considered to be a better alternative than the exponential growth model here.

It is true that the population growth of Muslims is higher in percentage than the population growth of Hindus, but the population gap between the two communities is so large that Muslims are not surpassing Hindus even after the faster growth rate.

Appendix 2

Islam, Muslims and Family Planning in India: Identified Research Tasks/Topics

The current situation

- Is there any organized effort among Muslims against family planning? Where? By whom? What is their motive?
- What has been the impact on the Hindu birth rate after the right-wing appeal to Hindus to produce more children?

Factors influencing family planning among Muslims

- Literacy
- Income
- Age of marriage
- Male bias
- Concern for security in old age
- Polygamy

Impact of availability/delivery of health services

• What is the impact of these services on acceptance of family planning?
• What is the level of availability of these services in Muslim areas?

Knowledge, Attitude and Practice (KAP)

Level of KAP (including fears and apprehensions) among Muslims compared with others in different regions.

• Factors affecting the acceptance/non-acceptance of family planning.
• Ratio of Muslims who believe Islam is against family planning. The basis of their belief. Their sources of information and influences.
• Why have so many Muslims (45%) adopted family planning in spite of the universal belief that their religion is against it?
• If Muslims are opposed to family planning, do they have different attitudes towards the following:
    • Terminal methods
    • Temporary methods
    • Natural methods
    • Spacing methods/breastfeeding

Role of the ulama/(scholars)

• What is the attitude of the ulama/Imams/madrasas in family planning? What is their role in it?
• Are there liberal scholars who could be mobilized?
• Are there case studies or success stories of family planning among Muslims? Where? What were the problems faced?

Outreach/Field Health Workers

- What training has been given to the staff to carry out family planning tasks? Has the training been evaluated?
- A KAP study of the staff in this context. Do they know the real Islamic position on family planning? Have they made any efforts to explain the real position to the community?
- Are Muslim medical and para-medical staff more effective in persuading Muslims to adopt family planning? Will more Muslim staff help?

Information, Education and Communication (I.E.C)

- What efforts have been made by the government, NGOs, scholars, media, to allay the belief that Islam is against family planning?
- What communication efforts have been made so far to popularize family planning among Muslims in particular?
- Has any literature on the subject specifically been produced for Muslims? What literature? And where? What was its impact? Analysis of the literature, its content, language, distribution and impact.
- Have any seminars, workshops been organized?
- What conscious efforts have been made to remove misconceptions/fears about family planning among Muslims? By whom? When? Where?

Media

Awareness generation is the most critical factor in creating a supportive environment for family planning. For this, the following information needs to be obtained:

- Nature of media coverage by
  - Muslim press
  - Hindu press
  - Mainstream press
- Impact of media coverage on Muslims, and on Hindus, in the context of family planning. Their knowledge and practice of family planning.
- Has any analysis been done of coverage of the subject by various other media, like electronic and outdoor media? By whom? When? What are the findings?
- In the age of new media, what role is social media playing in the context of family planning?

Appendix 3

SWOT Analysis of Indian Muslim Situation for Future Family Planning Campaign

The SWOT (Strengths, Weaknesses, Opportunities and Threats) analysis that has been attempted shows that the weaknesses and threats identified can be easily overcome and the strengths and opportunities suitably built upon.

Strengths

- Ample evidence available from the Quran and Hadith to show that Islam is supportive of the concept of family planning
- Nearly 45 per cent of Indian Muslims have already accepted family planning
- Some liberal Muslim individuals/NGOs are already motivated towards this end

Weaknesses

- Inadequate/erratic reach of delivery of health/family planning services
- Lack of conscious efforts by the government machinery to reach the Muslim target audience
- Lack of literature specifically designed for the Muslim audience
- Paucity of Muslim staff at health departments and centres
- Lack of special training of field staff to reach out to Muslim target groups
- Political evasiveness

Opportunities

- Presence of large Urdu press/Muslim press
- Availability of liberal Muslim scholars/theologians
- Pro-family planning position already adopted by those Muslim countries held in high esteem by Indian Muslims
- Fairly wide reach of health and family planning services (though there is scope for improvement in the backward Muslim areas)
- Increasing NGO participation in population matters
- Increasing public concern about population issues

Threats

- Possibility of bigoted clergy's opposition
- Existing propaganda by some fanatical organizations that Islam is opposed to family planning and that there is an organized fundamentalist conspiracy to increase the Muslim population. This is proving counter-productive since it provides a rationale in the Muslim mind for such a thought, wherein the thought did not exist earlier

- Unstable political situation in various states, which discourages political leaders from taking a clear, unambiguous and vocal stand for assertive implementation of family planning.
- The surcharged emotions of the Muslim community post the Babri Masjid demolition in 1992, after which even an innocuous welfare scheme can be misunderstood and misinterpreted among the community. This has greatly aggravated in the last decade of high pitched organised anti Muslim rhetoric.

On balance, we find that the opportunities and strengths far outweigh the weaknesses and threats. What we need is intensive strategic thinking to evolve a successful operational design for successful family planning in the country. With good intent and positive political will, we can create a model India can be proud of.

Abbreviations

ASHA	Accredited Social Health Activist
BJP	Bharatiya Janata Party
CBR	Crude Birth Rate
PBUH	Peace be upon him
CSOs	Civil Society Organizations
FPAP	Family Planning Association of Pakistan
FWP	Family Welfare Programme
GDP	Gross Domestic Product
ICDS	Integrated Child Development Services
ICPD	International Conference on Population and Development
IMR	Infant Mortality Rate
IUD	Intra-uterine Devices
JSK	Jansankhya Sthirata Kosh
JSSK	Janani Shishu Suraksha Karyakaram
KAP	Knowledge, Attitude and Practice
MCH	Maternal and Child Health

MLA	Member of Legislative Assembly
MMR	Maternal Mortality Rate
MoHFW	Ministry of Health and Family Welfare
MP	Member of Parliament
MTP	Medical Termination of Pregnancy
NAR	Net Attendance Ratio
NCP	National Commission on Population
NDC	National Development Council
NFHS	National Family Health Survey
NFPP	National Family Planning Programme
NFWP	National Family Welfare Programme
NGOs	Non-Governmental Organizations
NHP	National Health Policy
NIHFW	National Institute of Health and Family Welfare
NPP	National Population Policy
NRHM	National Rural Health Mission
NRR	Net Reproduction Rate
NSSO	National Sample Survey Office
NUHM	National Urban Health Mission
OBC	Other Backward Classes
OPHI	Oxford Poverty and Human Development Initiative
ORG	Operations Research Group
PFI	Population Foundation of India
PHC	Primary Health Centres
PMSSY	Pradhan Mantri Swasthya Suraksha Yojana
PPP	Public-Private Partnership
PrSBS	Private Sector Banks
PuSBs	Public Sector Banks
RCH	Reproductive Child Health
RHPs	Rural Health Practitioners
RMNCH+A	Reproductive, Maternal, Newborn, Child and Adolescent Health Strategy
RSS	Rashtriya Swayamsevak Sangh

SC	Scheduled Caste
SRH	Sexual Reproductive Health
SRS	Sample Registration System
ST	Scheduled Tribe
STD	Sexually Transmitted Diseases
S.W.O.T.	Strengths, Weaknesses, Opportunities and Threats
TFR	Total Fertility Rate
TMFR	Total Marital Fertility Rate
UNDP	United Nations Development Programme
UNFPA	United Nations Population Fund
VOs	Voluntary Organizations
WHO	World Health Organization

Acknowledgements

The journey of the book

The idea of this book was born in a surprise development when Country Director, UNFPA, India, Tevia Abrams visited me in my office in 1994 accompanied by his programme officer, Ena Singh. He said he wanted me to write a strategy paper for family planning among the Muslims in India. This was a strange request as I was neither a Islamic scholar nor a family planning expert, never having worked in the health ministry either in the state of Haryana, my service cadre, or in the central government. Not sure what I would write, I tried my best to excuse myself, but Tevia wouldn't budge. The offer was also financially attractive - thirty times my take-home monthly salary of 5,000 rupees! Seeing his adamance, I agreed to do it, but an inner voice said I should do it pro bono. He insisted that I get paid. So we settled for a remuneration – one rupee! I requested him to send me a formal proposal on which I would get the approval of the Government of India.

295

That settled, I started looking around for ideas. I had no clue what would be the outcome. When I started the project, I was under the impression, like everyone else, that Islam is against family planning. But what I discovered during my research was an eye opener. I found that the reality was just the opposite. Islam was not only not against family planning but was actually the pioneer of the concept. What helped me understand the Islamic position was a fascinating book titled Family Planning in the Legacy of Islam by Prof Abder Rahim Omran of the greatest Islamic University, Al Azhar, Cairo.

It took me five months, instead of the stipulated one, to complete the paper. When ready, it caused quite a few ripples because of its unusual findings and recommendations. I sounded many Ulama and Imams to make sure I don't end up getting fatwas against myself. Contrary to my apprehensions, I found extraordinary support from them. As I was also holding charge of Administrator Punjab Wakf Board, I decided to organise a national seminar on Rights of Women and Children in Islam, with Imams and teachers of madrasas to test the ground. The three-day seminar was a terrific success as it greatly enthused the participants, and gave me a clue how to approach the subject of family planning - through the rights route.

I was asked to present my research paper at several conferences and lectures. There again I persisted with my decision not to accept any fee or honorarium. This decision proved providential. Five years later, I was staying with my daughter in her hostel in London when I received a call from one Dr Qureshi, President of Muslim Doctors Association of UK, who said he wanted to 'discuss' my paper. I got the feeling that the tone was somewhat threatening. Not wanting to get beaten up in London, I tried to wriggle out saying I have my flight back early next morning.

The guys arrived at the airport with a few books in hand. The opening sentence was such that I have remembered it all these years. "Mr Quraishi, family planning is a western conspiracy against Islam. They hire, through UN agencies, mercenaries like you to write such papers." Well, the charge would have stuck. I was indeed "hired" by a UN agency, UNFPA. If I had accepted even a rupee, I could be considered a mercenary. I did not collect even the one rupee that was agreed upon. This gave me the moral authority to pounce back on them. They went away sulking, promising to send me some more literature later, which would help me change my mind. They never did.

In 1998, when the BJP came to power, I thought my paper would be a great hit as they were critical of the Muslim population growth. When I expressed this hope to a friend in Chandigarh, a renowned political analyst, he disabused me of all illusions with his unforgettable remarks, "You must be silly to entertain such a fancy notion. Do you think they really want Muslims to do family planning? They only want to use this as a stick to beat them with! You are stealing their stick and expect them to be happy?" He proved prophetic. The Ministry of Health and Family Welfare completely ignored the paper.

For a long time I thought I must upgrade the paper to a full-fledged book. It has taken over twenty years for this vision to become a reality.

While the book debunks the myths that Muslims procreate prolifically for whatever reasons, political or religious, it seeks to motivate the Muslims to adopt family planning willingly and proactively, irrespective of the right wing calls for procreation war. It also suggests strategies to accomplish this task effectively.

I consider this book my humble contribution to the cause of national development.

I must acknowledge the under-mentioned persons who contributed in the conceptualisation and culmination of this work.

Tevia Abrams, the then Country Director, UNFPA, who sowed the seed of the idea in my mind. Ena Singh, also of UNFPA, who provided the initial resource support. Venkat Srinivasan of UNFPA who consistently inspired and helped me with the literature.

Frederika Meijer, Country Director UNFPA for her enthusiastic support during her tenure.

Poonam Muttreja, Executive Director, Population Foundation of India (PFI) who was there for me ungrudgingly any time I needed information, which was often. Alok Vajpayi of PFI for unstinting research support and reviewing the book thoroughly and helping me with extremely useful suggestions. Pravin Jha of PFI who helped me with the original chapters on demography and later in fine tuning these.

M.Z. Khan has been inspiring me in all my academic pursuits and has given valuable inputs for the book, particularly the policy perspective in chapter one.

I am extremely grateful for the expert comments by the doyens of demography in India, namely, P.D. Kulkarni of Jawaharlal Nehru University, Leela Visaria, professor emeritus, Gujarat Institute of Development Research, K.S. James, Director International Institute of Population Studies, and Abusaleh Shariff, the renowned economist and Member Secretary of the Justice Sachar Committee, who drafted the monumental report on the conditions of the Muslim community in India's development story.

Special thanks are due to the great mathematician Dinesh Singh, former vice chancellor, Delhi University and Ajay Kumar, assistant professor of Mathematics in the School of Basic and Applied Sciences, KR Mangalam University, Gurugram for developing the mathematical model that shows that the Muslims can *never* overtake the Hindus. This should provide a closure to the mythical propaganda around this debate which has been a polarising issue to drive a wedge between Hindus and Muslims.

My thanks to Maulana Mumtaz Qasmi, who was the President of Imams Organisation of Punjab, Himachal and Haryana who mobilised the Imams and Islamic scholars for the National Seminar on the Rights of Women and Children in Islam and became the link between me and the Ulama. He later led the Imams' movement for

Pulse Polio programme in Gurgaon, which helped the district top the country. Imtiyaz Khizr, the media officer of Punjab Wakf Board, was always helpful with the information I required.

I am grateful to my niece, Najma Ansari, in Johannesburg for reviewing my chapter on Islamic Edicts and providing the Arabic text of the verses from the Holy Quran which I have quoted. My sister, Rasheda Hussain, helped me improve the chapter with her great knowledge, insights and nuances. The help of Sachi Poudyal in creating JPEG of the Quranic verses and repeated proof reading was commendable. Jawed Jamil, professor of Islamic Studies, Yenepoya University, and a pioneer of NGO efforts for promotion of family planning among Muslims in Saharanpur, UP, for his review of the chapter and valuable suggestions.

I am grateful to Davendra Kothari, the renowned demographer, for agreeing to write the forewords. There could have been no better authorities on the subject to do the honours. My gratitude to Professor Tahir Mahmood for penning the Foreword from the point of view of the Muslim law.

I am most grateful to my brilliant young research associate, Sayari Misra, in Durgapur whom I am yet to meet because of Covid lockdown, who, in just six months, did amazing work for the completion of the book that has been on my table for years.

I am happy that I could convert the lockdown due to Covid19 into an opportunity by keeping myself bound to my desk and completing the work in five months that I could not in 25 years! A lesson: there is an opportunity to grab in every problem.

Finally, my gratitude to Swati Chopra, Executive Editor, HarperCollins India, for encouraging me to take up this work in right earnest and to publish it in record time. Her contribution in making this book reader-friendly is unquestioned. Rinita Banerjee did a painstaking job of copy editing which I gratefully acknowledge. And thank you Saurav Das for your very pleasant cover design.

About the Author

S.Y. QURAISHI joined the Indian Administrative Service in 1971 and rose to become the seventeenth chief election commissioner of India. He introduced a number of electoral reforms, such as the creation of a voter education division, expenditure monitoring division, the India International Institute of Democracy and Election Management, and launched the National Voters Day. In October 2017, he, alongside Kofi Annan, was appointed ambassador of democracy, by International IDEA (Institute of Democracy and Electoral Assistance), Stockholm. He is the author of *An Undocumented Wonder: The Making of the Great Indian Election* (2014) and edited *The Great March of Democracy: Seven Decades of India's Elections* (2019).